William Arthur Bishop wrote this biography as a result of
the promise he made to his father before he died in 1956.
The author's own career in the RCAF began when he was
presented with his wings by his father at Uplands, Ottawa,
1942. He subsequently served overseas as a Spitfire pilot with
the First Canadian Squadron 401. Bishop's biography of his
father recreates the man about whom Arch Whitehouse
wrote in *The Years of the Sky Kings*, "There never was so
relentless a fighting airman in any war."

Books of Merit

The Courage of the Early Morning

BILLY BISHOP

THE COURAGE OF THE EARLY MORNING

A BIOGRAPHY OF THE GREAT ACE OF WORLD WAR I

By William Arthur Bishop

Thomas Allen Publishers

Toronto

Library and Archives Canada Cataloguing in Publication

Bishop, William Arthur, 1923–
The courage of the early morning : a biography of Billy Bishop,
the great ace of World War I / William Arthur Bishop.

First published: Toronto : McClelland and Stewart, 1965.
ISBN 978-0-88762-739-2

1. Bishop, William A., 1894–1956.   2. Fighter pilots—Canada—Biography.
3. Great Britain. Royal Flying Corps—Biography.   4. World War, 1914–1918—
Aerial operations, British.   I. Title.

UG626.2.B5B57 2011   940.4'4941092   C2010-908133-1

Cover design: Sputnik Design Partners Inc.
Cover image (airplane): Canadian Aviation and Space Museum—
CSTMC/Collection, Image CASM-13418
Cover illustration (soldiers): Dan Kangas

Published by Thomas Allen Publishers,
a division of Thomas Allen & Son Limited,
390 Steelcase Road East,
Markham, Ontario L3R 1G2 Canada

www.thomasallen.ca

ONTARIO ARTS COUNCIL
CONSEIL DES ARTS DE L'ONTARIO

Canada Council
for the Arts

The publisher gratefully acknowledges the support of
The Ontario Arts Council for its publishing program.

We acknowledge the support of the Canada Council for the Arts, which
last year invested $20.1 million in writing and publishing throughout Canada.

We acknowledge the Government of Ontario through the Ontario
Media Development Corporation's Ontario Book Initiative.

We acknowledge the financial support of the Government of Canada
through the Canada Book Fund for our publishing activities.

11 12 13 14 15   5 4 3 2 1

Printed and bound in Canada
Text Printed on a 100% PCW recycled stock

To all those who wore wings in the Allied cause in two World Wars, and to those who still wear them in the cause of freedom

For he had that courage which Napoleon once said was the rarest—the courage of the early morning.

— *Montreal Gazette*

Billy Bishop was a man absolutely without fear. I think he's the only man I have ever met who was incapable of fear.

— Colonel Eddie Rickenbacker

Contents

Acknowledgements

Without the help of the Royal Canadian Air Force this work would not have been possible. I will always be grateful to Air Marshal Hugh Campbell, Group Captain G. F. Jacobsen and Air Commodore Donald Blane for their assistance and co-operation.

The help of Wing Commander Ralph Manning, the RCAF Air Historian, must be especially cited. Thanks also to his associates Arthur Heathcote, R. V. Dodds, H. A. Halliday and Archie Paton, and also to his predecessor Frederick Hitchins.

A number of the surviving 1914–1918 fighter pilots assisted in various ways. My thanks to Lord Balfour, Keith Caldwell, Lord George Dundas, Spencer Horn, C. "Mike" McEwen, S. L. G. Pope, Alec Wilkinson and Graham Young.

Two veterans of the trench warfare of the First World War, Colonel George A. Drew and Douglas Kittemaster, generously lent their assistance.

The staff of the Air Historical Branch of the Air Ministry in London opened its doors wide to me. L. A. Jackets, head of the branch, and his assistant, W. H. Martin, were extremely helpful. They even provided me with an office as headquarters.

I am also grateful to the staff of the Imperial War Museum and to F. S. White of the Air Ministry Library at Whitehall.

Group Captain G. F. Hannifin of the Royal Aircraft Establishment, Farnborough, was most helpful in explaining the characteristics of the S.E. 5 aircraft on display there.

Special thanks are due also to H. H. Russell, one of the foremost research experts on World War I aviation, who helped me in research when I was in London.

At the Musée de L'Air in France, Rougedin Badille was kind enough to show me that prize collection of aircraft.

Kenneth M. Molson, curator of the National Aviation Museum, Ottawa, was of particular help in suggesting many sources of information, including the Cross and Cockade Society of First War historians. My thanks to those of its four hundred members who so willingly proffered information of every description.

I wish to thank Major C. C. J. Bond for preparation of the maps which appear on pages 71 and 197 of the text.

Many of my close friends also assisted in this work. I am indebted in particular to Lord Shaugnessy whose keen socio-political insight is well known, and to a former business associate Frank deB. Walker, RCAF director of public relations overseas during World War II.

To all these and to many others who helped in different ways, I wish to express my appreciation for their generous assistance, interest and support.

WILLIAM ARTHUR BISHOP

THE WESTERN FRONT, 1917

O N THE MORNING of Friday, March 24, 1917, Lieutenant William Avery Bishop, formerly of the Mississauga Horse, latterly of the Seventh Canadian Mounted Rifles and now the newest reinforcement of the Sixtieth Air Squadron of the British Third Brigade, stood on the carpet before General John Higgins, the brigade commander. (The carpet was figurative: no such luxury existed in the battered farmhouse that served as headquarters of Filescamp aerodrome, fifteen miles behind the front lines at Arras.)

It was fortunate for Bishop that he had so recently come to Filescamp that he did not yet know the airmen called this distinguished soldier "Old-Bum-and-Eyeglass"—because he had been shot in the former and wore the latter. Bishop, with his irrepressible small-town Canadian sense of humour, would not have been able to keep a straight face at a moment when his career hung in the balance.

Bishop had lost no time in coming to the general's attention. While Higgins and other visiting dignitaries watched, Bishop, returning from his first patrol over enemy lines, had crashed a new

Nieuport scout practically at the general's feet. The precious machine was wrecked, but Bishop walked away wearing a slightly embarrassed grin.

General Higgins, a career soldier whose service in numerous campaigns, including the Boer war, had earned him the D.S.O. and a row of other ribbons, gave the blond-haired lieutenant with the penetrating blue eyes an admonishing glance. Then he peered gloomily through his monocle at Bishop's undistinguished dossier. Bishop had been in uniform for five and a half years, ever since he entered Canada's Royal Military College at the age of seventeen. He had been on active service almost from the day World War I started. But entries on the credit side of the dossier on the desk before General Higgins were few: he had suffered a slight shrapnel wound during a tour of duty as a Royal Flying Corps observer; he had achieved consistently high marks at target practice but had never fired a shot in action, except for a few exasperated bursts of machine-gun fire in the general direction of enemy trenches at extreme range. On the "crime" side, Bishop's record contained more entries: a series of breach-of-discipline, conduct unbecoming-of-an-officer, encounters with authority and an unusual ability to get involved in mishaps and accidents.

General Higgins closed the file and looked at Bishop.

"How much solo time have you got, Bishop?"

"Nearly twenty hours, Sir."

"Hmmm. You should have learned to fly in that time."

"There was an eddy, sir. A gust of wind swirled around a hangar and threw the plane out of control."

"I was on the field, Bishop."

"Yes, Sir."

"There was no wind."

"No, Sir."

"Afraid I'll have to order you back to flying school."

It was a severe sentence. True, Bishop's high spirits (he was barely twenty-three years old) had led him to treat the discipline of the British services with less than reverence. It was also true that he had not been able to master the niceties of flying an airplane, especially in the matter of taking off and landing. But he had worked hard to get his wings as a fighter pilot and to reach the front lines in France. He knew, as he stood before General Higgins, that additional training was unlikely to improve his flying ability, and that the general's decree might end his career as a fighter pilot—before it had well begun.

That noontime in the officers' mess of Filescamp aerodrome, Bishop consoled himself with a few shots of cognac chased by champagne. His own gloom was in keeping with the atmosphere of the mess. The traditional cheerful chatter of men who faced death as a way of life was conspicuously absent from the other officers of 60 Squadron downing their drinks around Bishop. Their despondency had nothing to do with Bishop's dismissal, which was indeed a trivial matter compared with the other misfortunes that beset 60 Squadron at that moment. The Squadron's top fighter, Albert Ball, had been promoted to flight commander of another unit, and for weeks now 60 Squadron had been suffering severe losses to German fighter pilots. The most recent and tragic casualty was Evelyn Graves, the squadron commander, who had been shot down and killed behind enemy lines. The airplanes causing such havoc to 60 Squadron were a group of new Albatros fighters that formed a *Jagdstaffel* (hunting pack) based at Douai, about the same distance behind the German lines as Filescamp was behind the British trenches. The Albatros had little advantage in top speed over the Nieuport, the machine flown by the British pilots. But the Germans had two great advantages: the Albatros was equipped with two machine-guns, the Nieuport with one; and the German machines were piloted by experienced air fighters, whereas 60 Squadron's casualties in the past few months had left it with only five experienced pilots.

On the enemy side, the German *Jagdstaffel* II was manned by airmen of much greater experience, and led by the man who had

shot down more planes than any other pilot to date: Baron Manfred von Richthofen. The Baron was a year older than Bishop, and
strikingly similar physically—both were rugged, sturdy men, short
and wiry. Like Bishop also, he was a cavalry man who had escaped
the mud and misery of ground warfare by joining his country's air
force. Both had survived dangerous and inglorious apprenticeships
as aerial observers before graduating to the more dangerous—and
more glorious—role of fighter pilots.

But there the parallel ended. By a grim coincidence as the clock
in 60 Squadron's officers' mess was about to strike noon, twenty-
five miles to the northeast and 5,500 feet above the shell-torn earth,
Manfred von Richthofen was winning his thirtieth victory in the
air. It was his first fight as a full lieutenant, and, on returning to
base, in his usual meticulous manner he filed this report "Request-
ing acknowledgment of Victory":

> *Date*: March 24, 1917.
> *Time*: 11.55 A.M.
> *Place*: Givenchy.
> *Plane*: Spad with Hispano motor. The first I have
> encountered.
> *Occupant*: Lieutenant R. P. Baker, 16th Squadron, RFC,
> wounded taken prisoner.
>
> I was flying with several of my gentlemen when I observed
> an enemy Squad passing on front. Aside from this Squad there
> were two new one-seaters which I had never seen in the air
> before, and they were extremely fast and handy. I attacked one
> of them and ascertained that my machine was better than his.
> After a long fight I managed to hit the adversary's gasoline tank.
> His propeller stopped running. The plane had to go down.
>
> BARON MANFRED VON RICHTHOFEN

Baker's 16 Squadron was stationed at an aerodrome adjacent
to Filescamp, but Bishop, nursing his brandy and brooding in the

officers' mess, knew nothing of Richthofen's latest triumph. He knew only that his own career was at a new low point—and he knew he had no one to blame but himself.

Into the 60 Squadron mess hobbled an airman whose jaunty manner and cheerful grin seemed to disperse the gloom. He was Major Jack Scott, the new squadron commander appointed to replace Evelyn Graves. Of all the occupants of the mess, Scott would seem to have the least cause for cheerfulness. It was remarkable that he could walk at all, even with the help of two canes. He had been crippled in a crash early in the war, and although he was under orders not to fly, he had no intention of accepting a role he described as "non-playing captain of the team." So he simply disregarded the order and took his regular turn on patrols.

Scott was a protégé of one of Britain's most powerful elder statesmen, Lord Birkenhead, and a close friend of one of Britain's most influential young statesmen, Winston Churchill. Both these friends had tried to persuade Scott to take an important headquarters job more suited to his physical handicap, but Scott had stubbornly refused.

Scott now made his halting way to the bar beside Bishop and ordered a drink. "Sorry, Bish," he said quietly. "However, I've persuaded the brass that we're so shorthanded that you'd better stick around until your replacement arrives."

"How long should that take?" asked Bishop.

"Couple of days, probably. So you can go on tomorrow's patrol, anyway."

The next day, March 25, 1917, in a cloudless sky, four silver Nieuports climbed to nine thousand feet in diamond formation and crossed the German lines between Arras and St. Léger. The rear man was Bishop, who searched the sky warily; the tail man was always the most inviting target to an attacker.

The patrol had been flying for about half an hour over the trenches when the leader spotted three small dots to the east. The specks grew larger and larger until the Nieuport pilots could identify the sweeping wings and bullet-shaped snout of Albatros fighters. To Bishop's surprise his leader made no motion to turn away as the German fighters wheeled around behind the patrol. Instead he gradually slowed his speed to allow the enemy machines to overtake them all the faster.

Just as the Germans closed within firing range, a hundred yards behind, the Nieuport leader pulled to the left in a tight climbing turn. The patrol followed. Bishop was a split second slower than the rest. It cost him about fifty yards in distance. Suddenly an Albatros shot underneath him and pulled up under the leader's tail. Bishop looked through his telescope-shaped Aldis sight and as the Albatros filled his field of vision he pressed the firing button.

To his elation, the smoking tracer bullets streaked into the cockpit of the enemy machine and seemed to strike sparks all around it. Immediately the Albatros dived vertically. Bishop pushed down the nose of his own machine and gave chase.

The Albatros dive might be a ruse. Grid Caldwell, a veteran fighter and the left flank man of the formation, had warned Bishop of the German tactic of diving away as if hit, only to escape by levelling off near the ground. Sure enough, the enemy plane levelled out after diving a thousand feet. From forty yards away Bishop fired again. This time he saw his bullets strike all around the pilot. Once again the enemy machine dived towards the ground and once more Bishop chased after it.

His speed indicator showed he was diving at two hundred miles an hour, but the enemy plane seemed to be diving even faster. Bishop continued firing in short bursts, when the fight ended suddenly as the German plane crashed nose first into a field.

Elated by his first victory, Bishop pulled his Nieuport abruptly out of its dive. His engine coughed, sputtered; Bishop pumped the throttle desperately but the engine refused to work. Now he could hear the rattle of machine-gun bullets all around him—a signal that he was over enemy territory.

Furious at his own carelessness, Bishop tried to reconcile himself to a forced landing behind the enemy lines. The pilot of a plane with a dead engine and a thousand feet of altitude has time for only a few seconds of thought. Bishop had to face the bitter fact that the best he could hope for was survival—and a billet in a German prison camp for the rest of the war. In the back of his mind were unpleasant stories he had heard of Allied airmen being shot by enemy infantry after surviving a forced landing. Even more imminent was the hazard of a bad landing on a rough field. Bishop put his plane into the shallowest angle of descent short of stalling. He peered over the side of his cockpit and was horrified to see that the field that was inexorably rising toward his wheels was covered with shell holes.

Bishop made one of the rare good landings of his career. Somehow the plane threaded its way between deep craters and came to a stop undamaged. He leaped out of the plane and ran for the nearest shell hole. Seeing four drab figures slogging their way toward him, Bishop grabbed hold of his Very pistol. He had no intention of resisting capture—but he also had no intention of being shot by his captors without putting up a fight.

When the infantrymen were within a few feet of him, Bishop gave a shout of joy. They were not German infantrymen in field-grey uniforms, but English soldiers in mud-stained khaki. They helped him out of the crater and explained that the field had been captured from the Germans only a few hours before. The enemy trenches were only three hundred yards away, and already the Germans were pot-shotting at Bishop's exposed Nieuport with rifles and machine-guns.

After his four rescuers led him through the barbed-wire entanglements to the British trenches, counter-fire from those trenches silenced the German gunners and saved Bishop's plane from further damage until darkness came.

He sent a message to Jack Scott at the airfield explaining his plight and asking for a tender to bring back his mired plane. But by nightfall on the first day no help arrived. This is Bishop's own description of the events of the next few days.

> The first night was frightful. I slept, or rather tried to sleep and failed, on the ground in the pouring rain. A battle started before sunrise and the guns—Oh Lord! You can't imagine the row. At first light I saw the cavalry forming up for a charge, and remembering that not many months before it had been my ambition to gallop into battle on horseback, I murmured to myself "there but for the grace of God . . ." It was ironic, too. There I was, crowded in the mud helplessly looking at my helpless ultra-modern airplane while nearby men on the oldest of all battle transport were carrying on.
>
> It was a cruel scene, too. The cavalry could not penetrate the enemy lines through the wire entanglements. The brave beautiful horses struggled eagerly and then desperately to get through. Riders and mounts were sitting ducks for enemy fire and many went down and lay struggling in the mud and wire. Then the cavalry got the order to withdraw and those who could helped their wounded horses to their feet and led them back at a plodding run while the infantry on our side covered the retreat as best they could. This must have been one of the last times cavalry was used in battle.

As the sun came up two enemy scouts criss-crossed overhead and Bishop suddenly realized "They're looking for *me*!" They were indeed. When one of the German pilots spotted the bogged Nieuport he dived at it with his guns chattering. A few bullets tore through the Nieuport's fabric skin. The German had to pull out of his dive low over the British trenches. The Tommies threw everything they had, including a chorus of derisive shouts. Bishop saw one officer deliberately aim and empty his service revolver at the belly of the swooping Albatros.

The plane escaped, signalled the second plane which had been circling at a safe distance, and together they flew off toward their own base. Bishop was sure they would return with reinforcements and he decided to try to start his Nieuport. To his surprise and joy the engine roared into life at the first swing of its propeller. (His mechanic later explained to Bishop that the long dive and sudden pull-out had flooded the cylinders with oil, which drained out during the night.)

Bishop climbed into the cockpit, revved up the motor and picked his way among the shell holes, seeking a stretch of level mud long enough for a take-off. He spotted such a stretch and pushed the throttle wide open. The Nieuport strained forward as if eager to free itself of the clutching mud. The plane gained speed, bounced once, bounced twice . . .

Bishop's shout of triumph was drowned by a horrible grinding crash. The second bounce of the wheels had dislodged a lump of mud and thrown it into the wooden propeller, which smashed into splinters. Disgusted, Bishop switched off the motor and climbed out of the cockpit.

He trudged through the mud until he stumbled on a British anti-aircraft battery. When he told the young lieutenant in charge what had happened, the latter said cheerfully: "Oh, yes, we saw the Hun crash and confirmed the kill. Then they asked us what happened to *you*. Seems you're on the missing list."

"Looks like it," said Bishop gloomily, "I sent a message asking for a tender to come up for the plane, but I suppose they didn't get the message."

That night he borrowed a Ford from the anti-aircraft lieutenant and tried to drive back in the general direction of Filescamp over roads that at best were axle-deep in mud, at worst a seemingly endless series of shell holes. For twelve of the most exhausting and frustrating hours of his life he tried to find a way through the labyrinth of destruction, but when the grey dawn broke he and the battered

Ford were back at the anti-aircraft position. He arrived just in time for the opening barrages of another artillery battle. The gunners helped Bishop drag his crippled plane to a safer position under the guns.

It was a thoroughly depressing day for Bishop. By now his replacement would have arrived at Filescamp, and he and his plane were apparently written off ingloriously. He was among strangers who were too busy fighting their own war to give much time to this grounded and pathetic aviator.

Bishop could not know, of course, that things were not as dark for him as they seemed. Just over the horizon, as sundown approached, a rescue convoy was picking its way towards him. And over the transatlantic cable the Canadian Press news service was sending a report that would appear in Canadian newspapers, including the *Sun* of Owen Sound, Ontario, which modified it slightly to read:

"Lieutenant William Avery Bishop, son of our respected County Registrar, Will Bishop, has been credited with shooting down an enemy fighter plane in France."

CADET

TO OLDER RESIDENTS of Owen Sound, Billy Bishop, his brother Worth, and his younger sister Louie were not so much the children of Registrar Will Bishop, as the grandchildren of "Old E. W.," the laziest man in town. It was a constant source of wonder that any man as shiftless as Eleazar Wilson Bishop could produce a son as energetic as Will and grandchildren as lively as Billy, Worth and Louie. The only explanation could be that the second and third generations took after Grandmother Sarah Bishop.

In the nineteenth century many a Canadian community had its remittance man, a character in which the town took a wry pride, a feckless younger son of a titled, wealthy or merely proud English family who banished the black sheep to "the colonies" with an allowance large enough to keep him alive but small enough to ensure that he could never pay the fare back to the ancestral roof. In Owen Sound Eleazar Bishop assumed the role of the local remittance man, but it was a fraudulent title. In the first place he was not English, but of German Pennsylvania Dutch ancestry, and in the second place his remittance came not from abroad but from his wife's dogged capacity for hard work.

In the small town of Unionville, northeast of Toronto, there was no accord between the emigrant Pennsylvania Dutch and the

United Empire Loyalists who had fled to Canada rather than support the American Revolution. So when Eleazar Bishop, the German leatherworker's son, eloped with Sarah Kilbourne, the English loyalist's daughter, both families disowned them.

The young couple tried their luck in the North—and found none. In 1855 they settled in the boom town of Owen Sound, Ontario. This port on Georgian Bay, the world's largest fresh-water bay, had been founded only fifteen years earlier with the arrival of the railroad connecting Georgian Bay, Lake Huron, Lake Michigan and Lake Superior ports with Toronto, Southern Ontario and Montreal. The first Welland Canal was not built until 1870, and at this time Owen Sound was a link connecting by rail and ship the world's trade with the Great Lakes and the interior of Canada and the United States. The town's boosters were beginning to call Owen Sound "the Liverpool of Canada."

It was difficult for any man with a minimum of energy and enterprise not to succeed in Owen Sound in the eighteen fifties. But Eleazar Bishop was uniquely equipped to be the exception. First he tried operating a hotel. But his casual attitude toward collecting the accounts of his guests, plus a tendency to treat friends at the hotel bar, soon put him into bankruptcy. Next he opened a saddlery and leatherworking shop—the trade he had learned from his father.

Eleazar was a skilled leatherworker, but impatient of the drudgery of catering to customers' wants. Instead of stocking utilitarian saddles, bridles and other items of farm and home-stable use, he devoted his time to designing and making elaborate pieces of luggage that had no market in the frontier lake port of Owen Sound. When Eleazar's leatherworking shop went into bankruptcy too, a masterpiece of leather craftsmanship in the shape of a gentleman's hatbox was one of the few assets salvaged. It was to become Billy Bishop's sole legacy from his grandfather, and although he never used it as a hatbox it served a useful purpose in his later life, as we shall learn.

When Eleazar failed for the second time his wife, Sarah, took over as the family breadwinner. She let it be known in town that she would accept any domestic work, however menial. She sewed and scrubbed, mended, cleaned and cooked from dawn until late at night to support her husband and three children. Eleazar accepted this turn of events philosophically. He spent the rest of his long and happy life on the porch of his home, whittling, cultivating his magnificent crop of snow-white whiskers, and dispensing good advice to the many townsfolk who paused to pass the time of day with him.

Sarah not only supported her family by hard work, but when her youngest son, Will, graduated from high school she was able to send him to Toronto to study at Osgoode Hall, the famous law school of Upper Canada. Before he left Owen Sound, Will Bishop became engaged to a girl who undoubtedly reminded him of his mother.

Margaret Louise Greene was born in New Orleans. In 1855 William Greene, her father, had graduated from Dublin University with a medical degree and returned to County Down to practise. But the disease that lay like a blight over the county and over most of Ireland was one no doctor could cure: the effects of the potato famine which in eight years had caused the death of a million Irish men, women and children and had driven nearly two million to seek new lives in the Americas. In 1855 the exodus was still on, and Dr. Greene and his bride, Sarah Crothers, joined it, intending to settle in Canada. But when their ship reached New Orleans Sarah could go no further. She was ill from the hardships of the nightmare voyage, and she was pregnant.

Dr. Greene tried to obtain a licence to practise medicine, but was told that he would have to serve an internship and pass an examination in American medical procedures. So while his wife awaited the birth of their daughter, Margaret Louise, and slowly recovered her strength afterward, Dr. Greene, a tall, rugged and handsome Ulsterman, worked at any casual job he could find in the bustling city of New Orleans.

Sarah was still far from strong when the couple and their infant daughter set out on the long journey to Canada. They settled in the pioneering farming district of Jackson's Point, fifty miles north of Toronto on the shores of Lake Simcoe, and William Greene became a country doctor.

One night in the second winter after their arrival, Dr. Greene was summoned to attend a woman in childbirth. It was a difficult delivery, and when it had been accomplished successfully the doctor and the new father celebrated with a few glasses of Irish whiskey. Belatedly anxious to return to his own ailing wife and infant daughter, Dr. Greene decided to take a short cut across the frozen Black River. Midway across the ice broke under him, and the icy water soon stilled his struggles. When his body was found Sarah collapsed. She never recovered from this final misfortune, and died within the year. A sister who came from Owen Sound for the funeral took the infant Margaret Louise back to live with her.

Margaret Louise, an Irish pixie of a girl, and Will Bishop, son of the town's "remittance man," grew up together. They were married soon after Will returned to practise in Owen Sound and Will staked his future by building an elegant Victorian home for his bride. They moved into it just before their first son, Worth, was born in 1884. A second son, Kilbourne, was born two years later. He died suddenly at the age of seven and the Bishops mourned until, on February 8, 1894, their third son was born, an eleven-pound baby with a full head of blond hair and bright blue eyes. They named him after his father, William Avery. The last child, Louie, was born a year later.

In 1896 Will Bishop's fortunes took a sudden turn for the better. In the national election of that year he worked as an organizer for Sir Wilfrid Laurier's Liberal party. When Laurier won, Bishop was rewarded with the post of county registrar.

He took the position, and the dignity that went with it, seriously, and dressed the part in dark coat and waistcoat, striped trousers, cutaway collar, pearl-grey bow tie and soft pinched black homburg hat. His manner was stern and overbearingly correct, but many an Owen Sound youngster who followed the dignified figure on his way to and from the white stone courthouse knew that he had a habit of filling the pockets of his immaculate coat with deliciously sticky sweets. And one grateful Owen Sound mother credited Will Bishop with smuggling poison into the cell of her condemned son so that he could take his own life and save her the shame of having him die on the gallows. Will vehemently denied it, but the legend remained as long as he lived.

Billy Bishop grew up so absurdly like his father in appearance, posture and even mannerisms that it was inevitable that his proud mother should turn him out as a replica of his father, in neat dark suits, white collar and tie. That was enough to give Billy a rough time from his schoolmates, who invented a game known as "tearing off Billy Bishop's tie." But Billy's behaviour provided them with other reasons for victimizing him: he scorned rough sports like hockey, football and lacrosse in favour of swimming and riding. Moreover, he spoke with a slight lisp which seemed to fascinate the girls, and—worst sin of all—he actually seemed to enjoy feminine company and attention. He was undoubtedly the only pre-teenaged boy in Owen Sound who enjoyed attending classes at Miss Pearl's Dancing School.

If Billy Bishop had grown up a generation or two later he might well have become a prime example of what child psychologists would call a victim of mother-possessiveness or father-fixation—or worse. Not to mention a younger brother complex. But there were no child psychologists in Owen Sound at the close of Queen Victoria's reign, and the only effect on Billy of a temperament that other boys regarded as "sissy" was that he learned, of necessity, how to defend himself stoutly with his fists against his tormentors.

On one memorable Monday morning he had to defend himself against the resentment of no fewer than seven boys whose parents had held him up as an example of virtue by reading an item in the Owen Sound *Sun*: "A concert was given at the residence of Mr. W.

A. Bishop on Saturday afternoon last. An excellent musical and literary program was carried out and a speech filled to overflowing with good humour was delivered by little Billy Bishop."

But even the most cynical of Billy's non-admirers had to admit there was one thing in his favour: he was no teacher's pet. He was, in fact, an indifferent student. After a string of bad reports Billy's parents, deeply concerned, consulted Thomas Murray, his school principal. Their concern was particularly deep because their oldest son, Worth, had been the top student at Owen Sound high school, later graduated from the Royal Military College at Kingston with the highest standing ever attained by a cadet, and became the youngest engineer ever to enter the federal government service.

Principal Murray, who was no admirer of Billy Bishop, told the latter's parents: "As far as I can see, the only thing your son is good at is fighting."

Will Bishop decided that if his younger son's talent was physical rather than intellectual he should be encouraged to develop his athletic side. He bought Billy a life membership in the YMCA on Poulet Street. Billy tried to work up some enthusiasm for athletics, and even entered the Y's cross-country race and trained quite strenuously for it. But when he could finish no better than second, he abandoned strenuous sports.

Meanwhile, though, he had discovered a much more desirable facility at the Y—the billiard room. He began cutting afternoon classes to sharpen his skill with the cue, and occasionally picked up pocket-money by playing pool against habitués of the town's disreputable pool halls. The Bishops' neighbours shook their heads and murmured gloomily that young Billy was a chip off old Eleazar, and wasn't it sad for Will, who had worked so hard to make something of himself. Of course there was the compensation that Billy's older brother, Worth, was a prodigy for learning, and his sister, Louie, was growing up a fine young lady and moved in the town's best society.

Billy's boyhood pursuits were not *all* decadent, of course. A few years later when Billy Bishop became the Allies' greatest air hero and millions of people heard the name Owen Sound for the first time, the townspeople forgot his early love of playing pool, and reminded each other of his uncanny skill with a gun. Billy's father had given him a .22 rifle one Christmas and offered him twenty-five cents for every squirrel he shot. Will Bishop did not expect the offer to cost him much. He knew it was extremely difficult to kill a wary squirrel high on a tree with a single, low-powered .22 bullet, but the very difficulty would give Billy good practice, and might even scare off some of the squirrels that damaged the fruit trees in his garden by gnawing their bark.

That offer was to cost Will Bishop many dollars. Soon Billy could boast modestly that his rate of slaughter had reached "one bullet—one squirrel" accuracy. When the surviving squirrel population no longer invaded the Bishop garden, Billy expanded his operation into other gardens and orchards, at the standard rate of twenty-five cents per squirrel. The *Sun* recorded the phenomenon of the scarcity of squirrels in town, and dubbed Billy "the Pied Piper of Owen Sound."

Another appropriate recollection of the people of Owen Sound was "the time Billy built and flew an airplane." It was rather less an achievement than that, but it contained enough of a grain of truth to justify its recollection by his admiring fellow residents. The modest fact was that in 1909 the papers were full of the achievement of John McCurdy, who flew an airplane off the frozen surface of Baddeck Lake in Nova Scotia, and thus became the first British subject to fly a powered heavier-than-air machine. Billy decided to build a plane of his own. He studied newspaper photographs of McCurdy's *Silver Dart* and assembled his own version, using boards, bedsheets, an orange crate, cardboard and much strong string.

Laboriously he hauled it to the roof of the family home, took his place in the orange-crate cockpit, and skidded down the steep roof into space. His descent was more a nosedive than a flight. The 28-foot fall demolished the machine, but Billy scrambled out of the wreckage with no more than a bruised knee and a scratched ear. Actually the incident is worth recording only because it happened to be the first of many violent contacts between the earth's surface and aircraft piloted by William Avery Bishop, near-disasters which became known simply as "Bishop landings."

The only witness to Billy's first flight was his sister, Louie, his long-suffering supporter-defender in various adventures and mis-adventures. She helped him out of the wreck, tended his bruises, and helped him hide the scattered remnants of his aircraft before it could be discovered and lead to punishment.

A few weeks later Louie asked Billy for a favour in return for hushing up the airplane incident. A girlfriend of hers would be entertaining a house guest from Toronto next weekend. Would Billy take her dancing on Saturday night?

"I don't need any more girls," said Billy ungallantly. "I've got enough."

Louie knew this was true, but she wheedled. "Margaret is a lovely girl and belongs to a prominent Toronto family," she said. "We *have* to see that she enjoys her visit to Owen Sound."

Billy was unimpressed. "I'll take her for two dollars—provided I like the look of her."

Louie arranged to have the girls over for tea on the veranda of the Bishop home. Billy could look at Margaret from behind the curtains of the dining-room windows without being seen.

Billy liked what he saw. Margaret Burden was a vivacious girl with auburn hair and hazel eyes, quietly but beautifully dressed. "She's class," Billy told himself, peering at her from behind the curtains. But later when Louie confronted him he assumed an air of indiffer-ence. "She's not so much," he said. "It will cost you five dollars."

Thus unromantically did Billy Bishop meet the girl he was to marry. It was a strangely democratic confrontation of the grandson of the least successful merchant of Owen Sound and the granddaughter of the most successful merchant of all Canada. In the same year that Eleazar Bishop was opening his doomed leather shop, Timothy Eaton was taking over the bankrupt stock of a dry-goods merchant in Toronto and opening his own small store on Toronto's Yonge Street. At the time when Eleazar's grandson took Timothy's granddaughter dancing, Eleazar had not earned a dollar for many a year—and Timothy had ceased counting his millions.

On his seventeenth birthday, in February, 1911, Billy decided to apply for entrance to Royal Military College, the Canadian equivalent of England's Sandhurst or the United States military academy at West Point. Billy had no desire for a military career, but he chose RMC rather than a regular university for several good reasons.

In the first place, entrance to RMC was by examination instead of general academic standing and Bishop felt he might be able to pass a test even though his scholastic record was mediocre. Furthermore, Billy's brother, Worth, had achieved the highest standing of any cadet in the history of RMC, and he felt that this would reflect to his credit. He was a superb rifle shot, and surely this should be an asset at a military school. Finally, he could ride a horse well, which should be an advantage in cavalry training. But an even more pertinent stimulus was Louie's needling: "You'll be lucky if you end up as a foundry hand. More likely you'll always be a grocery delivery boy." This was a reference to the fact that Billy had worked summers as a delivery boy for the local Loblaw store.

Tom Murray, the school principal, was even more discouraging. When Billy told him he planned to try the RMC entrance examinations, Murray told him bluntly that he hadn't got the brains.

But two or three of Billy's teachers did not share the principal's low opinion of Billy—or, more likely, the latter persuaded them into helping him after school. At any rate Billy left for Toronto, where the exams were held, so crammed with "instant knowledge" that he passed the tests and was accepted as a recruit at RMC.

Late one evening at the end of August Billy and forty other nervous recruits entered the ancient complex of stone buildings

on the banks of the St. Lawrence, where the mighty river flows out
of Lake Ontario, across the harbour from the city of Kingston,
Ontario. The college buildings had originally been the main dock-
yard of England's Great Lakes fleet in the War of 1812. The dormi-
tory to which Billy was assigned had once been a storehouse for
the shipbuilders. Later, when it was used as the winter quarters for
sailors, it was fitted out with all the accoutrements of a land-borne
warship and named "the stone frigate."

Billy soon learned that there was nothing romantic in being a
recruit at RMC. "We are," he wrote home gloomily, "the lowest form
of military life—of any life, for that matter."

A recruit has no privileges, he was informed by senior class-
men. A recruit will run at all times when on the parade square. In
Kingston on his afternoon off (there were to be few of these) he will
march, but always at attention, eyes front—no loitering or window-
shopping.

Infractions—and apparently almost everything a recruit did
could be interpreted as an infraction by ever-watchful upper class-
men—earned a sharp blow from a swagger stick across the rump,
or extra drill at six o'clock in the morning. And on the theory that
even the vigilant seniors must have missed some cadet crimes
during the week, each first-year man was soundly trounced every
Friday night.

A recruit was assigned to a senior as his "fag" or batman; in
effect a servant who tidied the senior's room, made his bed, looked
after his wardrobe and generally catered to his comforts. For Billy
this servitude took on a weird aspect. The senior who was his master was Vivien Bishop. They were not related, but because of the
coincidence Billy was required to kiss the older Bishop on the forehead and bid him "Goodnight, Daddy" every night.

Punishment at RMC was sometimes more macabre than merely
physical. Once when he was late for parade Billy was ordered to
clean out a Martello tower, a gun turret that was a relic of the old
navy days. The senior who inspected the finished job discovered

that Billy had overlooked a spider. He ordered Billy to eat it in the presence of his classmates.

Billy was profoundly depressed by the indignities of his first year, especially since he had been so much his own master until then. At any rate, he failed his examinations. Billy was too ashamed to face his family and friends in Owen Sound that summer. He begged his brother, Worth, then a rising young government engineer, to find him a job. Worth was then helping to build the unique lift locks at Peterborough, Ontario, on the Trent Canal navigation system. Billy worked there as a timekeeper, swallowed periodic doses of good advice from Worth, and promised solemnly to work hard and keep out of mischief when he went back to RMC.

He did too—for a full year. There were strong inducements, of course. Although he was accorded provisional second-year status, his failure in his first-year examinations meant that he would have to take an extra year to graduate, and a second failure would mean the end of his career. He passed that second test with something to spare.

But a whole year of good behaviour was all that Billy Bishop's ebullient high spirits could endure. His third year was an epic of rules broken and discipline scorned. His regular sorties—legal and illegal—into Kingston town to rendezvous with girls became the talk of the stone frigate. The RMC yearbook devoted a page to Billy's behaviour, with this opening scene:

Voice from cadet with telescope peering out of his window: "There's a red coat on Fort Henry hill. There's an umbrella too with a couple of people behind it. Wonder who it can be?"

Voice from the next room: "Come on, Steve, Bill Bishop is out. Let's swipe his tobacco . . ."

One evening early in the spring of 1914 Billy and a classmate arranged to meet two Kingston girls at Cedar Island, just across Deadman Bay from the college. Before they had embarked for the island they had already broken two college rules and one criminal law: they had left RMC grounds after dark without leave; they carried, and had already taken a few drinks from, a bottle of gin; and they stole a canoe.

A quarter of a mile from shore the canoe overturned. By clinging to it and swimming desperately, they managed to reach shore and to sneak back to their quarters. The other boy was so thoroughly chilled that he told Billy he would have to report to the infirmary.

"Well, change into dry clothes first," Billy told him, "and don't say a word about this." His companion promised, and Billy went serenely to bed. Unfortunately a staff officer had witnessed the whole thing. When the cadet in the infirmary was faced with this evidence, he assumed that Billy had also been informed that there was an eyewitness to the crime, and confessed. But Billy had admitted nothing. When he was unceremoniously routed from bed and paraded before Adjutant Charles Perreau he blandly denied the charge. When he was told that the other boy had admitted everything, he felt he was in too deep to change his story, and stoutly proclaimed his innocence. Perreau lost his patience and hurled at the defiant youth the most damning accusation that could be charged against a Gentleman Cadet: "Bishop, you're a liar!"

For his offence Billy was assessed twenty-eight days' "restricted leave," the equivalent of house arrest. It was the longest penalty of its kind ever imposed on a cadet up to that time. But worse was yet to come. In May, 1914, when he sat his examinations, he was caught cheating. Actually, he caught himself. He had hidden crib notes up his sleeve, and when he turned in his paper he absentmindedly handed in his notes with it.

With Billy once more up before him, Adjutant Perreau had only a few terse words for the culprit; the punishment would be held in abeyance during the summer holidays. There is little doubt that the adjutant was intensifying the penalty by making Billy worry about it all summer long. It was almost certain that the verdict would be dismissal.

As it turned out, Billy did not return to Royal Military College. (Not as a cadet, that is; but three years later, with a breastful of medals including the Victoria Cross, he was the honoured guest of the staff officers who not long before had described him, with some justification, as "the worst cadet RMC ever had.") Most of the senior cadets did not return, either. Before the start of the fall term, the First World War had broken out. Canada was woefully short of officers. Billy Bishop's military training, albeit incomplete, and his ability to ride a horse won him quick acceptance into the Mississauga Horse, a Toronto militia regiment.

CAVALRYMAN

T HE THOUGHT of becoming an aviator simply never oc-curred to any Canadian who joined up at the outbreak of war. Although two Canadians, Casey Baldwin and John McCurdy, as early as 1908 had made powered flights in heavier-than-air craft, and the great Alexander Graham Bell had put his genius into the design of pioneer Canadian planes, the coun-try's impressive war effort did not include the vestige of an air force.

Or rather, there was a vestige of an air force, a comedy of errors consisting of two men and one airplane that never got off the ground. The brief inglorious history of the first Canadian Aviation Corps was recalled years later by the Canadian military historian John Swettenham:

> The corps owed its enthusiastic if shaky start to Canada's unpredictable defence minister, Sir Sam Hughes. Hughes appointed as provisional commander Captain E. L. Janney, a 21-year-old aviation enthusiast from Galt, Ontario, who claimed flying experience in the United States. With five thou-sand dollars allocated by Hughes, Janney bought a Burgess-Dunne machine in Massachusetts and took off for Quebec.
>
> But meanwhile the eccentric Hughes had apparently for-gotten all about Canada's new air force. When Janney landed

to refuel at Sorel, Quebec, on his way to Camp Valcartier he was arrested as a German spy and detained on Hughes' order. Matters were straightened out, and Janney reached Valcartier where he first met his newly enrolled deputy, Lieut. W. F. Sharpe, a native of Prescott, Ontario. The plane was crated and stowed aboard the English-bound liner *Athenia*.

In England, Janney proposed forming a flight squadron at an estimated annual cost of over $116,000. The Canadian turned the proposal down, and to add to Janney's chagrin neither he nor Sharpe possessed any official status. Their appointments had not been gazetted—and they were not being paid.

In December, 1914, Janney had had enough of the army. He acquired an English plane which he planned to use in Canada for flying exhibitions, hoping to raise money to fit out a squadron of his own. Eventually he opened a private flying school near Toronto. No disciplinary action was ever taken against him for so summarily divesting himself of his commission, presumably since there was no record that he had ever taken the oath of allegiance.

Sharpe joined the Royal Flying Corps and was killed on his first solo flight in February, 1915—Canada's first air force casualty.

Meanwhile Canada's five-thousand-dollar airplane had vanished somewhere in England. Neither Janney nor Sharpe had taken any interest in it after it crossed the Atlantic. Sharpe had described it as an old machine, useless for military purposes, and had noted that it had been damaged in transit. A Canadian major reported seeing it lying on the road opposite the ordnance depot at Salisbury and said he had ordered it removed to a place of safety. It turned up next at the Upavon Central Flying School, and in December, 1914, the airplane was on the move again, to the Canadian Division at Larkhill. But for some reason the ordnance depot at Salisbury kept its propeller.

Nothing was heard of the airplane for several months, until a sergeant reported it was still at Larkhill. The report was passed along to Canadian authorities with the cautious comment: "What do you think?" Apparently the Canadians preferred not to think about it.

In May, 1915, there were rumours of a plane abandoned "somewhere on Salisbury Plain," and in June an officer who had been "rather successful in finding bicycles and other properties" in the Salisbury area was detailed to trace the machine.

The search was thorough but unrewarding. A contractor who was given the job of clearing up after the Canadians at Larkhill said he had found some airplane parts and sold them for scrap, but he could not be sure they came from the missing Burgess-Dunne. A few spare parts were found in a clump of woods near the Canadian encampment. At a garage in Salisbury the radiator was salvaged in good condition, and two inner tubes turned up, mysteriously, at the Bustard Inn. That is all that is known about Canada's first military aircraft.

Certainly aviation was the remotest thing from the mind of Lieutenant Bishop of the Mississauga Horse. When the First Contingent of the Canadian Expeditionary Force sailed from Quebec City on October 1, 1914—the largest armed force ever to cross the Atlantic until then—Bishop was not even among those present. He was in a military hospital with pneumonia plus an unidentified allergy. One doctor attributed it to the horses. Another thought it was the army food. Bishop, whose opinion wasn't asked, blamed the dust of the parade ground. Not that he really cared; he was comfortable and getting lots of attention.

A girl he had courted in Kingston ordered fresh flowers to be delivered to his bedside every morning. Bishop found this flattering, but dangerous to his romance with Margaret Burden, who visited him every afternoon. So he arranged with his sister to call at the hospital every day at lunchtime, and insisted on presenting her with the daily bouquet. Louie, who was studying law in Toronto, probably saw through his dilemma, but she accepted the flowers graciously and without comment, thereby saving her brother from embarrassing questions.

Soon after Bishop left the hospital he was transferred to an active service unit, the Seventh Canadian Mounted Rifles, then mobilizing in London, Ontario, under Colonel Ibbotson "Ibb" Leonard. Bishop was the youngest officer in the regiment—not quite twenty-one years old. Because of his skill in shooting and in dismantling and reassembling weapons he was put in charge of the machine-gun section.

A few weeks later Bishop's career nearly came to an untimely end. On a training exercise he had an accident that was reported thus in the local newspaper: "Lieutenant Bishop of the Seventh CMR was seriously injured and had a close call from being killed this afternoon when a horse he was riding suddenly reared and, losing its balance, fell backward on him, fracturing a rib and shaking him up very seriously. The horse escaped injury."

Early in June when the Seventh got its orders to sail for England Billy formally proposed to Margaret Burden. She accepted him, but at the romantic moment when he should have slipped the ring on her finger he realized in panic that he had forgotten to buy a ring. Margaret was gracious about the oversight. "Your RMC class ring will do for now," she said.

In Montreal a week later the Seventh and their seven hundred horses crowded aboard the cattle ship *Caledonia*. The Atlantic voyage lasted fourteen days, but seemed interminable. The *Caledonia* carried more men—to say nothing of more horses—than she had been built for. The sea was rough. The horses became seasick, and so did the men. Many horses died and had to be thrown overboard. The men lived under miserable conditions, and in constant fear of being sent to the bottom by torpedoes. Halfway across a thoroughly despondent Billy Bishop wrote to Margaret: "I wonder if I shall ever come back to you."

The last few days of the voyage were particularly harrowing. Off the coast of Ireland German U-boats attacked the convoy. The cavalrymen watched from the rails of the *Caledonia* as other ships around them were blown up and sunk. "I was petrified," Bishop later admitted. But the *Caledonia* bore a charmed life and sailed unscathed into Plymouth harbour in thick fog at four o'clock on the morning of June 23, 1915.

Five days later the Seventh moved into Shorncliffe military camp near the popular peacetime summer resort of Folkestone on the English Channel. That night the Canadians could see the brilliant flashes of artillery fire across the Channel in France. It was an eerie and frightening introduction to the reality of war.

But after a few days such distant dangers began to seem preferable to the comforts and safety of Shorncliffe. Bishop wrote home:

> They call Shorncliffe "military Hell." That's an understatement. The wind swirls in off the Channel constantly. When it brings rain the whole place becomes an incredible morass of muck, mud and mire with the special added unpleasantness that only horses in large quantity can contribute. Training becomes a travesty. Horses get stuck fast up to their fetlocks and when riders dismount they sink above their ankles. When it stops raining and the ground dries out for a few days we pray for rain again because the dirty dust is worse, if possible, than the mud. It gets into the tents—or such tents as the wind hadn't blown away. It gets into the eyes, ears, noses and other body orifices of men and of horses. It makes the horses so restless that we fear a stampede. It gives men a sort of *cafard* or desert madness. And to think that I had expected to go into battle astride a charger.

On one particularly grim day Bishop had succeeded in getting mired in the middle of the parade ground. Suddenly out of the low clouds a trim little fighter plane emerged. It landed hesitatingly in a nearby field as if reluctant to soil its wheels in the mud. The pilot apparently had lost his bearings. In a few minutes he got them and took off into the clouds.

"How long I stood there peering at the spot where the plane had disappeared I do not know," Bishop recalled later. "But when I turned to slog my way back through the mud I knew this was the only way to fight a war: up there above the clouds and in the summer sunshine."

That was wishful thinking, of course. Bishop had no reason to believe that it was possible for a Canadian cavalryman to apply for transfer to the adventurous Royal Flying Corps. What's more, he had no reason to believe that he had any qualifications as a fighter pilot. Apart from the homemade glider he had piloted on its first and only ill-fated flight, the closest he had been to an airplane was that day when one landed on a nearby field.

A few days later he and some fellow officers of the Seventh dropped in at the Grand Hotel in Folkestone. It was a favourite rendezvous for troops training in the area. Some of them favoured the Grand because it somehow managed despite wartime austerity to serve excellent food and drink. But what really attracted the young and camp-weary officers was the prevalence of girls and a dance orchestra. Bishop discovered the Grand very soon after he arrived at Shorncliffe and on many a night he sneaked away from camp for a couple of hours of relaxation. Colonel Leonard somehow learned of these sorties and kept tab on Bishop by placing a lighted candle in his tent and noting at next morning's inspection how much of the candle had burned before Bishop snuffed it out on retiring. Bishop saw through the ruse, and thereafter kept off the colonel's crime sheet by substituting his own candle.

But on this evening, with a legitimate pass, Bishop was less interested in girls and dancing than in the conversation of an airman who had landed his plane at Shorncliffe and started Bishop dreaming of going to war airborne.

"Look here, old boy," said the RFC pilot, "if you're so keen on it why don't you apply for a transfer?"

"How?"

"Next time you're in London drop in at the War Office and ask for a chap named Cecil—Lord Hugh Cecil. I don't know what his official job is but he seems to be able to wangle transfers for people who seem to be probable RFC types. He got *me* out of cavalry, for instance."

Bishop was cautious about putting too much faith into barroom conversations, and he filed the airman's suggestion in a remote corner of his mind. He forgot about it almost entirely in the events of the next few weeks. On a night bivouac exercise in a cold and persistent rainstorm he suffered a recurrence of the pneumonia that had plagued him earlier in Canada. It had put him into hospital for two weeks and when he was discharged, cured but feeble, he was given convalescent leave and departed for London.

He got a room at the stately Royal Automobile Club in Pall Mall, which had been converted into a haven for Canadian officers on leave. Bishop found the pleasures available to a young overseas officer so much to his liking that it was not until the morning he was due to leave for Shorncliffe that he remembered about Lord Hugh Cecil. He decided to risk the penalties of being absent without leave, and make his way to the War Office.

In the papers of Lord Hugh Cecil there is no record of an audience he gave a young Canadian cavalryman named Billy Bishop on a Monday morning in July, 1915. Nevertheless it was a somewhat historic event, since it got Bishop into the air force. To Bishop, Lord Hugh seemed a rather elderly lieutenant (he was forty-six at the time, and the rank was one of those bits of English understatement) who asked strange questions of applicants for transfer to the RFC.

Actually Lord Hugh was a man of considerable distinction. As the Member of Parliament for Oxford University he had formed the Hughlians, a group of progressive-minded rebels within the Conservative Party. A member of the Hughlians and a close friend of Cecil's was Winston Churchill, at whose wedding Cecil had been best man.

When Cecil was put in charge of recruiting for the Royal Flying Corps there existed no scientific criteria of the characteristics that made a good airman, and Cecil had to improvise his own questionnaire. This he now propounded to Bishop:

Lord Hugh: Do you ski?

Bishop: Yes. (He didn't, really, but he thought that to an Englishman a Canadian who did not ski would seem an eccentric.)

Lord Hugh: Can you ride a horse?

Bishop: I am a cavalry officer.

Lord Hugh: Doesn't always follow, but righto, you ride. How well can you drive a car?

Bishop (never having driven a car): Very well.

Lord Hugh: Can you ride a motorcycle?

Bishop (having done so once): Excellently.

Lord Hugh: How well can you skate?

Bishop (at last almost truthfully): Perfectly.

Lord Hugh: Did you go in for sports at school—running?

Bishop (deciding that the RFC wouldn't go back to Owen Sound to check, and anyway he *had* finished second in the YMCA cross-country): Yes, a great deal.

Those seemed to be all the qualifications Lord Hugh needed. Bishop asked himself: "What sort of game *is* this flying, anyway?" When he had become familiar with the series of improvisations that went into the organization of the early RFC, he came to this conclusion: "I can only believe Lord Hugh's cross-examination stemmed from the belief that you must ask the candidate *something*, if only to impress the young man with the importance of the occasion. Having no dossier on flight statistics on which to base a questionnaire, Lord Hugh was simply doing what he could to make the occasion seem important."

Next Lord Hugh tossed a bitter disappointment at Bishop: If he applied for transfer as a fighter pilot, it might be six months or a year before he could get in, but there was an immediate need for observers, or, as Lord Hugh put it, "The chap who goes along for the ride."

Bishop asked for a few days to think it over. He returned to Shorncliffe and a difficult interview with Colonel Ibbotson Leonard. In the first place Bishop was returning late from leave. In the second place he had to report to his commanding officer that he had applied for transfer without permission or consultation. Fortunately for Bishop, Leonard was an easygoing man. Bishop explained his dilemma over getting into the RFC immediately as an observer or waiting to be accepted as a pilot.

"Well, Bish, I'll tell you this," said Leonard. "If I were you, knowing what sort of pilot you're likely to be, I'd sooner trust somebody else to do the flying than do it myself."

Bishop was apparently impressed with this rather garbled piece of advice, for he wired Lord Hugh that he would report for training as an observer.

OBSERVER

"THIS FLYING is the most wonderful invention," Bishop wrote home when he made his first training flight after joining 21 Squadron at Netheravon on Salisbury Plain on September 1, 1915. "A man ceases to be human up there. He feels that nothing is impossible."

Actually Bishop's enthusiasm was a rather exaggerated compliment to the primitive old Avro two-seater trainer, which looked as if it had been strung together with wire. Its design was an adaptation of Sir Alliott Verdon Roe's pioneer tractor design. "Tractor" describes a plane pulled rather than pushed through the air by its propeller. The Avro had barely enough power to lift itself, a student and an instructor into the air with no armament whatsoever. Later Bishop admitted that in attempting to gain altitude "she struggled and shook and gasped like a freight train going up a mountain grade."

The history of aerial warfare was barely one year old when Bishop made that first flight, and the list of casualties by enemy action was negligible. On August 19, 1914, both sides made their first aerial reconnaissances across each other's lines over the battlefield in France. German and Allied planes passed within a few yards of each other, but because both were unarmed they could not do much harm to each other short of ramming.

In fact, the greatest hazard of airmen was rifle fire from the ground. On the day of the first reconnaissance Sergeant Major Dillings, an observer, was struck in the leg by a rifle bullet fired from the ground and became the first air casualty.

On August 25 Lieutenant H. D. Harvey-Kelly became the first Allied airman to bring down an enemy plane, by crowding it from above and forcing it to land. It came down behind the British lines, and when Harvey-Kelly landed to claim the crew as prisoners he was astonished to see the German observer kicking and punching the pilot. The observer, it turned out, was the superior officer and was punishing the pilot for his poor airmanship.

Soon after that the airmen started to smuggle weapons aboard their aircraft (neither side had yet authorized airborne armament). This armament included rifles, pistols, light machine-guns— and some pilots even took up bricks to drop on enemy planes. But the real value of aerial reconnaissance as a vital weapon of war first became apparent early in September, 1914, when British and French airmen returning from flights over enemy lines reported that the German army had overextended itself, and seemed to have walked into a pocket. On the basis of this information General Joffre, the French field commander, decided to attack. The result was the Battle of the Marne, which was the first engagement to turn the tide of German advance, repulsed a possible march on Paris, and forced the first retreat of the German army.

On September 7 Sir John French, the British commander, issued the first dispatch to mention the Royal Flying Corps—and incidentally to give the first RFC score against the enemy:

> They have furnished me with complete and accurate information which has been of incalculable value in the conduct of operations. Fired at constantly by friend and foe, and not hesitating to fly in every kind of weather, they have remained undaunted throughout. Further by actually fighting in the

air they have succeeded in destroying five of the enemy's machines.

The lessons of the Battle of the Marne caused the British high command to change its attitude toward military aviation abruptly. Where once the generals had regarded the airmen as wild young desperadoes and the airplane as a dangerous toy, the airman now assumed a serious place in war strategy. By the time Bishop joined, the RFC was working hard on new techniques and new equipment.

British reconnaissance planes were now being equipped with one-way wireless to signal the artillery batteries and direct their fire, and cameras were mounted to photograph enemy positions for scrutiny by the battery commanders. The one-way Morse signalling never developed into an efficient liaison between air and ground, largely because the observers never developed much skill with Morse.

"And no wonder," Bishop recalled. "To learn Morse we were sent off every afternoon with huge searchlights and divided into two groups about a thousand yards apart on the level plain. Our procedure was to memorize our messages before we went out and send them to the other fellows while an instructor watched and checked. They were always correct, of course. Then he would leave us with instructions to 'carry on,'—whereupon we would find the nearest haystack and sit behind it chatting and smoking and dozing while one member of each team kept flashing the lights in case anyone from the base turned a suspicious eye in our direction." It wasn't until two years later that Bishop, home on leave, saw Henry Ford first demonstrate two-way ground-to-air wireless at Dayton, Ohio.

Bishop found aerial photography much more interesting and challenging because it required great concentration and precision. Bishop gave a preview of the superb muscle-nerve-eye co-ordination that was later to make him the deadliest of aerial fighters, by taking photographs so expertly that the War Office used them as standards of excellence.

In December, 1915, Bishop was put in charge of all new observers who joined the squadron at Netheravon, and was responsible for their training. In later years when planes were perfected to the point where it was difficult to select and train men efficient enough to handle them, Bishop recalled mournfully that the airmen of 1916 were saddled with machines that were too primitive for the capabilities of the men.

The casualty rate among Bishop's students was high. Wings fell off planes, engines failed. Forced landings occurred daily. One pilot set a record of seventy-five forced landings, and many more came close to this record. The reason for this extremely high figure was very simple—there was no means of escape from a disabled airplane; the parachute was still a long way from becoming accepted as a reliable method of escape. Bishop could claim only one forced landing. His pilot was unhurt and Bishop hobbled away from the wreck with no more damage than a sprained ankle. "The haystack," he reported, "was demolished."

At Christmas, 1915, 21 Squadron's training was, in theory, completed, and it needed only its new planes to be ready for front-line service. The move to France was planned for New Year's Day. The men of 21 Squadron were given a week's leave. Bishop went to London with a fellow officer, Harry Kennedy. They tried to make every minute count. They went to matinees at the Hippodrome, to the durable revue "Chu Chin Chow," to dancing at the Four Hundred club, and held hilarious reunions with RMC classmates.

Christmas Day was spent at the liveliest hotel in London. "Merry Christmas," Bishop wrote his parents. "Much merrier, I hope, than it is here. Harry and I have decided not to call on anyone we know today as they will look at us in such a 'poor boy so far from mother' sort of way. Instead we are going to the Regent Palace Hotel to watch the gay life. It is full of people on 'weekend honeymoons' and the grill and restaurants are full of love girls and men intent on picking them up. It is one of the most amusing spots in town and the only place that does not look like a cemetery at Christmas."

Twenty-One Squadron was supposed to take delivery of its new improved planes in time for its departure to France on New Year's Day, 1916, but they had not arrived when the squadron crossed the Channel. ("Being flyers we crossed the Channel by water, of course," Bishop wrote home.)

The weather in southern England had been miserable. The January weather in northern France, at Boisdinghem, near St. Omer, reminded Bishop of his native Owen Sound on the shores of Georgian Bay. Cold winds and sleet storms blew in from the Pas de Calais. At times the planes had to take off and land in four inches of snow. Pilots and observers piled on all the bulky clothing they could lay their hands on—long leather coats lined with sheep-skin, leather helmets, waist boots and heavy gauntlets—but they still returned from the long patrols chilled to the bone. On his first flight over enemy territory Bishop's face was severely frostbitten. Even on clear and relatively mild days the weather was a hazard. The prevailing westerly wind meant that the homeward journey was a constant struggle against headwinds and dwindling fuel supplies. Many a pilot and observer had to walk back to their base after making forced landings with dead engines. The casualty rate of aircraft undercarriages and wings was depressingly high.

Anti-aircraft fire, which in the early months of the war was regarded as a noisy nuisance, now was becoming increasingly accurate. "It's perhaps more frightening than destructive," Bishop wrote home. "Without warning greyish-white puffs burst all around the machine, followed by a terrifying shriek of shrapnel fragments flying in all directions. You suffer a terrible moment of suspense while your pilot changes course to get out of the aim of the anti-aircraft gunners."

Once Bishop's pilot, Roger Neville, failed to get out fast enough and Bishop became one of the few airmen to be wounded by anti-aircraft fire. It was only a slight bruise on the side of his head, but a few inches difference in direction could well have killed him.

But now the Allied reconnaissance planes were encountering a new and infinitely greater danger—the "Fokker menace," new Fokker planes equipped with synchronized machine-guns firing through the planes' propellers. When Sir John French announced on September 7, 1914, that Allied airmen had shot down five enemy planes he did not specify what weapons or tactics were involved, but obviously they were the primitive ones: pistols, rifles, light unattached machine-guns, menacing manoeuvres, perhaps even bricks. Certainly no authentic gun-and-plane combination was attempted before April 1, 1915—nearly nine months after the start of the war. On that day a French pilot named Roland Garros, flying a single-seater Morane Bullet, with a fixed machine-gun pointed forward and firing through the propeller, streaked down behind a German observation plane, riddled it with bullets and sent it spiralling down in flames.

Garros had contrived a primitive device to enable him to shoot through his propeller without smashing the blades—metal collars attached to the blades in the line of fire to deflect bullets. The first time Garros tried his deflector gear he shot down an enemy plane by aiming his own airplane at the target. For a short time it seemed that the Allies had stumbled on a valuable secret weapon. But two weeks after he first used his deflectors he had to make a forced landing behind enemy lines when his motor failed. He was captured before he could set fire to the plane, and the invention fell intact into German hands.

It was turned over to Anthony Fokker, the young Dutch airplane designer who was building the Germans' best warplanes. (It was ironic that shortly before the war Fokker had offered his advanced designs to Britain, Italy and Russia. All three Allied countries turned him down, but the Germans encouraged him and provided facilities for research and production of Fokker aircraft.)

As a result, when World War I broke out German air strength was comparable to that of her three aircraft-building adversaries, Britain, France and Italy. "Fokker" was a menacing name to the Allies from the first day of the war. It became associated particularly with the Richthofen circus which was by all odds the most lethal formation of air fighters ever to take to the air in World War I.

Not until the war ended did the Allied airmen discover that Fokker, far from being an arch-villain, was a mild and peace-loving young man. In his autobiography he admitted that the feats of Bishop, Ball, Richthofen and other air aces filled him with awe. "Had I been an aviator, as I intended, I could never have joined that brave crew. They were of stouter stuff than I. Indeed, if all people were like me, the world would be long at peace." Fokker also revealed that after the war started Britain tried secretly to offer him $10,000 to leave Germany, return to Holland and start making planes for the Allies. "Perhaps I would have," Fokker wrote, "but the offer never reached me. The German secret service, which kept me under close surveillance, sidetracked the offer. It wasn't until years later when the German military structure had collapsed that a Berlin friend of mine in the secret service informed me of it."

When Fokker examined Roland Garros' metal bullet deflectors, he told the German air force officials that there was no real future for that type of device. The constant hammering would eventually damage the propeller, he felt, and worse, might also damage the engine itself.

But the basic idea that Garros had in mind—a device that would allow bullets to be shot through a whirling propeller—intrigued him. Using only that proposition, Fokker invented an "interrupter gear" that prevented an airplane's machine-gun firing when a propeller blade was in its path. All the pilot had to do was to keep his finger on the firing button while the target was in his sights, and bullets would stream uninterruptedly through the whirling propeller at the rate of six hundred a minute.

Ironically, the German High Command was highly skeptical when Fokker first demonstrated his interrupter gear. The generals ordered him to test it himself in aerial combat. Fokker, as we now know, was anything but bloodthirsty; but he accepted the challenge. For several days he cruised the aerial no-man's-land over the trenches without finding a victim. Then one day he spotted a French Farman plane near Douai. Fokker dived and caught the French plane squarely in his sights at two hundred yards' range. But he never fired his gun.

"Suddenly," he said later, "I decided that the whole job could go to hell. I had no stomach for this business, no wish to kill Frenchmen for Germans—let them do their own killing."

In spite of Fokker's failure to "test-fly" his invention, the German authorities decided to adopt it on an experimental basis. Oswald Boelcke, one of the Germans' top fighter pilots, became the first pilot to bring down a plane with an interrupter-controlled machine-gun. A few days later another German ace, Max Immelmann, claimed the second plane. From then on it was enthusiastically accepted, and for a time it gave the German air force such an advantage that it practically dominated the air over the front lines. Then, inevitably, the same chance that had delivered Garros' invention to the enemy worked in favour of the Allies. A plane fitted with Fokker's gear was shot down intact behind the British lines. Hastily the device was duplicated in French and English factories, and once more the opposing air forces fought on even terms.

One bitterly cold afternoon Bishop watched a Fokker shoot down a British observation plane in flames. With a hawk-like swoop the German pilot attacked his slower adversary from behind, poured bullets into it, then pulled up in a half-loop, righted his plane at the top of the loop and thus gave himself a head start in the direction of home and safety. It was a manoeuvre he had perfected by hours of painstaking practice, and it was forevermore to bear his name: the Immelmann Turn.

Immelmann was the first fighter pilot to establish an unmistakable identity, a trade mark, for himself. Well, perhaps not quite unmistakable. There was a story about an English pilot whose machine was crippled in combat but made a safe landing behind the German lines. The German pilot landed nearby, drew his revolver and said to the Englishman, "Sir, you are my prisoner." The other answered, "You are Immelmann, so I am not ashamed." The German answered, "I am sorry to disappoint you. I am only Boelcke."

Bishop, in those first weeks of 1916, was no more than a highly expendable observer. By mid-January the long-promised new planes were delivered—"a strange flying contraption known as the R.E.7 (Reconnaissance Experimental No. 7)," he wrote.

It was a machine designed to mount four guns, cameras, and all manner of other equipment including a 500-pound bomb lashed to the fuselage. The idea was to fly over the target, take a quick look over the side of the cockpit, pull the wire cable— and away the bomb would go. All that was wrong was that this machine stoutly refused to leave the ground when all this gear, plus pilot and observer, were packed into it.

The first time we tried to take up our R.E.7, Roger Neville gunned across Boisdinghem airport at least a dozen times into the wind, but the wheels never left the ground. Consultation between senior officers followed. They decided that we should try to become airborne *without* the 500-pound bomb. The wheels bounced a few times, but we still weren't in the air at the point on the runway where we would have to throttle down and turn around to avoid running off the field.

More consultation. They decided to move us to the larger field at St. Omer, ten miles away, in the hope that with a longer run the R.E.7 might consent to struggle into the air.

So Bishop lugged his four machine-guns aboard a truck bound for St. Omer, while Neville took the lightened R.E.7 into the air.

The bombs, by common consent, were left behind at Boisdinghem. On the longer field at St. Omer the R.E.7 finally took the air with its crew of two and armament reduced to a pair of machine-guns. These guns, however, gave Bishop little comfort. "It will always remain a question of reasonable doubt whether anybody could have fired the guns at an enemy," he recalled later, "because to fire a bullet into the clear you would first have to shoot through the maze of wires between the upper and lower wings which gave the R.E.7 the appearance of a bird cage."

Even with only a fraction of the equipment its designers had assigned to it on the drawing board, the R.E.7 was, in parlance of the RFC, "a pig—on a windy day a boy on a bicycle could pass it."

It was possibly the most dangerous plane ever accepted as operational by the Allies, for one reason. Between its top speed and the speed at which it stalled and spun out of control there was a margin of barely twenty miles an hour. It was designed to reach eighty miles an hour but seldom could be nursed to sixty, and it stalled at forty-eight miles an hour. This characteristic made take-offs, landings and manoeuvring in the air agonizingly difficult. Yet it was impossible to treat the R.E.7 gently. "When a pilot wants to change direction he has to *throw* the stick in the direction he wants to go—really slam it," Bishop complained. "Putting on rudder was done about as gently as throwing out the clutch of an automobile. The things were nearly as manoeuvrable as ten-ton trucks, but by no means as safe."

The RFC tried an emergency operation on the R.E.7, in the form of heavier and more powerful engines. But the experiment was a dismal failure. The new engines were too heavy for their supports, which snapped off with disconcerting frequency if the planes were landed at all roughly—as they usually were. The Suicide Squadron, as 21 was now dubbed, hastily switched back to the old underpowered engines.

For a time 21 Squadron was placed in semi-retirement by being withdrawn from the front and assigned to fly aerial cover over General Sir Douglas Haig's headquarters at St. Omer. It was a strategic target that housed not Haig and his staff, but visiting political dignitaries and even royalty from time to time. Bishop was dubious about the wisdom of defending it with 21 Squadron's lumbering aircraft: "Day in and out we beetled over headquarters and the adjoining town. Fortunately the enemy did not seem to know we were there, for what we could have done to defend the place I do not know. Presumably we would have tried to join issue with the enemy if he had come along and, I imagine, have been shot down ingloriously for our pains."

But in March, 1916, the Allies' need for air power was so desperate that the Suicide Squadron was recalled to front-line duty. Sir Douglas Haig, the British commander-in-chief, had decided to launch an unprecedented aerial offensive in hope of breaking the stalemate of trench warfare. On March 9, 1916, six R.E.7's from 21 Squadron were part of a formation of thirty-one aeroplanes that bombed Carvin Junction some twenty miles behind the enemy lines. It was the largest formation ever assembled for a raid. To enable the R.E.7's to lift the bombs they were stripped of their guns and ammunition. They had to fly deep behind enemy lines, find their targets, drop the bombs and make their undefended way back home.

Next day Bishop wrote to Margaret: "In the air you feel only intense excitement. You cheer and laugh and keep your spirits up. You are all right just after you have landed as you search your machine for bullet and shrapnel holes. But two hours later when you are quietly sitting in your billet you feel a sudden loneliness. You want to lie down and cry."

In April the Suicide Squadron moved to another aerodrome at Hesdin. Now the unit was assigned to observation in the area between Albert and Péronne—the Somme. This open country— the clumps of woods had long since been reduced to ragged stumps by shellfire—was the front on which the summer offensive would be launched. As the weather improved so the number of reconnaissance flights increased. A Prussian soldier complained in a letter to his parents that the "English will soon be taking the very caps off our heads."

In addition to fatigue and nervous exhaustion, Bishop was plagued with misfortune on the ground. Driving a tender loaded with equipment to repair a crashed machine a few miles from the aerodrome, Bishop collided with an army lorry and was severely shaken up.

A few days later he was inspecting his machine in the hangar when a supporting cable above him broke and struck him on the head. He was unconscious for two days and medical examinations showed that he had narrowly escaped a serious skull fracture.

Some days later he had a tooth pulled. It became infected and he had to stay in hospital for a week. Next Roger Neville cracked up the plane in a rough landing. Bishop was thrown heavily forward and cracked his knee against a metal brace. He could barely walk and the pain was severe, but he refused to be relieved of flying duty.

In spite of his apparent accident proneness, Bishop believed that having survived such incidents he had been granted some sort of immunity from fatal or serious injury. In a letter home he said fatalistically, "If I am for it, then I am for it and nothing can save me. But I firmly believe that I am NOT for it." And as if to emphasize this conviction he added, "I have the most fantastic luck under fire. The others call it the luck of the devil."

Actually Bishop's great fear was being made prisoner. "If I can barely live with British discipline, how could I live in a German prison camp? The other day a poor German pilot lost his way and landed on our side of the lines. He was only testing his machine at that. I felt terribly sorry for him when I saw the dazed look on his face. I would rather die fighting than be captured."

Bishop was due for three weeks' leave at the end of the month. No one yearned for it more—three weeks with no flying, twenty-one days of nothing but the joys of London. He was physically exhausted and his nerves were at breaking point. But one more major operation remained to be carried out. The exercise was an experiment in liaison work between the Royal Flying Corps and the infantry, which could be launched at the height of an attack. Smoke bombs and flash shells were to be used as markers and the reflection of pocket mirrors were to be used for signalling. It was the idea of the British Commander-in-Chief, and the airmen called it "Dougie Haig's show."

First there was a week of diligent practice. Mail bags were used in place of smoke bombs. Bishop so perfected his aim that he could drop the bag within eighteen paces of the target. A hit anywhere within sixty yards was considered accurate.

The full-scale performance was held on the morning of May 2, 1916, the day that Bishop and a group of others from the Suicide Squadron were to go on leave. It was a complete success and Haig sent a message of congratulation. But Bishop and his comrades did not wait to hear it. As soon as they had taken off their flying clothes they hailed the first available motor transport for Boulogne, where they boarded a boat for England.

Bishop's jinx sailed with him. During the short voyage bottles of champagne began furtively appearing, first from one kit bag, then from another. By the end of the Channel crossing spirits were high. A khaki mob surged on deck as the boat pulled into the harbour at Folkestone. There was much good-natured jostling in an effort to be first ashore. In this exuberant scramble, Bishop slipped on the gangplank and stumbled forward on the concrete pier with three other men on top of him.

He felt a sharp pain in his knee—the same knee he had injured in the crash landing with Neville. But Bishop refused to let this change his plans for a riotous leave. He denied himself none of the feverish pleasures that London and its people offered so eagerly to men on leave from the battlefields. He almost succeeded in forgetting that he had a crippled knee. "When I thought of it, it hurt like hell—so I stopped thinking of it." But late at night, after the festivities, the pain kept him awake. Bishop found that generous doses of brandy brought unconsciousness that passed for sleep. On the last day of his leave Bishop faced the bitter fact that he would have to get medical attention, and secretly he hoped that the doctor would find him unfit to return to France. With a feeling of deep guilt Bishop hobbled into the RFC hospital on Bryanston Square.

"It was almost a relief," he confessed, "when the doctors found that in addition to the cracked knee, which was my fault for neglecting, I had a severely strained heart—which was comfortingly blamed on the tension of the long patrols and on the continual changes in altitude and temperature."

The verdict: confinement to bed for an indefinite period of treatment and rest.

PILOT

I N MID-AFTERNOON a few days after Bishop had been bedded down he awoke from a drugged sleep and found himself gazing into the eyes of a woman who was bending over him. She was old and lean, with sparse hair severely drawn back to show unusually large ears. Her most remarkable features were her wide-set luminous eyes that appeared much younger than the rest of her, eyes that penetrated and probed and yet were kindly and reassuring. Bishop had met one of the three most important women in his life.

Lady St. Helier was at that time nearly seventy years old and already a legend in English and international society and politics. But an important chapter of the legend remained to be written, and young Bishop was to be part of it.

Years later the London *Times* published a memoir of Lady St. Helier that might have been written with Bishop in mind: "One might say that many a person's first intimation of approaching success was the discovery that Lady St. Helier knew all about him. She begged him to come and see her; she introduced him to those who might be useful to him. She made much of him. She put new heart into him."

The importance of this woman who so quietly entered Bishop's life, and so profoundly influenced it, is indicated by the celebrities,

dating back to the mid-Victorian era, who were proud of her friendship—Lord Randolph Churchill, Whistler and Millais, Tennyson
and Browning, Parnell, the ill-fated Irish patriot.

> But, [the *Times* memoir continued] the general society that
> gathered at her house can only be summed up in the word
> "everybody." She literally went everywhere, including public
> as well as private houses, and she knew everybody—not merely
> those of high station, but quite simple toilers and moilers. First
> in Harley Street, then in Portland Place she was almost world-
> famous as a hostess. Of her one could say that she did really
> have the world and his wife at her house.
>
> It was open house upstairs. Above the entertainment floors
> she had staying visitors, whom she called her "lodgers," and
> sometimes when the evening guests were leaving, they could
> see one or two of the "lodgers" discreetly mounting the stair-
> case towards their resting places....
>
> But she did not wait for people to be excessively well known.
> She recognized talent and genius while their possessors were
> still poorly rewarded by the world. I think she was the first
> London hostess of importance who sprinkled her gatherings
> with quite young people....
>
> Another tremendous originality in Lady St. Helier's method
> of entertaining was her mixing up the people who might be
> described as enemies in public. She refused to admit that a
> sound old Tory must not be invited to meet a Radical of dan-
> gerously advanced views, or that one of the old-fashioned crit-
> ics must not encounter the author or actress who had been
> his victim.

Lady St. Helier was independently wealthy. Her husband, a
judge of England's Probate Court, had left her an estate of half a
million dollars when he died in 1905, a few months after being created Lord St. Helier. But her role of society hostess was only part

of this remarkable woman's activities. She was an elected alderman of London County Council and a tireless fighter for legislation to better the lives of London's lower-paid workers, and of defective children.

When the First World War broke out she added to her other interests the organization of auxiliary services for the hospitals turned over to ill and wounded servicemen. In this last role she came that day in May, 1916, to the bedside of Lieutenant Billy Bishop.

"I saw your name on the register," she told him, "and I was sure that someone named William Bishop, from Canada, *must* be the son of my friend Will Bishop. And when I looked at you I was sure of it, you look very much like him."

Bishop stared at her uncomprehendingly. He thought the drugs he had been given must have affected his understanding of what this unusual visitor was telling him.

"My father's name is Will," he said, "but he lives in Owen Sound, a small town in Ontario ..."

"Then you *are* Will Bishop's son," said Lady St. Helier, beaming. She explained that before the war she had visited Ottawa and had been introduced to Will Bishop at a reception given by Prime Minister Sir Wilfrid Laurier. It was an indication of Lady St. Helier's boundless capacity for friendship, for "collecting people," as well as of her incredible memory for names and faces, that out of the scores of strangers she had met on an evening more than five years before, she instantly remembered the name and appearance of one of them—and remembered him, moreover, as "my friend."

When Bishop asked his father why he had not given him a letter of introduction to his charming and influential English friend Lady St. Helier, Will Bishop had no idea what his son was talking about. When Bishop went into detail, Will could conjure up only a vague recollection of having met Lady St. Helier.

By the middle of June Bishop was allowed to leave the hospital. At Lady St. Helier's insistence he became one of her "lodgers" in her four-storey mansion at 52 Portland Place. A strong bond of affection had grown between the young Canadian country boy and one of Britain's most sophisticated noblewomen during her regular visits to the hospital. She told him of her own only son, member of a Guards regiment, who had died of typhoid years before in India. In a rare sentimental moment this indomitable woman told Bishop: "You are the kind of grandson my son would have given me if he had lived."

Her voice was choked. She was close to tears. It was the first time Bishop had seen her show anything but cheerfulness and self-assurance. He tried to comfort her in the only way he knew, by saying with an impertinent grin: "Yes, Granny." From then on he called her "Granny"—and she introduced him to her vast array of friends as "my grandson."

Life at 52 Portland Place was much more exciting than in the hospital. But although Bishop knew he was fortunate to be there, he found it impossible to enter into the spirit of Lady St. Helier's perpetual house party. He was exhausted and dispirited.

"You need home leave," Lady St. Helier told him.

"Not a chance," Bishop said. "I've done nothing to deserve it. A few months ago when my father was ill I thought of applying, but it turned out I didn't need to."

"Your father was ill?"

"A slight stroke. But he recovered quickly. My mother cabled: 'Stay where you are. You've never done anything so well before.'"

Lady St. Helier laughed. "I still think you should have a holiday at home," she said. A week later Bishop was summoned before a medical board. The verdict came quickly: indefinite home leave.

Bishop suspected that "Granny" had pulled some of the numerous strings at her disposal, but he was too elated with the outcome to question how it had been arrived at.

Joyously Bishop boarded a ship for Canada, for a reunion with his family—and with Margaret Burden. The visit could only be described as uneventful. In a country busily mustering its manpower, men in uniform were everywhere, and even though the natty double-breasted jacket and jaunty cap of the RFC had rarely been seen in Canada, Bishop attracted few glances during the long journey from Halifax to Montreal to Toronto and finally to Owen Sound.

In his home town Bishop's arrival attracted a little more attention, in the form of a newspaper item that hinted he was something of a war hero, back home to convalesce from wounds received in action; Bishop was acutely embarrassed. "If 21 Squadron ever reads this," he told his parents gloomily, "I'll never hear the last of it." But somehow his proud mother and father regarded the fanciful newspaper report as no more than he deserved.

Margaret Burden's father, a stern and righteous man who had married into a wealthy family and was therefore suspicious of the motives of the young man who seemed interested in his daughter, had been less than enthusiastic over Bishop's courtship of Margaret. But now he gave his consent to the marriage. Margaret seemed to be as much in love as ever. Charlie Burden had hoped that the long separation would make her forget Bishop, but she had not looked at another man during his months at the front.

Billy and Margaret decided to postpone their wedding, however. He was determined to become a fighter pilot; he was realistically aware that as such his chances of survival were rather less than even, and he did not consider it fair to Margaret to make her a widow almost as soon as she became a wife. Bishop did finally present her with a proper engagement ring, however.

Early in September, 1916, Bishop returned to England. From the start everything went awry. When he reported to the War Office he was told that he could not collect his back pay until he reported to another medical board. The board's findings were disheartening: he was still unfit for active service. It would be at least a month before he would be allowed to return to France. Moreover his records had been lost, and this meant, for some reason Bishop could not fathom, that an application to train as a pilot was out of the question. That meant that when he eventually returned to the front it would be as an observer, with a new squadron, for by then

21 Squadron probably would not exist. The news from the front had shaken Bishop: the Suicide Squad had lived up to its name. It had been practically wiped out in the summer battles over the Somme.

Bishop lay on a bearskin rug in front of the fireplace at 52 Portland Place and grumbled to Granny St. Helier about War Office red tape. "Here I am, perfectly fit, and they won't take me back. They half promised that I could take pilot training, you know."

Lady St. Helier was sitting at an antique desk, writing letters. She had a unique method of turning out her correspondence. As each letter was finished she tossed it to the floor. From time to time a footman entered the room, gathered the scattered sheets and put them into the appropriate envelopes. Bishop never tired of watching this strange performance. Granny had explained that she evolved this system because her desk was so cluttered with letters, cards, invitations, London County Council reports and other assorted paperwork of an incredibly busy life that there was no room on her desk for her own letters.

"What can I do?" Bishop asked.

"Do about what?" said Lady St. Helier.

"You know—the War Office not accepting me for pilot training."

"Oh, I'm going to have a talk with Hugh Cecil and Winston Churchill," said Lady St. Helier casually.

"You know Mr. Churchill?"

"My dear boy, of course I know him—not that I've ever trusted him absolutely, or his father for that matter. Clementine Churchill is my great-niece, and I introduced her to Winston in this very room. As a matter of fact, their wedding reception was held here."

The wedding of Winston Churchill and Clementine Hozier in the spring of 1908 was, in fact, the highlight of the long and distinguished social career of Lady St. Helier. It was on a Saturday, and half of London lined the streets between St. Margaret's Church in Westminster and Lady St. Helier's house in Portland Place to cheer the young couple.

Churchill's proposal to Clementine Hozier was the coup of Lady St. Helier's matchmaking career, which had led to many of the most important matings in Britain's ruling classes. For years Churchill had been the most eligible—and most elusive—of bachelors. Time and again rumour had him engaged to one girl or another, but always the young statesman emerged unscathed. Then Lady St. Helier arranged an intimate dinner party that included her great-niece and Churchill.

"He didn't have a chance later that evening," Granny St. Helier told Bishop with a chuckle. "In fact, it was Clementine who kept Winston guessing for several weeks before she accepted him."

The Hoziers were far from wealthy, and their small house in Kensington was quite unsuitable for a fashionable wedding. So Lady St. Helier took over the arrangements. Clementine moved into 52 Portland Place four days before the wedding, was entertained at a glittering bridal tea, and left there for St. Margaret's Church. When the bridal party returned to Portland Place, rose petals from the bridesmaids' bouquets were strewn over the bride and groom instead of the traditional rice.

What Lady St. Helier said to Churchill and his erstwhile best man, Lord Hugh Cecil, Bishop never learned. But a few days later he was summoned back to the War Office. "Compared with the previous visit it was positively embarrassing," Bishop recalled. "Stiff formality was swept aside. Bureaucratic procedure became friendly co-operation. The brick walls of English protocol suddenly developed with open doors. My papers appeared from nowhere. I felt like saying, 'look, chaps, I'm only a lieutenant and observer asking for a chance to prove I can become a pilot.'"

But no influence could excuse Bishop from the necessity of a medical examination, and he became increasingly worried as the day of his appointment with the doctor drew near, only a few days after a medical board had ruled him not yet medically fit. He need not have worried. His own description of the ordeal suggested that Lady St. Helier's influence might, indeed, have penetrated into the medical service of the RFC: "After the doctor listened to my heart and banged my lungs and persuaded me to say 'aah' and 'ninety-nine,' he put me into a swivel chair, spun me around sharply, and suddenly invited me to spring to attention. Since I did not fall flat on my face I was presumed to be healthy and fit to fly."

A week later, on October 1, 1916, he was on his way to Brasenose College, Oxford, for a month of ground-school training at the School of Military Aeronautics. Bishop braced himself for a month of hard work. But he soon discovered that his training and experience as an observer put him at the top of the class in map reading, wireless and meteorology. He was one of the few in the class who had ever actually been in the air. He breezed through the examinations with high marks.

Next he went to Upavon Flying School on Salisbury Plain. Learning to fly, he soon discovered, was a casual and perfunctory process, which perhaps accounts for the large number of student pilots who crashed on their first attempt to solo.

The Farman "Shorthorn," one of the trainers used in those early days, was not a very great advance on the early machines of the Wright brothers, either in appearance or performance. Its fuselage, for example, consisted of open spars joining the wings and tailplanes. Instructor and pupil squeezed into a pod situated just ahead of the seventy-horsepower motor and its pusher propeller. In the event of a nosedive, the engine was almost certain to fall on the occupants, with fatal results. The Shorthorn barely topped sixty miles an hour, and a patient pilot could sometimes attain an altitude of three thousand feet in fifteen minutes.

The grim possibility is that some student pilots who crashed on their first solo flights did so because they had never actually been in control of a plane before. Instructors who were relative beginners in aviation themselves—but experienced enough to know how skittish and eccentric those early planes could be—were understandably nervous of trusting their lives to wholly inexperienced hands. Subconsciously some instructors kept a hand and foot on the dual controls throughout training flights. In most training planes the student was ahead of the instructor and could not see what the latter was doing. And a student had no way of knowing the difference in feel between controls wholly in his hands and those under the gentle guidance of a nervous instructor.

A young Scottish student pilot who took his training at the same time as Bishop suspected this was happening to him and accused his instructor of hogging the controls. The instructor indignantly denied it. The next time they went up on a training flight everything went off perfectly. After a smooth landing, the instructor praised the student for his progress.

"Congratulate yourself," said the student bitterly. *"I never put a hand or a foot to the controls!"*

Bishop felt that his own experience as an observer, a veteran of several missions over enemy territory, should again give him an advantage over student pilots who were starting from scratch. But from his first flight in a dual-control Farman trainer (disrespectfully referred to as a "Rumpty" because of its ungraceful lines) he discovered that "all the time I had been an innocent bystander."

"I tried very hard but it seemed to me that I just could not get the proper 'feel' of the machine. Sometimes my instructor would roundly curse me for being ham-handed when I gripped the controls too tightly, every muscle tense, in my anxiety to do well. That would send me to the other extreme and I would become 'timid-handed'—and when you go timid with a Rumpty she is very likely to fly you into the ground. She didn't like to be rough-housed, either, but she needed to be treated with a firm hand. My instructor and I both suffered tortures. So when suddenly one day—after I had logged just three hours of actual flying time—he told me I could go up alone, I had my doubts as to whether it was confidence or desperation that influenced his decision."

The moment when he climbed into the cockpit, alone for the first time, Bishop remembered as the loneliest moment of his life.

Off to one side stood an ambulance with its engine running. Bishop knew that in the aerodrome hospital a doctor and nurses were on standby duty, "with knives sharpened and needles at the ready." The aerodrome personnel went about their duties with all the unsmiling efficiency of undertakers' helpers.

Bishop waved a "ready" signal with a cheerfulness he was far from feeling and took off in a shallow, staggering climb.

Once in the air I felt better [Bishop wrote to Margaret that night]. In fact, I felt like a king. I wasn't taking any liberties. I flew as straight ahead as I could, climbing steadily. At last I had to turn, and I tried a very slow gradual one. They told me afterward that I did some remarkable skidding, but I was blissfully ignorant of a little detail like that. Suddenly an awful thought came to me: sooner or later, somehow or other, I would have to get that plane down to earth again. It would have been so much more pleasant just to stay up there . . .

At last I screwed up all my courage, shut my eyes and pulled the throttle back. The engine almost stopped. I knew the next thing to do was to put her nose down, so down it went at a steep angle. Too steep. I opened one eye and pulled her nose up a bit, then put it down again, and in a series of steps descended toward the ground. The watchers on the ground must have got the impression that my machine was walking down an invisible staircase.

Finally I levelled off and executed to perfection everything I had been told to do in order to make a perfect landing. The only thing wrong was that I did it forty feet off the ground! I hastily put her nose down again, and executed another perfect landing—from a mere eight feet up. This time I didn't have enough altitude for another nose-down manoeuvre, so I just sat there and suffered. The temperamental old Rumpty took matters into her own hands, and pancaked the distance to the ground with a spine-jarring "plonk!" There was no damage, except (momentarily) to my pride. Training machines were built sturdily to cope with pilots like me.

How did he survive two hundred flights into danger to become the greatest fighter pilot to survive World War I? It was a question that intrigued many of the airmen who flew with him—and the ground crew who worked overtime to keep his plane airworthy. Bishop was primarily a superb marksman, a gunner whose reflexes were uniquely attuned to placing bullets in a target. To him an airplane was little more than a mobile gun mount, and rather an unwieldy one—until the prey came into sight.

At that instant, by some alchemy, the clumsy plane became part of the gun and under Bishop's will, his to control and aim as he would a light handgun. Bishop was also endowed with extraordinarily keen eyesight, and continually searched the sky for his prey. He invariably saw the enemy first, and was himself seldom the victim of surprise. Indeed, he searched the sky so intently that the back of his neck was often raw where his uniform chafed from the constant turning. *Then* he was a peerless pilot who could do no wrong. But a few minutes later, the enemy vanquished or in flight and Bishop back over his own airfield, he was apt to smash an undercarriage or crack a wing in a landing even less delicate than his first solo effort. It was not, I believe, an inability to learn but an impatience with the comparatively unimportant process of getting to and from the element in which he was supremely at home.

There was, however, no sense of failure in Bishop that November day in 1916 when he climbed out of the cockpit after his first flight alone. "That is the greatest day in a flying man's life," he wrote. "Certainly I did not stop boasting about it for weeks. I felt a great pity for all the millions of people in the world who would never have a chance to fly solo!"

Bishop's jubilation was somewhat premature. He still faced an advanced course, including night flying, before he could claim his wings.

For this he was transferred to No. 11 Squadron at Northolt, a home defence station. Bishop apparently felt that having survived three hours of solo flight he had nothing more to learn, and immediately he ran afoul of the strict discipline with which Northolt's commanding officer, Major B. F. Moore, ran his station. Many years later Bishop's instructor, Squadron Commander (then Captain) Tryggve Gran, who took a lifelong pride in the fact that he had trained the great Bishop, gave a softened version of the twenty-two-year-old Canadian's conduct at Northolt: "He was full of *joie de vivre* and high jinks, and hated discipline, with the result that he was always in conflict with the squadron regulations."

Periodically the station's instructors and Major Moore met to review the progress and problems of the pilots-in-training. In the course of one session Captain Gran said, "and now, Lieutenant Bishop. . . ." Major Moore cut him short with an impatient gesture. "Don't trouble to report on Bishop," he said, "I've ordered his travel pass."

In air force jargon that meant that Bishop was being dismissed.

Captain Gran pleaded for another chance for Bishop. Gran was probably the only instructor at Northolt who would have dared argue a decision after it was handed down by Major Moore. But Gran was no ordinary airman. He was a Norwegian, and the only subject of a foreign neutral country accepted to serve in the Royal Flying Corps in World War I. This unique dispensation was a recognition of the fact that Gran had served gallantly with Captain Robert Falcon Scott's ill-fated second expedition to the Antarctic, which resulted in Scott's death on his return trek from the South Pole.

At any rate Bishop got a reprieve from Major Moore, a memorable tongue-lashing, and applied himself to the task of learning how to fly passably enough to win his wings. His last few hours of advanced training were spent in night flying.

The terrifying memory of night flying in 1916 planes with 1916 ground equipment remained with Bishop all his life. He would, he said, prefer to fight a dozen aerial battles against any odds—in daylight—than attempt one night takeoff and landing. "It was like being dumped into an unknown lake at midnight."

Bishop consoled himself with the knowledge that at the front there was no night flying. Dawn patrols, yes; dusk reconnaissance, yes. But the hours of darkness, so seasoned pilots had assured him, were traditionally spent in the pursuit of relaxation in the squadron mess or in the nearest town. With a week's graduation leave he went up to London, was duly congratulated and lodged by Lady St. Helier, and celebrated feverishly until his assignment came through. It was: Report to Suttons Farm, on the Thames estuary, for anti-Zeppelin night duty.

Little is remembered half a century later of the Zeppelin war into which Bishop was thrust at the end of 1916, and what is remembered is surrounded somehow by an aura of improbability, almost of grim humour. But in its own way this Battle of Britain was almost as crucial as the struggle that was to be fought a generation later. The statistics of the Zeppelin raids sound less than decisive, as military statistics go. In less than two years in 1915–16 one hundred and thirty Zeppelins crossed the coast of Britain in thirty-seven raids. They dropped 4,500 bombs, killed four hundred persons, mostly civilians; injured a thousand persons and caused six million dollars' property damage (including farm livestock).

Royal Flying Corps pilots flew two hundred sorties against the raiding Zeppelins and the few who sighted the dirigibles attacked them with a strange variety of weapons: incendiary bullets, then in the experimental stage; incendiary darts, which were so ineffectual that they never got out of the experimental stage; and hand-launched bombs. There is no certain evidence in the official record of the Zeppelin Battle of Britain that (a) any bombs were actually thrown in anger toward a Zeppelin or (b) that any bombs ever landed on a Zeppelin. But it is a recorded fact that thirty-one of the defending pilots crashed, several of them with fatal results, on the makeshift flare-lighted fields provided for home defence pilots. It was perhaps understandable that a belief developed, and gained support even in War Office circles, that the Zeppelins were surrounded by a layer of inert gas that prevented incendiary missiles from taking effect.

But the destruction and casualties caused by the Zeppelin raids were trivial compared with the damage they were doing to civilian morale and, even more important, to Britain's war production and transportation. In 1915 and 1916 the submarine blockade and heavy losses of men and material on the battlefield forced Britain into a situation where she could survive only by producing guns and ammunition, ships, planes and transport around the clock. But the sighting of one or two Zeppelins crossing the English coast would halt work in hundreds of factories and stop freight trains and truck convoys in areas many miles away from the airships' course. The reason was that British officials responsible for war production and home defence had not devised an effective selective warning system that could chart the course of the raiders and warn workers to douse lights and seek shelter only in areas of possible attack. As a result tens of thousands of workers refused to stay on the job once a Zeppelin alarm was sounded.

Fixed anti-aircraft batteries "defended" obviously strategic points, but many large cities were undefended. Not until later (too late to a large extent) did mobile anti-aircraft mounted on trucks stand at the ready to speed to places under attack. On March 5, 1916, the Zeppelin L-14, commanded by Captain-Lieutenant Bocker, hovered over the city of Hull from 12.05 midnight until 12.15, dropping bombs with deliberate aim on the city and the docks. The British and the German reports of this attack were essentially the same, although with different emphasis, of course.

The British report: "We counted seven high-explosive and thirteen incendiary bombs, four of the latter falling in the river. The main damage was to houses near the docks.".

The German report: "The most striking result was the collapse of whole blocks of houses, and these afterwards showed up against the snow as big black patches."

An hour later Captain Victor Schutze guided his Zeppelin L-11 over Hull and, again unmolested, dropped bombs on the city for twenty minutes. Schutze reported: "The town, though very well darkened, showed up under the starlight like a drawing. A few lights were moving on the streets. Buildings went up like packs of cards. With binoculars it was possible to see people running hither and thither in the glare of the fires. In the harbour ships began to move out."

Serious civilian disorders resulted from the bombings. The official British report admits: "Great feeling was aroused in Hull. That Zeppelins should be allowed to hover over the town without any attempt to attack them from land or from the air led to many forceful protests. The feeling was such that a Royal Flying Corps transport was attacked and damaged by a crowd, and a Royal Flying Corps officer was mobbed."

An indication of the concern of British authorities over the effects of the Zeppelin raids was an order issued to RFC pilots at two airfields: "A pilot having expended his ammunition in attack on a Zeppelin without apparent effect, and observing that the enemy airship continues on its way to the target, will ram said enemy airship." There is no record that an RFC night-fighter pilot ever actually carried out the suicide order, but years later Air Marshal Sir Robert Brooke-Popham, who was an RFC officer in World War I, said: "I certainly think a great many officers would have deliberately charged a Zeppelin if they had met it."

Bishop, who shared with one other pilot (an awesome veteran with all of forty hours of solo flying to his credit) the defence of a strategic fifty miles of the Thames estuary, repeatedly had nightmares in which a Zeppelin loomed ahead of his plane in the night sky. "The inevitable result was that I went down in an uncontrolled spin, while the Zeppelin cruised on toward London."

It was not until early in the morning of September 3, 1916—nearly two years after the first Zeppelin raid on Britain—that the first airship was shot down over Britain by a night fighter. The victory could not have come at a more opportune time for Britain. Emboldened by the lack of effective resistance, the Germans had been sending stronger and stronger forces. The armada that crossed the English coast on the night of September 2 was the largest yet—fourteen Zeppelins.

Lieutenant Leefe Robinson, who kept vigil at Suttons Farm field a few weeks before Bishop was assigned there, took off at eleven o'clock that night, his machine-gun armed with a new type of incendiary bullets. He succeeded in coaxing his plane to the extraordinary height of 12,900 feet and roamed the night skies over the Thames estuary until two in the morning when he sighted a Zeppelin, the LS II. Three drums of ammunition set the Zeppelin afire and it crashed at Cuffley and burned for two hours. Robinson won the Victoria Cross for breaking the Zeppelins' long invulnerability. In the next four raids five Zeppelins were shot down. By the time Bishop went to Suttons Farm the raids had dwindled to the point where the hazards of the assignment consisted of the ever-present dangers of night flying—and loneliness.

Bishop's second Christmas Day in England started off to be even more lonely than his first. In the hut on the aerodrome at Suttons Farm he and his fellow pilot cooked their own Christmas dinner, including a ten-pound turkey. "While the big bird roasted," Bishop said in a letter home, "it struck us how absurd it was for the two of us to tackle all that food alone. So we telephoned a local hotel on a sudden impulse and told the manager to send out any guests who seemed to have nowhere to go. Alas for our ten-pound turkey. The guests from the hotel kept coming until there were twenty of them. But by some miracle we managed to feed the hungry score and stir up a little jollity. But night shut in early, the guests departed, and once more we took up our wintry vigil."

By late February it became obvious that the Zeppelin raids were a thing of the past, and Bishop received his long-awaited transfer to a fighter squadron at the front. The commander of the Royal Flying Corps in France, General Hugh M. Trenchard, had asked for more pilots and more squadrons at the front in preparation for a spring offensive—even at the expense of the Home Defence squadrons.

Early in March, Bishop was told to report to the War Office for orders to proceed to France. His hopes of becoming a fighter pilot were to be realized. The night before he reported he met the leading British ace, Albert Ball, who was on leave in London. Ball, who had shot down twenty-nine enemy planes, enthralled Bishop with tales of his exploits.

Ball more than any other pilot symbolized the individual tenacity and bravery of the British airmen. He had attacked as many as forty German planes single-handed. It was due to the courage of individual fighters like him that the Allies had overcome the "Fokker menace" and had gained supremacy of the air in 1916.

The French, too, played a gallant part. Ball himself ranked Georges Guynemer, a short man, weak in physique, who some said suffered from tuberculosis, as the bravest of all. In one day Guynemer had shot down four German planes. By the end of 1916 he had brought down twenty-five enemy planes and his score was still climbing.

The Germans had suffered heavily and had lost their two top aces. Max Immelmann was killed in the summer of 1916. Oswald Boelcke crashed to his death in November that same year, when he collided with one of his own pilots. But before he died Boelcke had brought down the incredible total of forty Allied planes.

By early 1917, the Germans were preparing for an all-out effort in the air to regain their lost supremacy. In the vanguard of the attack was the man who had assumed Boelcke's mantle and who had been his protégé—Baron Manfred von Richthofen. A former cavalry officer and a fearless fighter, Richthofen had already brought down twenty-one Allied planes by the beginning of March 1917.

"There's going to be a whale of a scrap out there before long," Ball told Bishop. The following morning, when Bishop reported at the War Office, he could hardly believe his good fortune. He was to join 60 Squadron—the squadron in which Ball had served and which, to a great extent through Ball's efforts, had become the most famous fighter unit in France.

On the evening of March 17, Bishop arrived at Filescamp Farm, the home of 60 Squadron, located adjacent to the hamlet of Izel-le-Hameau. The farm had been requisitioned from its owner, Monsieur Tétus, for the duration. Its proximity to the front fifteen miles away meant only a few minutes' flying time to get over the lines, yet it was far enough away to be out of the range of no-man's-land. The field itself, while flat and open, was by no means ideal for landing and taking off. Monsieur Tétus, who continued to reside on the farm with his family (and the young maid who did not escape special attention from the pilots), had grown turnips on the field before it became an aerodrome. This made it hard and bumpy and many a pilot, Bishop in particular, used this as a welcome excuse on which to blame poor landings.

But to Keith "Grid" Caldwell, the swarthy New Zealander commanding C Flight to whom Billy reported on arrival, Lieutenant Bishop was just another eager, untested young pilot. He seemed likely to end up a casualty before the month of March was out.

And a week later, as we already know, Bishop sat beside his damaged plane in no-man's-land under the guns of an anti-aircraft battery, equally convinced that he had muffed his chance to become a fighter pilot.

In the afternoon the squadron tender arrived from Filescamp field, dismantled Bishop's Nieuport and took it in tow. By daylight it was comparatively easy to pick a route over the devastated land. Bishop noted in his diary: "Oh those villages, absolutely nothing left of them."

Eight miles from Filescamp the tender became hopelessly bogged down in the mud as darkness fell. Bishop and the mechanics worked half the night trying to get rolling. They finally had to give up and Bishop told the crew: "Get some sleep if you can. I'll walk back and send some help."

He arrived at Filescamp at 6 a.m. just as the first patrol was taking off. Jack Scott gave him a warm welcome.

"Got a call from General Higgins about you," he told Bishop.

Bishop's spirits sagged. "He's sending up my replacement?"

"Didn't mention that, as I recall," said Scott with a grin. "He said, 'give Lieutenant Bishop my congratulations—tell him good show and many more of them.' Didn't you know that you got a confirmed kill before your forced landing?"

An immense sense of relief flooded over Bishop. "You mean I don't have to go back for retraining? I can stay?"

"Looks like it," said Scott. "Get some sleep and you can take the next patrol."

"Sleep? I've had lots of sleep. I'd like to go up now."

"Righto," said Scott. "You can come now with Home, Caldwell and me. And Bish . . . take lead, will you? The rest of us are a bit bushed, what with being shorthanded with you holidaying up there in the trenches for the past three days."

Bishop knew that Scott was handing him an unusual honour, probably to bolster his self-confidence. In the happiest hour he had ever experienced, he led his more experienced squadron mates in an offensive patrol. They encountered no enemy planes, and when they were back in the mess, Bishop collapsed into a chair and slept soundly for sixteen hours. Far from having had "lots of sleep," Bishop actually had been awake for eighty-four hours.

60 SQUADRON, FILESCAMP FARM

THE DAY AFTER Bishop's triumphal return to Filescamp he and the other officers were invited to a musical evening in the sergeant's mess. Jack Scott noted in the squadron's diary: "It was observed that one of the few toasts proposed by the ground crew was to Bishop's health."

"Anybody who dives one of them Nieuports seven thousand feet needs to have his health worried about," Corporal Walter Bourne, Bishop's mechanic, later told him gloomily. He explained that the Nieuports were plagued by one dangerous fault. When pushed beyond normal speed, as in a dive, the lower wings tended to break off. There were two reasons for this defect, Bourne said. In the first place the scarcity of well-seasoned wood had made it necessary to use inferior wood in the Nieuport; and the design required too many screws in the main spar, so that the member was riddled with screw holes.

But Bishop decided that since his particular Nieuport had stood the severe test of what his fellow pilots called his "suicide dive," he would trust it to remain intact under his manhandling.

On March 30, 1917, five days after his first fight in the air, Bishop led a patrol for the second time. It was the kind of day on which the pilot of an underpowered, hard-to-handle 1917-model airplane was content to stay alive, without facing the requirement of maintaining close formation and engaging the enemy. A gale wind blew from the west toward enemy territory, an advantage to the German airmen which the RFC pilots came to accept as a matter of course.

The prevailing westerly wind meant that in the course of an aerial dogfight the drift of battle took the Allied planes deeper behind enemy lines. It also meant that Allied losses of planes and men were automatically higher. To return home, low on fuel or with a damaged plane, a pilot had to face both adverse winds and hostile ground fire. Because the German pilots rarely ventured over Allied territory, the British, French and later the Americans had to seek them out on their own home grounds. Forced landings almost always meant loss of the plane, capture of the pilot, and a "victory" for a German pilot.

With the exception of Alan Binnie, an Australian who was commander of 60 Squadron's A Flight but had "come along for the ride" as one of Bishop's flankers, the patrol was made up of novices.

One was E. J. D. Townesend, a classmate of Bishop's at RMC, who had joined 60 Squadron a few days before. The others were eighteen-year-old Frank Bower from the Northumberland Fusiliers, W. P. Garnett of the 3rd Royal Berkshires, and J. A. Milot, a French-Canadian major from the Canadian Pioneers—all completely new to the game.

With the wind tossing the planes about in the air, and with the inexperienced Bishop changing speed and direction without warning, the pilots had a hard time keeping their places in formation without crashing into each other. But Bishop managed to shepherd his patrol in the general direction of Vitry by following the winding Scarpe River.

Over Vitry, Bishop spotted a red Albatros two thousand feet below; he waggled his wings as a signal to the rest of the flight and dived. From sixty yards he fired a burst of twenty rounds, then to the right he saw another Albatros coming out of a cloud. As he turned toward it a flock of six Albatros fighters dived out of the overcast. It was Bishop's baptism in Richthofen's tactics. Seconds later bullets ripped into the rear of his fuselage. He pulled up sharply into a loop. When he levelled off he saw an Albatros on the tail of one of the Nieuports, pouring bullets into it. Slowly the machine faltered, then fell dizzily in a half-spin through the clouds below, carrying Garnett to his death.

Bower saw the sharp nose of an Albatros closing behind him and tried to turn out of its line of fire, but he wasn't quick enough. A bullet lodged in his stomach and he fought unconsciousness in an effort to stay in the battle. Then his engine started to vibrate as other bullets smashed into it. Coaxing his engine to keep him aloft, Bower headed back toward his own lines. Still fighting blackout, he glided through a barrage of anti-aircraft fire and landed on a field near Chipilly, behind his own lines. He managed to climb out of his machine, then fainted from loss of blood. Next morning he died.

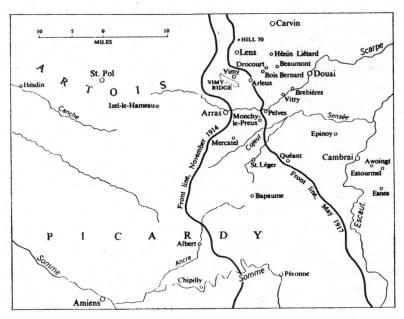

60 Squadron sector in 1917

Bishop and the other three pilots now found themselves under attack by six Albatros fighters. The ten machines whirled in circles, each trying to get into position to open fire. The mêlée of planes gradually lost height until all were in danger of ending the battle on the shell-pocked earth.

Finally the Germans broke off the fight. They were within gliding distance of their own aerodrome near Douai, where the Richthofen Jagdstaffel II was stationed. But Bishop and his three companions were in a serious situation. They were twenty-five miles behind the German lines; the fight had brought them down to one thousand feet, within easy range of anti-aircraft and machine-gun fire, and there was the danger that fresh planes might take off from the Douai aerodrome.

The gale from the west had increased. Flying homewards in the teeth of it, their speed was cut to fifty miles an hour. This made them perfect targets for the ground gunners, and shells began bursting all about them.

Using the clouds as cover, darting out of one and into another, they managed to reach Filescamp Farm. Their machines were shredded with bullet holes and shrapnel. The whole action had lasted an hour and a half, and the rest of the patrol regarded it with some amazement. Late in the afternoon Colonel George Pretyman, commander of the 13 Wing under which 60 Squadron operated, came over to the aerodrome to congratulate Bishop on leading a remarkable patrol. Bishop was not only surprised but embarrassed that a sortie in which he lost two out of six members should be regarded as "remarkable." "You can be certain we didn't do it on purpose," he told Jack Scott bitterly.

No narrative of this marathon patrol can convey the drama of the almost illegible pencilled note that Jack Scott scribbled at the bottom of the report that Bishop turned in when he landed at Filescamp: "At 1.20 P.M. Lieut. Bower and Garnett have not returned."

The next day Bishop won his second aerial victory, over one of Richthofen's squadron, while the four surviving pilots of his patrol were escorting photo reconnaissance planes ten miles northeast of Arras at fifteen thousand feet. He reported it tersely: "I went to the assistance of another Nieuport being attacked by an Albatros scout. I opened fire twice, the last time at fifty yards range. I saw my tracers hit his machine in the centre section and the Albatros seemed to fall out of control in a spinning nose dive." Bishop got double confirmation of this kill. Second Lieutenant L. H. Leckie noted, "I was behind Lt. Bishop and saw the Albatros go down." Jack Scott jotted on the report with his usual brevity: "The above is confirmed by anti-aircraft battery."

Bishop's report by no means told the whole story. Actually he had gone to the assistance of Townesend, his RMC classmate, when the latter was surprised by two Albatros scouts. Townesend was shot down and spent the rest of the war as a prisoner, and one of the photo reconnaissance planes was destroyed, but headquarters congratulated Bishop for "bringing five of the planes home safely— the photographs were a huge success."

April 1, 1917, was the first day of the bloodiest month the war in the air had witnessed. Both sides threw more planes into the air— and lost more—than in any similar previous period. On opposite sides of the trenches, Bishop's 60 Squadron and Richthofen's Jagdstaffel II bore the brunt of the fighting, and the score favoured the Germans by a wide margin. Richthofen shot down twenty-two planes during "Bloody April"—seventeen of them two-seater observation planes.

Bishop's score was twelve—all but two of them single-seater scouts that outgunned and out-powered Nieuports, and were manned by pilots who had many more hours of combat experience than Bishop.

On the afternoon of April 7, Bishop got his third Albatros— and his first sausage balloon. The big tethered gasbags that both sides used for observing the effects of their own artillery fire and the movement of enemy troops had seemed unworthy targets to Bishop. But Caldwell, whose wisdom and experience had made him the oldest survivor of 60 Squadron, had warned Bishop that balloons could be "the nastiest lot of all."

Not that Caldwell was a cautious man. On the contrary, he was "a wild New Zealand fire-eater," as one of his squadron mates put it, and the top morale-booster of the outfit. Only a few days before he had got into a dogfight with the redoubtable Richthofen at twelve thousand feet, in which both pilots had shot holes into each other's planes with near-fatal results.

What Caldwell had discovered was that the balloons, tethered by a cable at two thousand feet, were at an ideal altitude to be defended by "flaming onions"—whirling balls of fire hurled into the air by a rocket device. When a balloon was attacked, the ground crew would quickly winch it down and meet the diving enemy plane with barrages of rifle and machine-gun fire. In addition, enemy scouts had a habit of circling behind cloud cover above the balloons and darting down suddenly on a plane bent on attacking the "sitting sausage."

"Always be sure the chaps in the balloon's basket are alive, not dummies," Caldwell told Bishop. "The Hun has a trick of filling the basket with high explosives and detonating it from the ground when you dive in." (The Allies, incidentally, employed this device too, and probably used it before the Germans did.)

Soon after Bishop took off from Filescamp to attack his first balloon, Colonel George Pretyman telephoned Jack Scott from 13 Wing headquarters: "Dammit, Scott," he barked, "one of our observation balloons has just been shot down. Do something about it."

"We are, Sir," Scott assured him. "Bishop is on his way over to get one of theirs."

"Good God!" said Pretyman, "You don't think. . . ."

"I hope not, Sir," said Scott fervently.

Bishop was not guilty. He was at that moment attacking a balloon which, to judge from the bullets and balls of fire that whizzed by his wing tips, was definitely not "one of ours." As Bishop dived through this hair-raising hail of bullets and flame balls he heard the rattle of machine-guns behind him, felt his Nieuport shudder, and turned to see the snout of a red Albatros that was methodically chewing his tail planes with its twin Spandau guns.

He took the only evasive action possible. He pulled the nose of his Nieuport straight up in an almost vertical climb. The Albatros, taken by surprise, roared past underneath. Bishop quickly brought down the nose of his plane and found himself only fifteen yards behind the Albatros. At that close range he fired a burst of twenty rounds. The Albatros lurched on to its side, its nose went down and it crashed almost vertically into the ground.

Bishop now turned his attention to the balloon once more. During the few moments of the aerial duel, the balloon's crew had frantically winched it down, and now it was only five hundred feet up and descending as fast as the crew could reel it in. Bishop had orders not to attack under one thousand feet, but he had no intention of abandoning his quarry now. He aimed his plane's nose at the descending balloon, opened his throttle, and pressed the firing button. His Lewis machine-gun chattered as incendiary bullets poured into the gasbag, but without apparent effect. When he was fifty feet from the target—and little more than three hundred feet from the ground—Bishop came out of his dive. His engine sputtered and stopped.

It was the second time in a few days that Bishop had undergone this horrifying experience. But this time he was a little wiser. Corporal Walter Bourne, his ack-emma (aircraft mechanic), had tipped him off on how to correct the oiling up of the Le Rhône engine after a fast dive. With a very few seconds remaining before his wheels would touch earth, Bishop slowly pumped his throttle. One of the nine "jars" of the engine caught, then another and another. Twenty feet above the ground the Nieuport was alive. Bishop headed for home with throttle wide open. He was too low for anti-aircraft fire, but it seemed that every German soldier within sight had a rifle or machine-gun trained on his plane.

When he finally reached the British trenches he looked back. A mass of smoke and flame arose from behind the German lines. His sausage had finally caught fire. That afternoon Jack Scott received a wire: "Congratulate Bishop on fine feat today. Trenchard, General Officer Commanding, Royal Flying Corps."

But there was little cause for rejoicing in 60 Squadron that night. While Bishop was downing the balloon and the Albatros that afternoon, a patrol led by Alan Binnie had run into Richthofen's Jagdstaffel II near Mercatel south of Arras. Three pilots had been lost. Richthofen, promoted to the rank of captain that day, had led the attack himself, bringing down his thirty-seventh victim, nineteen-year-old Lieutenant George Smart from Manchester, who was killed when his machine crashed in flames. In the same fight M. B. Knowles was shot down and taken prisoner and C. S. Hall was killed in mid-air.

It brought the total casualties of the squadron for the first week of April to five. V. F. Williams had been killed on the second day of the month just after returning from leave, and Townesend was shot down behind the lines and captured.

That night Bishop wrote a bitterly emotional letter to Margaret: "Three more pilots lost today. All good men. Oh how I hate the Huns. They have done in so many of my best friends. I'll make them pay, I swear."

The Germans were, however, taking only partial revenge for the devastating night bombing attacks on Richthofen's base at Douai by 100 Squadron, also stationed at Filescamp Farm, adjacent to Izel-le-Hameau village. Richthofen wrote after the second raid: "I was in bed fast asleep when I heard, as though in a dream, anti-aircraft firing. I awoke to find the dream a reality. One of the Englishmen was at that moment flying so low over my quarters that in my sudden fright I pulled the blankets over my head. It would be too silly for a flying man to die by a rotten bomb."

Actually in two nights 100 Squadron dropped ninety-eight bombs on Richthofen's headquarters, destroyed four of his hangars, killed or wounded several of the German pilots and ground crews, smashed the landing field so it could not be used for several days, and damaged or destroyed many planes, including Richthofen's favourite red Albatros.

On the night of April 7 the Germans tried to return the compliment by bombing Filescamp Farm. Bishop, like his enemy counterpart Richthofen, found he was more nervous at being at the receiving end of a bombing raid than facing sudden death in plane-to-plane combat in the daylight skies. His remarks, by coincidence, were a close paraphrase of Richthofen's.

Bishop was in much less danger, however, as most of the German bombs fell harmlessly in fields. The aerodrome was hard to detect at night, as the only landmarks were the road and railway line which ran four miles to the north. Bishop's disturbed sleep did not prevent him from turning out for the dawn patrol. It was to be the greatest day in his life up to that time.

ACE

I T WAS EASTER SUNDAY, APRIL 8, 1917. The early sun was slowly burning off the night's mist as Jack Scott hobbled to his Nieuport, balanced himself by gripping the edge of the cockpit, handed his canes to a mechanic, and was boosted aboard by a member of the ground crew.

Scattered white clouds drifted lazily from the east as Scott led his patrol across the German lines near Vimy Ridge. For twenty minutes the flight criss-crossed the lines before Scott spotted an Albatros two-seater, far below. He dived and fired a short burst, but the German machine quickly dived away. Bishop, suspecting a trick, chased after it.

What happened during the next few minutes was described in the report Bishop wrote before 60 Squadron sat down to its Easter Sunday noon dinner:

> I dived after Major Scott on a two-seater opening fire twice as he was already diving. Then I engaged a single-seater. He flew away eastward after I had fired forty rounds at him. Tracers hit his machine in fuselage and planes. I then dived at a balloon from 5,000 feet and drove it down to the ground. It did not smoke. I climbed to 4,000 feet and engaged an Albatros scout, fired the remainder of my drum at him, dodged away and put a

new drum on, and engaged him again. After two bursts he dived vertically and was still in a nose dive when about 500 feet from the ground. I then climbed to 10,000 feet and five miles N. E. of Arras I engaged two single-seaters flying toward our lines. Three more machines were above and behind. I fired the remainder of my drum into the pair, one burst of 15 at one and the rest at the other. The former turned and flew away with his nose well down, the second went down in a spinning nose dive. My tracer bullets hit all around the pilot's seat and I think he must have been hit. Then I climbed and got behind the other three about the vicinity of Vitry. I engaged them and one, a double-seater, went down in a nose dive but I think partly under control. I engaged the remaining two and finished my third drum at them. They both flew away eastward.

How many planes did Bishop shoot down on that Easter Sunday? Some of his squadron mates insisted it was five; others claimed they saw four planes crash. Jack Scott said, "Let's not be greedy— let's settle for three." Bishop shrugged. The three official victories brought Bishop's total to six. This, in the French system of scoring, made him an "ace"—plus one.

The French introduced the "ace system," according the title to a pilot who downed five enemy planes. The Germans required a score of ten for "ace" status. The Americans at first used the French score but later raised the requirements to ten. The British, characteristically, stayed aloof from such things, and even when Bishop had registered seventy-two victories he was never officially referred to as an ace.

Corporal Walter Bourne's jaw dropped when Bishop landed his plane at Filescamp and crawled out of the cockpit, pale and dizzy. Bourne shook his head in disbelief. The Nieuport's fabric was riddled by bullet holes. The windshield was splintered, and the point at which the bullet entered it seemed to be directly in line with the pilot's head.

"How," asked Bishop's mechanic, "could a bullet hit *there* without hitting *there*"—and he tapped Bishop's flying helmet.

"Oh, it grazed me," said Bishop, showing a groove in the leather of his headgear. "By the way," he added, "keep that windshield for me." It was one of the few souvenirs Bishop took back to Canada when the war was over.

When Bishop had departed Bourne called to his assistant: "Carstairs! A can of blue paint!" The hangar mechanics heard, and were electrified. The last time the corporal had demanded a can of paint was when he had decided to honour 60 Squadron's greatest pilot, Albert Ball. Bourne's accolade had taken the form of painting Ball's propeller spinner red. Now the ack-emmas crowded around while Bourne solemnly applied the blue paint to the special spinner they fixed to the hub of Bishop's propeller. It was cone-shaped and appropriately vicious in appearance.

Jack Scott was propped against the door of his office as Bishop came in. "I've phoned old Boom Trenchard about our O.P. [offensive patrol], and he insists on coming over," said Scott. "Better get into a clean uniform."

"Old Boom Trenchard" was none other than General Sir Hugh M. Trenchard, officer commanding the Royal Flying Corps. (His nickname, obviously, arose from the fact that the general's voice could traditionally be heard a mile away.) When he arrived at 60 Squadron's mess he embarrassed Bishop acutely by declaring in a voice Bishop was sure could be heard clear to Izel, "My boy, if everyone did as well as you've done, we'd soon win this war."

Trenchard stayed for the celebration 60 Squadron staged that night and, mellowed by a generous amount of the Squadron's best champagne, watched benignly as Bishop, equally thoroughly lubricated, performed a tap dance on the piano and recited the airmen's favourite ballad:

Oh the bold aviator was dying
And as 'neath the wreck-age he lay, he lay,

To the sobbing me-chanics about him
These last parting words he did say:

Two valves you'll find in my stomach
Three spark plugs are safe in my lung, (my lung).
The prop is in splinters inside me,
To my fingers the joy stick has clung.

And get you six brandies and sodas
And lay them all out in a row,
And get you six other good airmen
To drink to this pilot below.

Take the cylinders out of my kidneys
The connecting rod out of my brain, my brain,
From the small of my back take the crankshaft
And assemble the engine again.

Bishop was roundly booed for his performance, and General Trenchard himself advised him, "My boy, stick to flying." Bishop blamed the pianist, Alan Binnie, who in turn blamed the piano. It was, he complained, "dried out."

"We can't have a dry piano in *this* mess," said Bishop, and poured a quart of champagne into the instrument. It was three o'clock in the morning before the weary, happy celebrants made their way to bed for a few hours' sleep before dawn patrol.

On that day, 60 Squadron found itself in a new role—as a direct arm of the ground forces. Until now the work of the air force had been co-ordinated with the overall offensive and defensive tactics of the ground forces in the plans of the commanding officers, but not in ways that were obvious to the airmen. They understood in a general way the need to knock down observation balloons and planes that came over to photograph troop movements and military installations. But most of the time the rank and file of fighter pilots had a somewhat vague knowledge of what the "poor bloody infantry" was up to. Essentially they were fighting a private war in the skies.

But now the British airmen on the Arras front were to play their part as a sort of airborne artillery in close support of the ground forces. The British and the Canadian Corps were driving for control of two ramparts from which they could dominate the Artois Plain—Vimy Ridge to the north of Arras and Monchy-le-Preux directly east of the cathedral city.

Artillery paved the way. The great cannon laid down a furious carpet of fire—a "creeping barrage"—in front of the attacking British and Canadian infantry to hammer the German infantry. Here and there stubborn machine-gun posts refused to yield and their efforts at times seriously slowed down the Allied advance. It became the duty of British fighter planes to search them out, swoop down and rake the gun posts with a rain of fire. It was a risky job. Artillery shells screamed through the air and machine-gun bullets peppered the planes as they dived. In spite of the danger, Bishop realized the importance of the job.

"I had reached a height of only thirty feet," he recalled of one incident, "so low I could make out every detail of their frightened faces. With hate in my heart I fired every bullet I could as I swept over, then turned my machine away. A few minutes later I had the satisfaction of seeing our line advancing and before the time came for me to return to my patrol our men had occupied all the German positions they had set out to take."

During that first week of battle, Bishop's blue-nosed Nieuport was a familiar sight along the front line. Time and time again the troops, crouching in the muck and mire of no-man's-land, saw the silver machine streaking down to harass the enemy in front of them.

Sometimes Bishop led as many as four patrols a day. And when not leading his flight, he was out flying alone, in search of Richthofen's scouts. But the hunting was poor. Only once did he encounter an enemy plane—a two-seater Aviatik observation machine—and that got away from him before he could get close enough to open fire. For twelve days he had no opportunity of adding to his score.

But Richthofen and his Jagdstaffel were not hiding. Bishop's flight ran into it one day when he was not leading the patrol. Only one man returned out of five planes—Graham Young, a bush-haired, moustached Scotsman from Perth. In a furious fight over Monchy-le-Preux, Alan Binnie, who was leading the flight, was badly wounded in his arm, forced to land behind German lines, and was captured. Two others, W. O. Russell and L. C. Chapman, were also forced down and captured, while another pilot, J. H. Cook, was killed.

After the war, Russell told of his encounter with Richthofen:

Unfortunately it can scarcely be termed a combat. By the time Richthofen arrived on the scene I had lost the use of my engine and so I had not the honour of putting up a show against him. Five of us were on offensive patrol in the neighbourhood of Douai in Nieuport Scouts at 12,000 feet. My flight comman-der suddenly dived. I followed him down and at 8000 feet I sighted two enemy planes on my right. I attacked one of these machines and then discovered to my horror that I had lost my engine. After descending another thousand feet I was attacked by two enemy scouts and I was obliged to make a zigzag descent to the ground and landed at Bois Bernard. A red scout followed me to the ground and I learned the pilot was Richthofen. Our flight was hopelessly outnumbered by Richthofen's squadron. I afterward met my flight commander, Capt. Binnie, in a German prison camp. He had accounted for four enemy machines before being hit in the arm while chang-ing his ammunition drum. He remembered nothing more until he woke up in a German hospital, although somehow he had landed his plane safely. Three of my companions were killed and I believe one succeeded in reaching our lines.

Richthofen's own claim of victory was less than insistent: His "request of acknowledgement of my 44th victory" merely stated: "Above Harleux, one of our observer planes was attacked by several Nieuports. I hurried to the place of action, attacked one of the planes, and forced it to land south of Bois Bernard."

In another battle with the Richthofen fighters, 60 Squadron's A Flight lost four men: Robertson, Languill, Elliott and Kimbell: all of them killed.

By mid-April, in fact, 60 Squadron had lost thirteen pilots within two weeks and, at the height of the offensive, Jack Scott had to call a halt to offensive patrols until the squadron could be brought up to strength and reorganized. This had to be accomplished quickly. The offensive was at its peak. Five days of bad weather—rain and fog that made flying impossible most of the time—gave the unit the respite it needed to absorb the new pilots as they arrived. Bishop found himself in the startling position of being one of the squadron's veteran pilots—and the one with the most planes to his credit after less than a month of solo fighter experience. Scott promoted him to full-time commander of C Flight when Grid Caldwell became ill while on leave.

None of 60 Squadron's three flights were up to the normal strength of six pilots each. Only Bishop and Young were left in C Flight. Bishop chafed under Scott's "no offensive patrol" order. He had not had a real air battle in twelve days. Then on April 20, the weather improved. Scott reluctantly agreed to allow Bishop into enemy territory to attack a balloon that was annoying Colonel Pretyman. Bishop did not find it—probably he didn't search very hard after he spotted a two-seater Aviatik observation plane, flying above him near Monchy-le-Preux. Bishop cautiously jockeyed his Nieuport until his propeller was no more than ten yards behind the Aviatik's tailplanes, and slightly below. He pressed the firing button and sent a dozen rounds into the big plane's belly. The burst seemed to have no other effect than to alert the observer-gunner, who swung his machine-gun around smartly and sent a stream of bullets flying around the Nieuport as his own pilot turned away. Bishop followed and again managed to manoeuvre directly underneath. This time he pulled his gun from its fixed position, grabbed the trigger and fired manually. Still no result. Bishop pulled away, then attacked again. He fired another ten rounds. Again nothing happened. Frustrated, Bishop tried a new tactic. He climbed above the two-seater, which now twisted and turned frantically to keep out of the Nieuport's line of fire. Bishop dived at right angles, aiming at the gunner. The gunner fired back and bullets whipped past the wing tips of the Nieuport. Bishop was still firing when his propeller was only five yards from the Aviatik's fuselage. Then he pulled up sharply to avoid a collision. As the planes passed each almost within arm's reach, Bishop leaned out of the cockpit and looked down. The enemy machine suddenly burst into flames, stalled, and spun out of control through a layer of scattered clouds below, trailing an ugly plume of black smoke.

Bishop flew back to Filescamp Farm, feeling less elated at his seventh victory than concerned with his poor marksmanship. Three times he had fired bursts at short range without scoring effective hits. He was aware that a pilot's very survival often depended on his shooting accuracy. He spent the rest of the day shooting at the practice target on the edge of the aerodrome.

That evening he talked with the three pilots who had been assigned to his flight that day. Young had already taken them on a practice formation flight and his report of their flying abilities was highly favourable. "They stick together well," he told Bishop, "and they're likely-looking fighters too."

There was the small intense Spencer Horn, with sleek hair parted in the middle, a former infantryman who had fought on the same ground he would now fly over. William Mays Fry, a short man with a quick wit and a willingness to learn all his more experienced comrades could teach him about aerial fighting tactics. "You'd think he'd been flying a Nieuport all his life," Young commented. A fellow-Canadian completed the trio. He was Jack Rutherford, wiry but strong. He had served with the 23rd Canadian Battalion before transferring to the RFC. Young told Bishop that Rutherford showed an uncanny sense of timing. He had landed the Nieuport for the first time so smoothly that it was difficult to realize it was his maiden trip in the machine.

Bishop grunted. His own landing technique had not improved noticeably. He took Young and his new flight members over to the mess for a drink. Jack Scott came in and hobbled across to the bar and slapped Bishop on the back. "Drinks are on you tonight, Bish," the squadron commander grinned. "Word just came in from Brigade—they've awarded you the Military Cross."

BLOODY APRIL

THE UNUSUALLY mild-mannered Jack Scott snorted when he read the opening sentence of Bishop's operational report on April 22, 1917: "While leading a patrol I dived to the assistance of Major Scott who was being attacked by five enemy single-seaters two thousand feet below."

"What the hell was I doing down there, cruising around alone?" he demanded.

Bishop grinned. It was true that Scott needed "assistance" because he had volunteered, against his better judgment, to become the bait in a trap of Bishop's devising. The trap required a special combination of good weather and cloud cover, which seldom arrived together in the April sky of northern France. On this day Bishop's flight—Young, Horn, Fry and Rutherford, with Scott tagging along—found the combination ten thousand feet above the city of Lens; two great pillars of white cloud hovered in a clear blue sky. Between the pillars was a snowy cavern a mile wide. Bishop and his boys circled to the southwest over Vimy Ridge. Jack Scott circled at eight thousand feet, waiting to be attacked.

At a time like that a man thinks of strange things. Scott counted the money in the pocket of his flying suit. Thirty francs. Not much to bribe a French farmer to shelter him if he should be forced down behind enemy lines.

Then he had no more time for idle thoughts. Five red Albatros planes were flying in formation toward the British lines, on a course that would bring the lone Nieuport into plain view. Scott needed all his phlegmatic courage to continue flying a casual course in apparent unawareness of the approaching enemy. "Blast it!" he muttered. "Where is that Bishop?"

Not until the five planes closed in on him with guns blazing did Scott turn to meet them. Bishop had seen the German planes even before Scott. He and his flight mates dived at full throttle into the formation. Bishop opened fire on the nearest machine from ten yards. Smoke spewed from it instantly and it plummeted down in a crazy spin. Bishop turned on the plane at his right, closed to within five yards and pressed the button. Bullets spluttered all about the pilot. His head fell forward and the plane turned on its side and dived out of control. Bishop had shot down two planes before his companions, who had started a few seconds behind him, could reach the scene. The remaining Germans fled. Young, Horn, Fry and Rutherford pursued them until they were out of sight. Bishop pulled up beside Scott to make sure he was all right. Scott grinned and waved his hand.

Bishop was well satisfied with the operation. Not only had his trap worked perfectly, confirming his theory that surprise was one of the most important elements of aerial battle, but his faithful target practice had paid off. His shooting eye was "in" again, as shown by two kills with two short bursts. On his way back to Filescamp Bishop made an important tactical decision: instead of endless twisting, turning and manoeuvring when in an air battle—which seldom seemed to produce decisive results and meant needless exposure to danger—he would confine his fighting method to quick darting attacks wherever possible.

Bishop had additional cause for satisfaction. His novice companions had performed admirably, and had stayed with him all the way during the swift encounter. Colonel Pretyman noted this fact in his official combat report: "The formation work during this patrol was excellent throughout. After the fight the formation were together again almost at once." Then he added a comment in tribute to Jack Scott, the sitting-duck decoy: "It is doubtful if there would have been a chance of engaging the enemy patrol if there had not been bait, (in the shape of Major Scott) which worked very well."

There was no keeping Bishop out of the air for the rest of that day. After lunch he took off, alone, in search of adventure. Four times he encountered Albatros scouts from Richthofen's circus—two pairs and two singles. As if the enemy sensed they were being hunted by a pilot who was on a winning streak, they used their superior speed to run away, and Bishop could get in only a few bursts at extreme range. In the late afternoon he led his flight on two more offensive patrols, but now the sky was clear of all enemy planes.

Next day Bishop scored another double, over his favourite hunting ground, Monchy-le-Preux. This was Bishop's terse report of the operation:

At 3.23 p.m. at 2,200 feet I attacked a two-seater doing wireless observation three miles east of Monchy-le-Preux, firing from a flank and above. My gun stopped and when I had remedied it I dived again and fired about 15 more shots. My gun stopped again and the H.A. (hostile aircraft) escaped. I then flew east towards Vitry and engaged another two-seater, firing at it from behind and above. After a short burst he seemed to be hit and dived. I dived after him firing all the way. He landed in a field near Vitry and I finished the rest of my drum on the ground. As far as I could see neither the pilot nor the observer got out of the machine.

At 6,000 feet I went to the assistance of another Nieuport attacked by three Albatros scouts. I attacked from behind and took one of them by surprise. He fell out of control and I followed him down and saw him crash.

It was now the last week of April, 1917, and both Monchy-le-Preux and Vimy Ridge had been secured—at a terrible cost in Canadian and British dead. The Germans, driven back to the line known as "the Switch," an offshoot of the Hindenburg Line between Drocourt and Quéant, directed heavy artillery fire toward the two ramparts from which they had been driven. They succeeded in slowing the Allied advance almost to a stop.

More and more German artillery observation balloons appeared along the front to help the gunners find the range, and 3rd Brigade headquarters ordered the fighter squadrons to concentrate on the "sausages." It was a task for which the pilots had little appetite. Bishop particularly disliked the operation that brought him within range of rifle and machine-gun fire. He had had his fill of this type of fighting during the ground strafing of the opening week of the battle. He willingly took his chances in duels high in the air, but he hated the thought of being killed by a lucky stray bullet fired from the ground.

Nevertheless the balloons had to be destroyed. So between offensive patrols the pilots were ordered out in search of them.

Bishop was never noted for strict obedience of RFC rules and regulations, but in the matter of "Balloons, orders re attacking of," he became a model of conformity, especially in respect of the order that balloons must not be pursued closer than a thousand feet to the ground. He reasoned that once an observation balloon had been winched down under attack by an Allied fighter plane it would not be sent aloft again for at least two hours, for fear that the plane might be waiting to return to the attack.

On April 27 Bishop did, however, shoot down his second balloon. But that was a mistake. Flying through clouds, he trusted to his own sense of direction instead of paying close attention to his compass. So he got lost. When he descended through the lowest misty layer of cloud he found himself directly over a German balloon. He dived at it, fired a burst, and climbed into the clouds again, followed by a scattering of ground fire. He flew on for a few minutes, then cautiously let his plane sink through the overcast—and almost landed on the broad round back of another balloon. He fired several short bursts into it before the ground crew could reel it in. Once more he disappeared into the clouds with bullets whizzing around the plane. Looking down, he could see the balloon blazing as the ground crew frantically tried to bring it to earth before the flames could reach the gondola, or collapse the gasbag and drop the crew to their deaths.

Bishop used his compass to get back to Filescamp. Corporal Bourne was, as usual, waiting for him when his plane taxied to a stop. Also as usual, he walked around the plane for a swift and expert inspection of any damage it might have suffered during the patrol. He whistled when he reached the tail, grasped it and jerked it loose.

"Pin shot through," he said grimly. "Another moment and it'ud have fallen off in the air." It was Bishop's turn to whistle.

Others in 60 Squadron did not share Bishop's phenomenal luck under fire. "Bloody April" was still taking its toll. Stedman, a young Indian pilot, was shot down and taken prisoner the day he joined the squadron. Clark, severely wounded in a dogfight with the Richthofen Jagdstaffel, wrestled his machine back to the aerodrome before he fainted from loss of blood. He died two days later. Henderson was so badly wounded that he was unable to continue flying. Losses for the month now stood at eighteen, one less than the total pilot strength of the squadron.

But there was some good news for 60 Squadron, too. It received a supply of modified Nieuports, fitted with more powerful engines said to deliver ten miles an hour greater speed. The steel cylinders of the Le Rhône engine had been replaced with "jars" made of aluminum which considerably lightened the load of the machine. In spite of their stepped-up performance they were still no real match for the power of the Albatros fighter. But some improvement was better than no improvement at all and the pilots of 60 Squadron were greatly excited with their new machines. Bishop wrote Margaret,

"I spent all day fussing with it. It is a beautiful grid with a glorious 120 horsepower engine."

On the day before the month ended, just before lunch, Bishop proved his new machine's mettle against the swifter Albatros—and vindicated his theory that success in the air depended on surprise and accuracy. At seventeen thousand feet over the village of Epinoy, twelve miles behind the Drocourt-Quéant "Switch," he spotted a lone red Albatros below him. He manoeuvred himself between the enemy fighter and the sun, then swooped down. From twenty yards he fired a burst of ten rounds straight at the pilot's head. The German plane spun down out of control. Bishop pursued, firing short, rapid bursts. After falling three thousand feet, the enemy fighter burst in flames.

Bishop levelled off and scanned the skies. He sighted a speck two miles away, and as he watched it increased in size. Again Bishop positioned himself between the sun and the approaching plane, which turned out to be another Albatros. As it crossed below him, he banked and dived. But he was a fraction too late. The enemy pilot saw him, rolled over on his back and plunged to safety. For several minutes Bishop circled in the hope that the German plane would return. Then, directly below, another Albatros appeared. Again Bishop chased it but once more the Albatros outsped the Nieuport and escaped.

As he flew homeward Bishop suddenly realized that for the first time during a brush with death he had not felt excited and nervous. Instead he had been icily calm and confident. In spite of being alone he had no sense of danger, only of being invincible and invulnerable. He credited this feeling to his new tactic of direct attack on the enemy, and to his shooting accuracy. To keep that accuracy at fine pitch he spent the rest of the afternoon firing at the practice target. In the mess that night another face was missing. Harry Cross had injured himself when he crashed returning from a late patrol. It brought the total casualties of the squadron for the month to nineteen.

"It doesn't do to think about these things," Bishop wrote home. In his own words those who survived "flew from sun up to sun-down and took their fun where they could find it."

Bishop, Horn and Young (who was inevitably called Old Young) found their fun that night in Charlie's bar at Amiens, the Picardy capital three hours drive from the aerodrome. Drinks were on Bishop that night. When he had turned in his report of the day's operation, Jack Scott read it, then crossed something off and wrote a word in. Bishop looked over Scott's shoulder, ready to put up an argument. He saw that the squadron commander had crossed out "Lieut." after Bishop's signature and written in "Capt." "It came up with the rations," Scott grinned.

Although Charlie's place was within sound of the front lines, the enterprising innkeeper somehow managed to serve excellent meals and vintage wines. The trio from 60 Squadron sampled the best of Charlie's fare in the upstairs dining room before repairing to the café, where there was always an abundance of friendly m'am-selles. Bishop, in merry mood, paid court to a pair of buxom dark-haired girls.

"Mesdames Richthofen and Von Bulow," he addressed them, bowing courteously. "Voulez-vous we buy you a drink?" The girls, whose English was limited to "please" and "thank you," accepted happily. Old Young, whose powers of persuasion were consider-able, cajoled from each of the girls a lacy purple garter, which in the tradition of knighthood he promised to attach to his wing struts as a tribute to the girls' beauty and charm. But Bishop had a bet-ter suggestion. In future any 60 Squadron officer who charmed a garter from one of the girls at Charlie's was to hang it on the wall of the mess with the lady's name and description (real or enhanced). "Then," he pointed out, "if he doesn't make it back from an O.P., someone else can always take his place." And so the "garter game" became a tradition of 60 Squadron from that night on.

But the night was far from over for the three revellers. After midnight they decided they had better start for home. The drive in pitch darkness was nerve-wracking. Bishop steered the rattling Ford along the narrow tree-lined road as best he could, then finally decided to defy regulations and turn on the headlights. He picked the wrong moment for it. They had just turned east at St. Pol along the road to Arras when they heard the drone of German night bombers overhead and seconds later machine-gun bullets spattered around the car.

"For God's sake, Bish, turn off those lights," Horn howled from the back seat. Bishop fumbled with the switch but it was stuck and the lights still blazed.

"The ditch," Old Young yelled, "head for the ditch."

Bishop turned the wheel sharply, and with a crash the Ford came to rest in a burrow four feet deep.

"Bish," Horn said quietly, as he rubbed his bruised forehead, "you landed that about as well as you usually do."

Bishop and his companions managed to get their battered car out of the ditch in time to return to Filescamp Farm for a few hours' sleep before morning patrols. At breakfast Jack Scott, who had been out on the first O.P., told Bishop cheerfully, "You've never seen so many Huns in your life, it's like shooting rabbits up there."

By nine o'clock C Flight was off the ground, climbing in the direction of Arras. Ugly greyish puffs burst all around the covey of Nieuports as they crossed the lines at eight thousand feet. At Vitry they turned north and climbed to eleven thousand feet, out of range of the anti-aircraft guns.

Climbing up from Douai to the east the patrol saw six red Albatros machines cross beneath, apparently unaware of the presence of the Nieuports. Bishop waggled his wings to signal the attack and dived.

In his eagerness he pushed the stick forward too roughly, and his plane was thrown beyond the vertical point; Bishop struck his head against the windscreen. This completely upset his aim and the Albatros at which he had been trying to fire escaped. The rest of the flight spread out in an aerial dogfight. When Bishop levelled off he found himself alone and out of sight of his companions. He fired a green light from his Very pistol to signal his position. Only Fry saw it, and he was so harried by two red planes that he was forced to keep turning and twisting or be shot down. Bishop circled warily, trying to find his flight. Then he spotted two giant grey-blue machines with speckled wings heading towards the British lines. He wheeled and chased them. As he drew nearer he recognized them as Gothas—the mammoth aeroplanes built to bomb London. They were the largest ships to fly up to that time.

Although they appeared slow and clumsy, they were well manned and heavily armed, and this pair seemed willing to duel with the lone Nieuport. Bishop slid under the tail of the nearer Gotha, but the other bomber pulled to one side and the two rear gunners opened fire. Bishop had to dive to gain speed. Again he manoeuvred under the first Gotha, pulled his gun down from the fixed position, and aimed right up at the big belly. "I felt," he said later, "like a mosquito chasing a wasp."

His attack might not have been so bold had he known that one of the Gotha's three machine-guns was mounted on a cross rail in the back cockpit and could be fired through an opening in the floor. Had the gunner been more alert, he would have had a dead shot at the Nieuport underneath.

Bishop's attack was a failure in any event. After fifteen rounds his gun jammed. He pulled furiously at the toggle, trying to clear the stoppage. This momentarily diverted his attention from the two enemy planes, and one of the gunners aimed a burst at the Nieuport. Bishop saw bullets rip into his wing tip and he angrily broke off. He flew back to Filescamp Farm, made a rough and hasty landing, and waved frantically for Bourne to come on the double. Bishop kept the motor running while Bourne leaned across him and pried out the cause of the trouble, a defective bullet. Bishop was in the air again in less than a minute.

Back over Vitry at fifteen thousand feet, there was still no sign of his patrol and Bishop began to worry, remembering the fate of other 60 Squadron flights in combat with Richthofen's pack. Then, far below, he spotted three grey enemy two-seaters flying in single file, the unmistakable formation for artillery-observation work. He dived to attack.

Some sixth sense warned Bishop to look behind—just in time. The two-seater convoy was a trap; out of the sun six scarlet Albatros fighters closed in on him. The leader's fluttering red wing streamers identified him: Baron Manfred von Richthofen, the highest scorer of all fighter pilots.

BISHOP *VERSUS* RICHTHOFEN

B ISHOP AND RICHTHOFEN had met in the air before, but always in mêlées of ten or a dozen planes and they had exchanged only passing shots. Now each was fighting in his favourite way: Bishop alone, Richthofen surrounded by members of his hunting pack. On this day their scores stood: Richthofen 52 planes in eight months of combat; Bishop 12 planes in five weeks.

As Richthofen's flight swept toward him, Bishop pulled back on the stick and climbed straight up. The Nieuport's wings shuddered and the engine growled in protest. As the machine slowed almost to a stall Bishop pulled over on his back, then aimed his plane in a full-power dive at the Albatros fighters, firing wildly. The Nieuport plunged straight through the formation, then zoomed up and attacked from below. From one thousand feet above, Bishop dived again and repeated his upward zoom, firing without aiming. Three times he repeated the manoeuvre, and each time the German planes scattered. Finally Richthofen, frustrated by the darting attacks, signalled his flankers to break off and the red planes dived in different directions, too fast for pursuit.

Bishop turned his attention to the two-seaters which had so nearly led him into Richthofen's trap. They were still visible, continuing their slow, unconcerned game of follow-the-leader. He approached them from the side, so that they must fly across his nose like cumbersome ships-of-the-line. The observers in the rear cockpits sighted the blue-nosed Nieuport and converged their fire on it. Bishop aimed at the observer of the middle plane and silenced his gun with a short burst that riddled the fuselage. He saw the machine turn on its side and fall away out of control. The German plane bringing up the rear dived steeply out of range. The leader of the trio simply disappeared. Bishop followed the wounded machine, which continued its spin until with a violent explosion it crashed into a farmhouse, "destroyed in the most satisfactory manner," Bishop's log reported.

The pursuit had brought Bishop to six thousand feet, farther to the south near Monchy-le-Preux, where the Richthofen formation had regrouped. Bishop sighted the red Albatros fighters again, attacking two British photographic reconnaissance planes. The outnumbered and outclassed two-seaters were putting up a stout resistance but they were being methodically peppered by the Richthofen planes.

With a slight advantage of height Bishop dived into the midst of the German formation, spraying a long burst of fire, then pulled up steeply as the Albatros scouts turned out of the path of his bullets. He stayed well above the German planes, content to harass them but without any intention of getting into close combat with such renowned fighters at odds of five to one. Several times he repeated his dive-and-zoom tactic. And once more Richthofen's flight, unable to corner the annoying Nieuport, made their way towards Douai, where one by one they glided down and landed.

Bishop turned west toward the British lines. He had just crossed over when he came upon a pair of German two-seaters spotting for the artillery. He flew headlong at them, firing as he went.

One of the two-seaters broke off. The other fought back. He and Bishop came at each other at a combined speed of more than two hundred miles an hour. Bullets whipped by the Nieuport as Bishop saw his own bullets strike around the engine of the German machine. When only thirty yards separated the two planes the German pilot broke off, much to Bishop's relief. Suddenly it dived steeply, smoke billowing out from the engine. The second machine, which had stayed out of the fight, dived after it.

It was now after eleven o'clock and the sun was high in a clear blue sky. Bishop had very little ammunition left, but he decided to cruise above the lines at a comfortable height of ten thousand feet in the hope of getting one last chance at an enemy plane before returning to the aerodrome. A lone two-seater Aviatik hove into view. Bishop pulled his Nieuport into a vertical dive, waited until he was twenty yards away, then opened fire. The observer returned the fire and a stream of bullets tore into the wing of the Nieuport.

On his second attack, Bishop pulled up underneath where the observer could not fire at him, then took careful aim at the Aviatik's belly. The two-seater shook violently as Bishop fired from ten yards away, then nosed over. Bishop emptied the rest of his drum but without effect. The German pilot was able to level out his machine a hundred feet from the ground and land safely in a field near Lens at the foot of Vimy Ridge.

With no ammunition and little fuel left, Bishop flew cautiously among puffs of anti-aircraft fire and landed at Filescamp. In one patrol he had engaged thirteen German machines in nine separate combats.

"Comment I think is unnecessary," Jack Scott added to the combat report, "except that Captain Bishop seemed to have destroyed one enemy aircraft and forced two others to land."

No less a personage than General Trenchard arrived for lunch to deliver his congratulations in person. "He said some things I shall always treasure," Bishop wrote to Margaret.

But he was less happy about his own performance. "I don't know what was the matter with my shooting this morning," he complained. "The Huns seemed to be continually diving away and escaping me."

Over at Douai, Richthofen was equally glum. All morning he had been hounded by the irritating Nieuport with the blue spinner that had refused to come down and fight it out with his formation, and what's more, had robbed him of a two-seater that was a sure kill. Richthofen was due to go on leave the next day, and he was eager to add to the spectacular score of victories he had amassed. The day before, April 29, he had shot down four planes. One of his victims was Capt. Frederick Barwell of 40 Squadron which operated from the same field as Bishop's 60 Squadron, and used the identical improved Nieuports.

On the night of April 29 [Richthofen's biography relates], he was busy celebrating with his father the great day that he had had in the air. Not only was 52 an unheard of number of victories at that time, but the downing of four enemy planes was a feat he had never achieved before. Since his brother Lothar had downed two, the brothers could say they had in one day wiped out one complete English flight.

Richthofen, Sr., joined in the big dinner and glowed with pride. At eight o'clock in the course of the dinner the baron was called to the extension telephone in the mess hall. He found himself in communication with the grand headquarters of the High Command, the Holy of Holies of the All Highest War Lord. The following message was read to him: "I heartily congratulate you on your marvellous success. The Fatherland looks with thankfulness upon this brave flyer. May God further preserve you. Wilhelm."

Richthofen had vowed to equal that day's score on his last day before going on leave. As Bishop took off from Filescamp for his second sortie, accompanied by Jack Scott, Richthofen with four other red Albatros planes left the ground at Douai. They met near Drocourt, east of Lens, at two o'clock—as if by appointment.

Scott and Bishop plunged into the middle of the five red planes. Richthofen and one of his flankers turned straight across the Nieuports and broke around behind them. Richthofen was the first to open fire.

A sharp burst from his twin Spandau guns raked Scott's engine. Scott jerked his machine to the left and climbed out of the line of fire. At the same instant Bishop swerved to his right as Richthofen and his wing mate shot by above him. Then another Albatros flashed by in front of him, and another. He was surrounded by scarlet planes.

He pushed his stick forward as he saw Richthofen dive at a right angle toward him. Bishop was banked over on his side as a stream of bullets smashed into the fuselage behind his seat. One of them pierced a fold of his flying coat. "The best shooting I have ever seen," he recalled later. He had no time for admiration now. He rolled his machine to the right as Richthofen sped by his nose, then pulled his Nieuport into a tight turn. Scott was nowhere to be seen but his own fate now occupied Bishop as bullets whipped around him. He twisted his machine to the left as once again Richthofen dived at him. He tried to get into position for a burst but Richthofen fired first. His bullets smashed the Nieuport's instrument panel and oil drenched Bishop's face.

For the first time in his fighting career Bishop lost his temper. Angrily he pulled back on the control stick and lurched upwards, shot straight up in the air, kicked the rudder bar, banked over and lunged down at Richthofen's Albatros. At sixty yards he opened fire. The Albatros rolled over on its back, then headed for the ground.

High above now, Bishop saw three Nieuports coming to his rescue. The rest of the German formation fled, and Bishop was free to dive after Richthofen's plane which was speeding down vertically, black smoke streaming from it. For one triumphant moment Bishop thought he had achieved the impossible: that the invincible Richthofen had fallen to his gun.

But it was Richthofen's old ruse. After diving four thousand feet he flattened out, smoke ceased to pour from his motor's exhausts, and he flew off eastward with a defiant waggle of his wings.

Bishop now searched the sky for Scott, with no success. In an unhappy frame of mind he crossed the lines, slowly descending. To his right he saw another plane flying toward him. He watched it cautiously, then he gave an involuntary shout of relief. It was Jack Scott's familiar silver Nieuport. The two pilots flew side by side at wingtip distance, waving and grinning as they glided down for a landing. Scott had managed to coax his limping machine out of the battle without being followed by Richthofen's men. He himself had narrowly escaped the baron's bullets, but his engine was damaged and he was coaxing it to keep running when Bishop found him.

"The C.O. and I got mixed up with five really good Huns this afternoon," Bishop described the encounter to Margaret. "We chased them away, but oh heavens did they shoot well. Seven bullets went through the back of my machine within six inches of me and one within an inch. I can only console myself with the thought that a miss is as good as a mile."

It was a fitting end to "Bloody April."

With Richthofen's departure on extended leave—he would not make another combat flight until the middle of June—much of the fire went out of the German fighter pilots who confronted the British squadrons based at Filescamp. And perhaps because the opposition was less savage, Bishop and his companions felt a letdown too. In the air Bishop had to make a conscious effort to be as eager and alert as ever, but on the ground he was irritable and listless. There were dark shadows under his eyes, and he looked older than his twenty-three years. "Here it is—only two o'clock in the afternoon and I am dead tired already after only four hours flying," he wrote Margaret.

There were good reasons for Bishop's condition. It was just over forty days since he had first flown across enemy lines as a pilot, and in that time he had fought nearly forty battles. He had watched half a dozen men with whom he lived—with whom he had eaten breakfast the same day—shot down. He himself had destroyed fourteen planes and the men who flew them. He had played hard when he wasn't fighting—few RFC pilots took more pride than Bishop in the Allied airman's traditional ability to perform on a minimum of sleep and a maximum of social drinking.

There was another and less romantic reason for Bishop's indisposition. Like other Nieuport pilots he suffered chronically from stomach upsets known as "the complaint"—the result of spending several hours a day in an atmosphere partly composed of castor oil fumes.

When rotary engines like the Le Rhône were first introduced it was discovered that petroleum oils were not suitable because the rotary design caused excessive dilution of oil by gasoline. Castor oil, however, proved to be almost insoluble in gasoline and for this reason it was used in the Le Rhône.

Jack Scott, who kept a paternal eye on his pilots, recognized the signs of nervous fatigue in Bishop and ordered him to take two weeks leave at the end of the first week of May.

That was all the tonic Bishop needed. That night he wrote to Margaret: "It will be wonderful to have the feeling that there is really a good chance of living for a few days." He had five days of flying left before he went on leave, and he made a secret resolve to bring his score up to twenty before he left for England. On May 2 his flight escorted a covey of photo-reconnaissance planes into enemy territory without resistance.

It was not until they were on their way home that Bishop sighted what appeared to be the only German machine in the sky that day. With a wave of his arm he signalled Fry to take over the patrol, and dived to the attack. But the German pilot saw him in time to get out of range.

Bishop was climbing to rejoin the patrol when he saw five two-seater machines across the Drocourt-Quéant Switch. He turned in their direction and closed the gap without being observed. As usual the reconnaissance machines were flying in line. Bishop singled out the rear one and attacked from underneath in the "blind spot" where neither the pilot nor observer could see him. He was twenty yards away when he fired his first burst, and no more than five yards from the enemy when he pressed the button again. The second burst killed both the pilot and observer. The machine spun down with the engine full on and buried itself nose first in a field near Monchy-le-Preux.

As he climbed away he heard the rattle of machine-gun fire underneath him. Bullets ripped through the fabric of his wings. He banked steeply and saw that one of the two-seaters had manoeuvred into position to give its observer a good shot at him. Bishop tilted his Nieuport, got the gunner into his sights, and opened fire at twenty yards. His bullets struck the side of the German machine but missed the observer. Another burst struck the engine. The enemy plane plunged down, trailing smoke, but Bishop was forced to break off his attack as three Albatros scouts suddenly appeared above him. With his ammunition nearly spent, Bishop decided to be content with his two victories. With a quick half-roll onto his back he dived west with the throttle wide open, levelling off at reduced speed once he had crossed the lines, and twenty minutes later landed at Filescamp Farm.

His double kill banished his fatigue. Half an hour later with his plane refuelled and with fresh drums of ammunition aboard, he was back in the air again. On that flight and on another sortie that afternoon Bishop got into seven fights, four of them while doing "lone stuff."

These are Bishop's official reports of the first afternoon flight:

(1) At 12.15 east of Lens at 8,000 feet I attacked two hostile aircraft doing artillery-observation, firing twenty rounds into

one. They then escaped. Watching five minutes later I saw only one H.A. there, the other evidently having been forced to land.

(2) At 12.15 east of Monchy at 6,000 feet I attacked two H.A. doing Art-Obs [Artillery Observation] but only succeeded in driving them away.

(3) At 12.40 over Monchy at 9,000 feet I attacked from underneath a two-seater returning from our lines; I fired a whole drum into him but there was no apparent result.

(4) At 1.05 over Pelves I attacked the same aircraft as in (2) and fired a drum at one of them from long range. No apparent result. I returned to the aerodrome as I had no more ammunition.

After lunch Bishop stretched out for a rest and was annoyed to find when he awoke that he had slept "all the way to tea time."

Fry, as deputy leader of C Flight, offered to take the evening O.P., but Bishop insisted on leading it himself. For the fourth time that day C Flight took to the air. The five Nieuports climbed towards the Drocourt-Quéant Switch. It was a beautiful evening for flying. From Drocourt at twelve thousand feet the pilots could see the glistening dark-gold Channel, and beyond it the coast of England. Below the checkerboard pattern of what had been farm fields in peacetime was slashed by zigzag lines that were the trenches.

Two Albatros scouts abruptly intruded into the pleasant scene, the sun glinting on their red wings. Bishop and Fry dived, Bishop taking the rear machine. But his shooting was at long range and ineffectual. Then his gun jammed. He pulled at the toggle furiously and freed it just as an Albatros closed in on his tail.

He banked in a turn to the right and the Albatros overshot. At once Bishop banked to the left, dived and pulled up underneath the enemy plane. He fired twenty rounds wide of the mark and the German nosed down swiftly out of his reach. Even with the throttle pushed all the way forward his Nieuport couldn't match the Alba-tros's speed.

The patrol had split up in the fight and Bishop now found him-self alone. But not for long. As he peered into the sun, he caught a flash, the reflection of a wingtip, and in a moment another Alba-tros fired at him. Bishop turned left and climbed, the Albatros shot by him, and with a quick manoeuvre he dropped back under its tail. But the speed of the Albatros took it out of effective range of Bishop's long bursts. Bishop cursed the comparative slowness of the Nieu-port as he flew north toward Drocourt, changing ammunition drums as he went. His search for the rest of his patrol was interrupted by a mêlée of airplanes several thousand feet below. He hurried to join the fight.

Six Albatros scouts were attacking a trio of lumbering British observation planes. Bishop's attack dispersed the German fighters and they stayed out of effectual range. Bishop continued to fire in the general direction of the Albatros scouts to prevent further attack on the reconnaissance planes. He circled over them for fif-teen minutes. No enemy scouts returned, and when the two-seaters finished their job Bishop escorted them back across the lines.

The sun was beginning to set as Bishop touched down at Files-camp Farm, but that was no excuse for his unusually clumsy land-ing. Bourne looked disgustedly after Bishop as he jauntily walked away from his machine to the mess. "An hour's work," he muttered, examining two damaged wheels.

The rest of the patrol had returned, safe and triumphant. Fry and Horn had each shot down an enemy machine. Bishop was delighted at the news; the achievements of his Flight meant almost as much to him as his own success. In any case he had accounted for two enemy planes himself that morning, and during the day had engaged a total of twenty-three German aircraft.

A PLAN
IS HATCHED

I N THE MESS that night, the pilots of 60 Squadron were entertained by a troupe of professional performers from the London variety stage, who were touring the battlefields as part of an Army Service Corps program to maintain the morale of British fighting men. The presence of a bevy of pretty and merry young girls certainly had that effect on the battle-weary pilots of 60 Squadron. When the party broke up a couple of hours before dawn a few more purple garters had been added to the growing collection on the walls of the mess.

Unfortunately for C Flight it was its turn to take the dawn patrol. Bishop and his men, operating under the handicap of monumental hangovers, were grateful for once that the only incident of the patrol was an indecisive skirmish with a flight of five enemy scouts. But there was one thing about the enemy group that caused the weary eyes of the RFC pilots to open wide in astonishment: leading the four red Albatros planes was a silver Nieuport—with the black crosses of the German air force painted on its sides. At first they thought it must be a Nieuport the Germans had captured and adorned with their own insignia. Later they learned that the "Nieuport" was the first model of a new German machine, a

Siemens-Schuckert, a faithful copy of the Nieuport in almost every detail.

Twice more that morning Bishop led the flight on uneventful patrols. At lunch Jack Scott had welcome news. The all-out effort was over. "Only one or two jobs a day for a while. The colonel has decided to give us a slight rest."

For the first afternoon in two weeks Bishop did no flying. He decided to spend it at target practice—lately he had been dissatisfied with his aim. But Jack Scott persuaded him to take a drive up to the line to "see the war."

From the air Monchy-le-Preux was merely a dark spot between the Scarpe and the Cojeul rivers. At ground level it was a shocking sight to Scott and Bishop, a dead ruin of jagged remnants of buildings and streets deep in rubble. The only indication that peaceful people had once lived there was a lone building, a tavern, that somehow still stood intact and defiant. On its wall was a huge faded poster proclaiming the virtues of Aperitif Byrrh.

Monchy had seen the fiercest fighting of the spring push. The British infantry was still clearing the town. The dead lay everywhere. On the side of a road the two airmen came upon the body of a German soldier unceremoniously propped up against an abandoned cart, still fully dressed in battle regalia—greatcoat, bucket helmet and a rifle clutched in one hand. Bishop nudged Scott: "What a trophy!" he said. "If we take him back it will prove to the mess that we were really at the front."

Before Scott could react to the ghoulish suggestion, shells whined and burst all about them. The Germans were laying down a barrage. Bishop and Scott took cover in the nearest dugout. For an hour and a half they did not dare move from the shelter as shells whistled overhead, some exploding not more than fifty yards away. When the barrage ended they agreed that they had seen enough of the war from the soldier's viewpoint and hastily returned to their car.

"You're a bloodthirsty one, Bish," Scott said as they drove back along the narrow road to Arras, "wanting to haul that body back."

Bishop retorted, "I'm sure he wouldn't have minded." But Scott's distaste for the idea made Bishop aware of his own callousness. He had been completely unmoved by the lifeless form of the German soldier. It was to him simply an enemy who was dead— the best condition for an enemy.

"I sometimes wonder if you will approve of the bloodthirsty streak that has appeared in me this last few weeks," he wrote to Margaret. "I simply can't help it. I detest the Huns and they have done in so many of my best friends; I hate them with all my heart."

But this feeling of bitterness was not deep-seated. It was a mood that came upon him when he was depressed and brooded on the friends he had seen shot down. Usually he respected the tradition of chivalry among the airmen of both sides. Germany's first great ace, Max Immelmann, had been known to break off a fight when he saw his adversary was wounded. When Oswald Boelcke, the German ace, was killed in October 1916, British airmen flew over Cambrai where the funeral was held and dropped wreaths inscribed: "To the officers of the German Flying Corps in service at the front: We hope you will find the wreath but we are sorry it is late in landing. Weather has prevented us from sending it earlier. We mourn with his friends and relatives. We all recognize his bravery."

Similarly the Germans paid their respects when Major Lance George Hawker, one of the first British airmen to win the Victoria Cross, was killed in a fight with Richthofen. The Baron himself dropped a message behind the British lines expressing the wide admiration of German airmen for him as "an exceptionally brave airmen and a chivalrous foe."

"We have a wonderful arrangement with the German Flying Corps," Bishop wrote his mother. "If a machine goes down behind the German lines, as soon as possible a German machine will come back and drop a message telling whether the pilot is killed or wounded and how badly. We do the same for them."

The reality of this spirit was illustrated that night at Filescamp Farm. A German *oberleutnant* who had lost his way was shot down by Fry close to the aerodrome. He was taken prisoner and escorted to 60 Squadron officer's mess. There he was royally entertained, served copious quantities of champagne, and although he spoke no English, and Bishop and his comrades were reduced to classroom phrases of "Mein Herr" and "Ja wohl," the fallen enemy joined whole-heartedly in the festivities. Ruefully he showed his captors a pair of tickets for a show in Cambrai that very night. Some m'am-selle in that city would not be guilty of consorting with the enemy, at least on this occasion. Sixty Squadron and their captive both seemed sorry when a British army squad came to take the German pilot away. Fry, as his conqueror, promised to drop a message over the German's aerodrome announcing that he was unhurt.

At one o'clock Bishop and Fry, who had returned from his errand, were having lunch when Jack Scott hobbled into the mess dining hall.

"Just got a phone call," he said, "couple of Huns over Monchy shooting things up. Off you go, you two, and chase them off."

In a few minutes Bishop and Fry were over the ridge at twelve thousand feet. They spotted a pair of two-seaters in the distance. The Germans saw the two Nieuports and went into a shallow dive towards Vitry. Bishop and Fry gave chase with engines under full power. From fifty yards away, both opened fire on the rear plane. The observer's gun went silent. One more short burst from Bishop and the enemy machine nosed over, performed a weird cartwheel and crashed in a field. The Nieuports now turned their attention to the second enemy machine, but it had fled far out of range.

Bishop and Fry returned to the aerodrome to resume their interrupted lunch. Bishop took a mouthful of mutton. "This meat is cold," he complained. "We weren't gone *that* long."

The brief encounter brought Bishop's score up to seventeen. With less than three days left before he went on leave, he spent as much as five hours a day in the air. For the first time since he had joined 60 Squadron, there wasn't an enemy plane to be seen for two days in a row.

On the evening of May 6, when Bishop returned from the last
O.P. of the day, a strange dark-green single-seater plane was parked
on the Filescamp field. It was the latest British fighter, the S.E. 5
(Scout Experimental). It was longer and heavier than the Nieuport
and reputed to be much faster. The new plane was equipped with
a Hispano engine, which was stationary and liquid-cooled. What
interested Bishop particularly was the plane's two guns—a Lewis
mounted on top over the wing like the Nieuport, and a Vickers
over the engine cowling in front of the pilot. The important difference between these two guns was that the Vickers was belt-fed, the
Lewis drum-fed.

The pilot of the S.E. 5 was waiting for Bishop in the mess, a
short dark-haired man who carried neither goggles nor flying
helmet. Bishop recognized him at once—Albert Ball, the highest
scoring British pilot. Ball had flown over from his own aerodrome
at Vert Galand, twenty miles south of Filescamp, especially to talk
to the young Canadian. Ball hoped to enlist him as his partner in a
daring scheme.

Bishop, sipping a brandy and soda, listened with mounting fas-
cination as Ball, who had waved off the offer of a drink, unfolded
his plan: "It's occurred to me that it's awfully inefficient always to
wait until enemy planes are in the air to attempt to destroy them.
My idea is to pull off an attack—you and I, on the aerodromes
around Douai. We'd go at first light, when the Hun planes are out
of the hangars and being prepared for takeoff. It's never been done
before so the surprise element should let us get away with it—I
think. I've been hearing quite a bit about what you've been doing
lately and you're the chap I'd like to have along."

It was a long speech for Ball, usually a man of few words. Ball
was introspective and deeply religious, but in aerial combat he was
a coldly calculating and ruthless enemy. After shooting down a
plane (he was officially credited with forty-three but the total was
probably much higher) he used to retire to his hut and play mourn-
ful airs on his violin for hours. Sometimes he could not sleep for

the agonizing memory of killing his fellow men, and he would emerge in pyjamas and walk in a circle around a flare on the aerodrome, playing the violin as if performing some weird religious rite.

By coincidence, Ball and Bishop devised identical battle tactics. The official history of the RFC in World War I relates: "Ball relied above all on the surprise that comes of daring. He would, single handed, fly straight into a formation, throw it into confusion, shoot one or two opponents down, and be away before the others had time to recover. A few pilots exceeded his score, but none achieved his successes with such calculated indifference to the odds against him." Like Bishop also, Ball did not wear goggles in the air. Both men were convinced that their shooting was more accurate without goggles.

That night in 60 Squadron's mess Bishop eagerly agreed to Ball's proposal. They would draw up final plans when he returned from leave. "I wish I had an S.E. 5 like yours, though," said Bishop.

"Don't," said Ball. "I'd prefer a Nieuport any day. The S.E. isn't as hot as it looks. Too heavy, doesn't get up as quickly, and its extra speed never got off the designer's blueprints."

"But two guns . . ."

"I'm going to take one of mine off to reduce weight for our show," Ball said. "And fit a smaller windshield to cut down wind resistance. By the way, if you have the time I wish you'd go up to the Austin people. I've designed a plane that I think is what we need to catch up with the Hun's fighters, and they're building it for me, but taking their own time about it. I'd like you to have a look at it and see what you can do to make them get a move on."

"God," thought Bishop, "a pilot who designs his own plane!"

Bishop was to start for London next day after lunch. That gave him a morning's flying to add to his score of seventeen. He had set twenty as his goal and obviously could not reach it. He took off alone after a late and leisurely breakfast and climbed to ten thousand feet north of Vitry. Above him a green-and-red Albatros was circling lazily, apparently unaware of Bishop's approach. The latter climbed until he was one thousand feet above the Albatros then started to stalk his prey, keeping the sun at his back. As the German continued circling Bishop fell in behind him. He nudged his Nieuport under the Albatros until the range was ten yards, then aimed at the spot directly under the cockpit and fired twenty rounds. The burst blew a gaping hole in the plane's bottom. The riddled pilot never knew what hit him. The Albatros skidded past Bishop's machine with no more than five yards to spare, then hurtled earthward in flames.

Bishop returned to Filescamp with no intention of going up again. He turned his plane over to Bourne. "She's all yours for a couple of weeks, Walter," he said. "Treat her gently and for God's sake don't let any of those ham-handed pilots touch her." Bourne grinned at Bishop—the champion wheel-smasher of 60 Squadron calling other pilots ham-handed!

Bishop walked to Filescamp's "office" for his travelling papers. The clerk-sergeant told him that a neighbouring squadron of photo-reconnaissance planes had telephoned asking for a fighter escort, but 60 Squadron had no pilots at the ready.

"Tell them I'll take them over," said Bishop, and yelled at a puzzled Corporal Bourne to bring his Nieuport out.

The formation was attacked by two red Albatros fighters as soon as it crossed the Switch. Bishop, flying high above the two-seaters, dived at the tails of the German planes. One of them spotted the blue-nosed Nieuport and fled. The other was not as lucky. Bishop closed to fifteen yards and opened fire. His bullets were right on target. The enemy machine seemed to stop in mid-air, then fell like stone.

Over the Switch, heavy anti-aircraft fire enveloped the British planes. The gunners had the range, and the leader of the two-seaters decided that it was impossible to do a satisfactory job of photo-reconnaissance while dodging heavy fire. He signalled his flight and Bishop to start back toward the British lines. On the way back the group ran into wave after wave of anti-aircraft shells. It was the heaviest—and most accurate—that Bishop had ever experienced. He felt his plane lurch and, looking back, saw fabric fluttering from a gaping hole in his tailplane. Then a shell burst right under him and pieces of shrapnel thudded into his engine. The Le Rhône immediately sputtered and lost power. Bishop desperately coaxed it during what seemed an interminably long limping flight back to Filescamp.

Two of the reconnaissance planes were so badly shot up that they could not be flown again. Bishop's Nieuport, with most of its tail missing and its engine damaged by two direct hits, would need major repairs. Bourne could only look at the wreckage and shake his head. "I was," Bishop admitted in a letter home, "thoroughly frightened. Nothing could have made me take a plane up again that day. My leave came not a minute too soon."

He had finished his first tour of duty as a fighter pilot with nineteen victories.

A PRICE
ON HIS HEAD

BISHOP REACHED LONDON at dusk and went immediately to Lady St. Helier's house in Portland Place.

Granny St. Helier's warm welcome raised his spirits immediately. He was anxious not to waste a moment of his leave, and proposed to go out in search of excitement and entertainment. But Granny fed him and packed him off to bed. He was awakened late next morning by a pretty maid, who brought tea, a telegram and the morning paper.

The telegram was from Jack Scott and brought good news: Bishop had been awarded his second decoration, the Distinguished Service Order. (The citation, which came later, read: "For conspicuous gallantry and devotion to duty. While in a single-seater he attacked three hostile machines, two of which he brought down, although in the meantime he was attacked by four other hostile machines. His courage and determination have set a fine example to others.")

The newspaper news shocked Bishop: Ball had been killed in action, only a few hours after he and Bishop had plotted a surprise attack on enemy aerodromes. The notice of Ball's death mentioned that the surviving British airman with the highest score was the Canadian, Captain William Avery Bishop. Bishop was genuinely surprised to find he had become something of a celebrity. It was his first taste of fame and it embarrassed him. Particularly a clipping from the Owen Sound paper his father had sent him. With more pride than accuracy it announced:

"This Owen Sound boy, a son of Mr. and Mrs. W. A. Bishop, has made a record for himself as an airman. On Easter Sunday he bagged seven enemy planes."

He tore it up. Heaven help me, he thought, if the chaps in 60 Squadron ever saw *that*.

He was even more apprehensive when Granny St. Helier proudly exposed him to London society. "At this moment," he wrote to Margaret, "I am trying to screw up courage to go into the next room. Princess Marie Louise is there and about four other Lord and Lady somebody. I am much happier right here telling you I love you."

It was a much more confident and composed Billy Bishop who finished the letter late that night: "I spent the evening talking to Princess Marie Louise. I made a great hit. Under the influence of champagne I told her one of the most brilliant lies of my career. I told her Louie was named after her, which so pleased her that Lady St. Helier has today received an order to bring me to see her father, old Prince Christian. Tomorrow I am asked to lunch with Sir F. E. Smith, the Attorney General, and the night after to dine with Lord Beaverbrook, so it helps having more Huns to your credit than any other Britisher."

But Bishop was shrewd enough to learn quickly how to exploit his sudden celebrity. Granny arranged for him to dine with Bonar Law, Chancellor of the Exchequer—the Canadian who later became Britain's "unknown" Prime Minister. On the afternoon of the dinner, Bishop was introduced to a beautiful, young—and impressionable—actress at tea in the Savoy. He decided that an evening in her company would be far more enjoyable than dinner with a senior member of Britain's war cabinet. He telephoned

Bonar Law's office, identified himself as Captain Bishop's secretary, and regretted that the captain would be unable to keep his engagement—he had been recalled unexpectedly to the front.

Lady St. Helier found out about it and lectured him severely. Bishop was boyishly defiant. "If you're going to become somebody that people look up to—and it seems that you might be—then you must learn to act the part. For instance, to keep appointments with your betters. And to keep your hairbrushes clean. I found yours in the bathroom in disgraceful condition."

This completely deflated Bishop's pride. He promised to behave, and was on his best conduct at dinner with Lord Beaverbrook. The elfin Canadian-born publisher who was one of Britain's top strategists of World War I talked to Bishop of a plan then being discussed by the War Cabinet to form a separate Canadian air force. Bishop, as the leading Canadian airman, would be in line for an important post. "I feel," said Beaverbrook, "that Canadians would be happier if they were running their own show instead of being under the discipline of British military tradition."

Bishop listened politely and tried to appear enthusiastic. But in truth he had not found British discipline in the RFC in the least disagreeable. If and when the Canadian flying corps was formed he would, of course, be quite willing to become a C.O., provided it did not keep him out of the air. At any rate, he would save up the conversation to spring at some appropriate moment on Jack Scott, who himself had friends in the highest places . . . "Oh, by the way, Jack, Beaverbrook told me when I had dinner at his place . . ."

On May 22, 1917, Bishop returned to France. His leave at Portland Place, his exposure to the hierarchy and his role as a bit of a celebrity had instilled in him for the first time a sense of identity and responsibility. There was something else on his mind. Since Ball's death, through all the feverish activities of his two weeks in London, Ball's plan kept nagging at his thoughts. Perhaps it was still possible; perhaps he could do it alone. On the boat back to France he decided to talk it over with Jack Scott.

He did not have to wait long. As he walked down the gang-plank the familiar face of the squadron commander beamed from the pier. "Welcome back, Bish. You're famous. The Germans have put a price on your head!"

Spring was late coming to northern France in 1917, but it was suddenly in full bloom when Bishop returned after his leave and Filescamp Farm was more like a summer resort than a battle station. In the orchard birds trilled in the blossom-laden fruit trees. Beside the officers' mess young men in smart white flannels played on a new tennis court.

"Always before I had known France in winter or dreary spring," he wrote to Margaret. "Now it is the most beautiful spot you can imagine. I went up and flew around for an hour just for the pure enjoyment of it."

Even having a price on his head did not disturb him. He could not take the threat very seriously; nor, in truth, did Jack Scott. The report came from a captured enemy pilot that two *oberleutnants* had each bet the other that he could end the career of the pilot of the blue-nosed plane. They did not seem to be trying very hard to win the bet, however. The afternoon he rejoined 60 Squadron Bishop twice crossed into enemy territory (in his old Nieuport which Walter Bourne assured him had been "fixed up better than new.") On both occasions no enemy planes appeared.

There were new faces at Filescamp—and missing friends. In the two weeks Bishop had been absent, five pilots had been lost, but none were from Bishop's C Flight, which was in fact at full strength of six pilots for the first time since Bishop had been its leader. The newcomer was a wiry dark-haired youth, D. R. C. "Black" Lloyd.

"Good man in a scrap," Fry assured Bishop. And Lloyd proved it the first time Bishop led his flight on patrol, by bringing down an enemy plane. Bishop was much less happy with his own marksmanship. Over Drocourt, a circus of Albatros fighters flew right into their midst. Bishop and Lloyd singled out one of the enemy fighters and Bishop opened fire first, but even from as close as forty yards he could see no effect from his first burst.

Lloyd's single burst hit the enemy machine's engine and it burst into flames. Bishop devoted the afternoon to firing at the white target on the edge of the aerodrome and after three hours of work he felt more confident.

Not all the additions to the aerodrome were newcomers. Grid Caldwell was back from hospital and had taken over command of B Flight. The burly, aggressive New Zealander, who only a month and a half before had introduced Bishop to air fighting, could hardly believe that his protégé had caught on so quickly and successfully.

The commander of A Flight was E. W. "Moley" Molesworth, a nerveless, balding Irishman who had transferred from the Royal Munster Regiment and was the squadron's most experienced member, with the exception of Scott. The three flight commanders were quartered together in a Nissen hut surmounted by a sign proclaiming it to be the Hotel de Commerce. Another sign on the door announced: "Welcome all comers," but the only guest it attracted was an unwelcome one—Bishop's dog, a large, black, part-Airedale who was, as Bishop admitted, quite the smelliest dog he ever knew. Grid tried sprinkling him with face powder, but this only produced an even more offensive odour, and the dog was ordered to find sleeping quarters elsewhere.

The three flight commanders rotated the duty of taking the O.P.'s and like the rest of the pilots in the squadron, enjoyed one day off in every three—a policy instituted by Jack Scott at the end of the spring offensive. But Bishop, intent on adding to his score, spent his days off hunting alone. He also explored the possibilities of making his lone raid on the German aerodromes, though Jack Scott's first reaction had been unfavourable.

Four days after he came back from leave Bishop shot down a single-seater Albatros scout near Vimy Ridge. It was his twentieth victory, and it was won against odds of six to one. This success restored his confidence and he spent more than four hours over the lines that day by himself. But it was not until the following afternoon that he had his next encounter in the air. Crossing the lines east of Monchy, at eight thousand feet, he saw British anti-aircraft shells bursting beneath him. At first he thought the gunners had mistaken the Nieuport for an enemy plane. Then he saw that they were signalling the position of a German two-seater, a yellow-and-red Aviatik. Bishop attacked from the flank and opened fire. At once two Albatros fighters came to the Aviatik's rescue. Before he could turn toward them, another Nieuport dived on them, firing wildly, and forced them to break off.

Bishop renewed his attack on the two-seaters, took careful aim at the gunner in the rear, intending to put him out of action first. But that proved unnecessary—the observer's gun had jammed. Unopposed, Bishop raked the two-seater from engine to tail. The machine fell on its side, went into a spin with the engine full on, and crashed into the Scarpe River.

That was about the last time for some weeks that 60 Squadron was to see a German two-seater flying alone. The enemy now introduced a new tactic: reconnaissance planes roamed in flights of three or four, at a height of three thousand feet, just on their own side of the lines. When British fighter planes attacked, the Germans would dive down and away, and anti-aircraft batteries would open up against the pursuing British planes. Consequently going after reconnaissance planes became as unpleasant and dangerous a task as going after observation balloons. To the disgust of 60 Squadron, it was given the assignment of dealing with the decoy two-seaters.

"It's not so much the danger, although that's nothing to sneeze at," Bishop wrote to Margaret, "but it's hard on the nerves—and on the legs. We never know when a call from the front lines will come and that damned Klaxon horn will give out with the two blasts that are our signal to scramble out to our planes."

The sorties provided poor hunting for 60 Squadron. The only apparent results were extensive damage to the Nieuports. Bishop cornered Scott in the mess after a nerve-wracking day: "If I've got to shoot at Hun planes practically at ground level I'd rather do it at one of their aerodromes where at least the anti-aircraft wouldn't be ready and waiting for me. What do you think?"

"What the hell does it matter what I think? Just let me know when you're going to do it."

Next afternoon, to relax after a trying day of chasing elusive two-seaters and dodging anti-aircraft shells, Bishop went for a lone flight toward Vitry and Brebières. There was not a cloud—or a plane—in the sky, and it was a relief to float up there at ten thousand feet, out of range of the murderous anti-aircraft fire he loathed. He turned for home and dinner—and immediately sighted two Albatros scouts. The enemy pilots, no doubt also with dinner in mind, were spiralling down toward their aerodrome at Epinoy.

Bishop put the Nieuport's nose down and opened the throttle wide to try to catch them. One was slower in getting down and Bishop had time to get into position to attack—behind and just below the Albatros. The German pilot saw him at the last moment and as Bishop opened fire he pulled up in a tight climbing turn. It took Bishop unawares and seconds later the Albatros got on his tail. Bishop veered sharply and regained the advantage. Both got in short bursts that did no serious damage. But the Nieuport's greater manoeuvrability gave Bishop a fraction of a second's advantage each time. When next he got on the Albatros' tail he pulled the Lewis gun down the rail, sighted through the ring, and from ten yards let go a volley of fifteen rounds.

The German pilot crumpled in his seat. The plane continued on an even keel, gradually losing height. For a moment Bishop watched as it slipped to the ground. At the edge of the aerodrome it crashed and burst into flames.

Flying back to Filescamp for a late dinner, it dawned on Bishop that although the fight had taken place near to an enemy airbase no plane had risen to help the Albatros. He attributed this to the fact that the presence of a British plane at such a place would be totally unexpected. He made up his mind to launch his planned attack on an enemy aerodrome immediately.

The next day, Friday June 1, 60 Squadron continued its futile and hazardous chase of German two-seaters. "What a complete waste of time," Bishop complained to Jack Scott at lunch. "My mind's made up. I'm going after those aerodromes tomorrow morning, rain or shine."

"Good luck," said Scott.

All afternoon Bishop practised his shooting. Afterward, he checked each round that went into his two ammunition drums. He oiled his Lewis gun. He pored over maps, checked every detail again and again. Walter Bourne checked out the Nieuport's motor and controls.

Early that evening Bishop scrawled on the mess blackboard: "Early call—Capt. Bishop—3.00 A.M." He left the mess just as a party was getting under way, and slept so soundly he didn't even hear Grid Caldwell's noisy arrival from the mess.

Bishop could scarcely have picked a worse time for his raid than that morning of June 2. Heavy clouds hung at five hundred feet and sprinkled the aerodrome with a light drizzle. He gulped a cup of scalding tea and pulled his flying suit over his pyjamas.

Bourne, the only other man out on the aerodrome at that hour, already had the Nieuport engine running. Bishop climbed into the cockpit, still sleepy. Bourne held out his hand under the drizzle as a silent gesture of disapproval. Bishop shrugged without speaking. Bourne pulled the wheel chocks away and waved. Bishop smiled and waved back.

The drizzle became rain as he climbed and he could hardly see through the windscreen. Over Arras the ceiling was a little higher. He turned to the right, saw that he was headed along the Cambrai road, then climbed to just under the clouds.

He experienced a loneliness such as he had never before known. He had a hollow feeling in his stomach—which he suddenly realized was hunger. He wished he had eaten some breakfast before he left.

THE *AUDACE*
OF IT

BEFORE FIRST LIGHT six Albatros scouts and a two-seater had been wheeled out of the hangars of Estourmel aerodrome, the base of Jagdstaffel V. The scouts' engines were warming up. One pilot was already in his plane preparing to take off. The others were straggling across the field from breakfast in the mess.

Without warning a silver Nieuport with a blue nose streaked over the roof of the hangars, spraying bullets among the waiting planes.

Bishop had no idea where he was. He had lost his way in the cloud and had flown further into enemy territory than he intended. When he descended from the overcast he found himself over a deserted aerodrome. So he hunted around for another field and a few minutes later he sighted the shadowy shapes of hangar buildings away to the right. The aerodrome that Bishop had found was Estourmel, near Cambrai, although he did not know it at the time. In fact in his report he stated it to be either Esnes or Awoignt. He came down to two hundred feet and turned towards them. As he drew near he saw the line of machines and went into a shallow dive. His first burst carried him to the far edge of the field, where he pulled his Nieuport into a tight climbing turn. He could see men running on to the field and a machine-gun opened fire at him from the ground. Bullets ripped his wingtips. He swerved to dodge the bullets that crackled all around him. The Albatros pilot who was already in his plane had gunned his motor and was gaining speed for takeoff. Bishop went after it.

The German fighter was only ten feet off the ground when Bishop pressed the firing button from sixty yards' range. Without enough speed to dodge the attack, the Albatros took the full blast of a burst of fifteen rounds, sideslipped, and crashed. Another Albatros started to roar across the field. Bishop fired at it from a hundred yards and missed, but the attack so unnerved the pilot that he crashed into a tree at the edge of a field, tearing off the right wings. Bishop fired one last volley into the wrecked machine, then hauled back on the control stick and climbed.

Two more machines now started to take off in opposite directions. ("There won't be any wind at that time of the morning and the planes will be able to get off in any direction," Grid Caldwell had warned. "In that case I'll just have to streak for home," Bishop had replied.) But he had no choice but to stay and fight it out.

One Albatros flew away from the aerodrome and hovered at a safe distance, but the other made straight for Bishop, who turned as the German pilot closed in behind him. The enemy tried to follow, taking a fast shot. Bishop saw an opening and fired. Twice the machines circled around each other, but neither pilot could get in a position for a decisive burst.

Once again as in many another battle, the Nieuport's sole advantage over the Albatros—its manoeuvrability—came to Bishop's rescue. He got underneath and at a slight angle to the Albatros, and finished his first drum of ammunition in a long burst. It struck the fuselage just in front of the pilot and put the engine out of action. The Albatros crashed four hundred feet from the aerodrome.

Bishop was now intent on making his escape. No doubt the aerodrome he was attacking had sent an alarm to other nearby fields, and Heaven knew how many fighters were swarming toward the scene. One comfort was that no more planes were attempting to take off from the field.

For the moment he had forgotten the fourth enemy plane, which so far had stayed clear of the fighting, but it now was bearing in. The German pilot opened fire at three hundred yards' range. Bishop saw the flashes from the twin Spandau guns, and turned away sharply. His own ammunition drum was empty.

Changing an ammunition drum while flying a plane was a tricky job at best, and to do it while dodging the bullets of a skilled and tenacious pursuer was a difficult feat of sleight-of-hand. Bishop had practised the procedure endlessly—minus the enemy plane, of course—and somehow he managed it now without giving the Albatros pilot a fatal advantage. Bishop had no intention of continuing the dogfight. His aim was to get away from there as quickly as possible.

But to make his escape he would either have to shoot down the Albatros or chase it away. He pointed the nose of his plane in the general direction of the other machine, pressed his thumb on the Lewis gun's firing button, and kept it there. The German pilot had undoubtedly never had the entire ninety-nine rounds of a Lewis gun's ammunition drum thrown at him in one prolonged burst. He broke off the fight and dived toward his aerodrome.

Bishop did not wait to see his opponent land. He turned west and climbed with all the power he could coax from the Le Rhône engine. His gun was smoking from the stress of firing a whole drum of ammunition without interruption. When it had cooled after a few miles, Bishop disconnected it from its mount and hurled it overboard. It was now dead weight and he would need all the speed he could muster.

For the first time that morning the clouds had broken, and here and there shafts of sunlight shone through. Bishop knew that such cloud formations made ideal lurking places for enemy scouts, and he kept a wary watch as he flew from patch to patch. Three miles west of Cambrai he sighted four enemy planes cloud-hopping in the same direction, two thousand feet above him. At first he caught only fleeting glimpses of the planes through the clear patches. Further west the clouds disappeared and the five planes were flying in a clear sky.

Bishop had never been in a tighter spot. The Germans did not appear to have seen him—yet. But at any moment one of the pilots might look down—and four planes with eight guns blazing would dive on the slower unarmed Nieuport. Bishop tried to keep his position directly under the enemy formation, in what he hoped might be a blind spot. Cautiously he followed their manoeuvres: as they turned, he turned. The general direction of the formation was taking him further and further south. He knew that he would soon have to make a break for it. He counted ten slowly, then dived in the direction of the front lines at full power. When he looked back the German planes were continuing their patrol—the enemy pilots never became aware of his presence.

His dive brought Bishop down to a thousand feet, and as he crossed the enemy lines anti-aircraft fire straddled the Nieuport. He dived, climbed and swerved to dodge the flying shrapnel. Time and again he heard a sharp snapping sound of shrapnel ripping the tight-stretched fabric of his plane. One of the lower wings, already damaged in the attack on Estourmel, now looked like tattered clothing flapping on a clothesline in a high wind. The barrage suddenly and mercifully ceased as he crossed the lines near Bapaume.

Bishop turned northwest towards Filescamp Farm. It was exactly fifteen minutes after five. The sky was calm and crystal clear and oddly haunting. The exhilaration of the early morning battle was gone. Bishop began to feel ill: "I flew in a daze. I was feeling queer at my stomach. The excitement and the reaction afterwards had been too much. My head was going around and around, and something had to happen. For the only time in my life I thought I was losing my senses. It was a horrible feeling and I also had the sensation that I would suffer from nausea any minute. Nothing mattered except the struggle to bring the plane safely to earth."

At half past five Bishop was over Filescamp Farm and feeling a little better. The aerodrome was still asleep, just as he had left it an hour and a half before. It seemed impossible that since then he had experienced the greatest adventure of his life.

Jubilantly, he fired off light after light from his Very pistol to signal his triumph and arouse the slumberers below. A crowd of ground crewmen led by Corporal Walter Bourne ran to greet him as he climbed out of the cockpit holding up three fingers and calling out rather incoherently, "Three of them taking off, one in a scrap—wicked ground fire—missed the other one."

Bourne as usual turned his attention to the plane as soon as he saw Bishop was unhurt. He took in the innumerable holes and slashes in the wings, fuselage and tail, and uttered an incredulous whistle. "Beats me how the thing stayed in one piece, sir!"

Jack Scott reported Bishop's early morning sortie to his immediate superior, George Pretyman at Wing Headquarters. By mid-morning the news had spread across the Western Front. General Higgins, the brigade commander, wired congratulations, and so did the commander of the Flying Corps, General Trenchard, who wired Bishop that the raid was "the greatest single show of the war." And before the day was out the army commander-in-chief, Sir Douglas Haig, had added his own congratulations.

Maurice Baring, whose essays and books on the RFC remain classics, made this note of Bishop's exploit in his diary: "Think of the *audace* of it." And Molesworth, who arrived back from leave that afternoon, described it in a letter home: "Our stunt merchant's star turn was shooting up an aerodrome. You can imagine how the fat old Huns ran, as nothing like this ever happened to them before. I believe his name has been put in for something big in the decoration line."

THE GAME

MOST of the aerial activity now centred around the battle lines to the north. A British air offensive was launched to soften up the enemy for a ground attack against Messines Ridge near Ypres. The Richthofen circus, which had been noticeably missing on the Arras front for the past month, had been moved north to Courtrai. But the tide had already changed. The Royal Flying Corps now had supremacy of the air.

To the south along the Drocourt-Quéant Switch the Germans continued their tactics of using low-flying two-seaters just inside their own lines to lure British fighter planes into anti-aircraft range. German scouts meanwhile contented themselves with watching for stragglers.

British fighter squadrons still maintained patrols along the front east of Vimy-Arras-St. Léger, where a month before the bloodiest fighting in aviation history had taken place. But "Hun hunting" became more and more frustrating. The Germans seemed determined to avoid a fight.

After the excitement of his raid on Estourmel Bishop found the regular uneventful patrols boring. So on June 8 he ventured alone toward Lille, where he hoped to find more action. He had climbed to twelve thousand when he saw six red Albatros scouts neatly arrayed in a three-layer formation. As he had done the first time he encountered that type of formation, he dived to attack the upper-most pair.

Those two pilots were so busy looking below for any luckless British planes that might venture into their trap that they did not see him coming. He opened fire from twenty yards. A burst of fifteen rounds sent one enemy plane down streaming smoke. Bishop continued his dive and escaped before the other pilots could gather their wits.

For the next week 60 Squadron seldom so much as sighted a German aircraft over the Arras front. The squadron, frustrated by this elusiveness on the part of the enemy, decided on a show of defiance—a "circus" of its own. Bishop led a formation of fifteen Nieuports after dinner one evening. They roamed the Switch at will and no German plane challenged them. What 60 Squadron did next was possibly the most blatant display of arrogance of the war in the air. The fifteen planes put on a display of aerial stunting directly over the German aerodrome at Epinoy, peeling off formation into stall turns, loops and rolls. The Germans at Epinoy preferred to watch the exhibition from the ground.

"We must have looked like a bunch of berserk eagles," grinned "Black" Lloyd. "We should have charged the damned Huns admission."

Next day Lloyd was killed in a fight with two Albatros scouts east of Monchy-le-Preux. Bishop was deeply affected. It was the first fatality in C Flight since Bloody April. Bishop's state of mind changed abruptly from impatience at the enemy's inactivity to hatred for the Germans who had killed his friend. That night he wrote to Margaret: "I am thoroughly downcast tonight. The Huns got Lloyd today, such a fine fellow too, and one of our best pilots. Sometimes this awful fighting in the air makes you wonder if you have a right to call yourself human. My honey, I am so tired of it all, the killing, the war. All I want is home and you."

For nearly a month since returning from leave in England he had been fighting steadily. He seldom took the one-day-off-in-three to which he was entitled. Instead he flew alone with the objective, as he frankly admitted later, of increasing his score of victories. He was disappointed that he had been able to add only seven enemy planes in four weeks, and that included the raid on Estourmel.

With Lloyd's death, some of the zest for the chase went out of Bishop. On June 18 he took his first leave since his return to France and went to Amiens for three days' rest.

Amiens was hardly conducive to rest. The city was a favourite short-leave headquarters for the troops in the region. The Picardy capital offered an abundance of opportunities for revelry at oases like Charlie's bar and Des Huitres. Fighting men, released for a few hours or a few days from the brutality (and as often the boredom) of war, crowded into the inns and cafés in pursuit of wine and women.

In Amiens Bishop met Ninette. By his own description she was beautiful, kind and affectionate. His story was that he had met her in a pharmacy. Later he admitted that while this was true, he had followed her into the pharmacy. When they had become well enough acquainted to exchange confidences (a matter of a few hours) Ninette confessed that she had seen him on more than one of his previous visits to Amiens, and wanted to meet him. "But I am not the kind of girl who goes to Charlie's bar," she pointed out virtuously, "so when I saw you walking down the street today I turned into the apothecary's, hoping you would come there too."

Bishop's affair with Ninette was no mere garter-gathering adventure. It was too serious, for example, to reveal to Horn, Caldwell and other members of 60 Squadron who habitually roistered with him at Charlie's—but serious enough to make him decide to tell Margaret. In just what terms he explained Ninette to his fiancée is not known. Margaret apparently "understood," and certainly it made no difference to their relationship. But the "Ninette letter" was the only one of hundreds Bishop wrote her from overseas that Margaret did not keep. In later years Bishop remembered his affair with Ninette as being more therapeutic than romantic. "If it hadn't been for Ninette," he said, "I don't think my nerves would have held." (Years later when Bishop and Margaret were visiting France, Bishop was seized by an overwhelming desire to visit Amiens— and Ninette. Margaret wisely realized that the "beautiful, kind and affectionate" French girl of 1917 probably looked somewhat different now, and to preserve her husband's illusions she persuaded him to abandon the idea.)

When Bishop got back to Filescamp Farm refreshed in body and spirit, he found that his Nieuport had been thoroughly overhauled and even fitted with a new skin. The repeated patching of bullet and shrapnel damage to wings, tail and fuselage had added to the weight and detracted from the smoothness of the faithful old machine with resulting loss of speed—the quality Bishop valued most in a plane. He celebrated the renovation of his plane by shooting down five enemy planes in as many days, and running his score to thirty-one. In the process he achieved a couple of minor "firsts" in his own career as a fighter pilot. One plane fell to the shortest burst he had ever used to down an opponent—ten shots. Another was destroyed at the longest range—over a hundred yards.

On June 29 the moderately good weather came to an end and rain, mist and heavy low clouds made flying impossible. As usual on such occasions, a sort of wet-weather madness seized the occupants of Filescamp Farm. The protesting farmyard animals were seized and painted in assorted colours, and the largest pigs were smuggled into comrades' sleeping quarters.

The well-decorated mess at Filescamp Farm was as much of a "home away from home" as anyone on the Western Front could ask for. On the east wall, which was covered with brown canvas, Old Young had practised his artistic skill by sketching life-sized figures of the alluring m'amselles from the French magazine *La Vie Parisienne* in charcoal. And to further overcome otherwise Spartan surroundings, there was a large fireplace at the south end with a two-foot railing supporting a padded seat around it. And the bar, ably attended by one Corporal Dayne, was open at all times. It was an ideal arena for comfort or frolic.

As the bad weather continued the pastimes in the mess became increasingly violent. The gramophone endlessly ground out the hit tunes from "Chu Chin Chow," the musical that had become as much part of life in wartime London as air raids and rationing. Bishop endured "Chu Chin Chow" for three days and nights and then, in desperation, invented a new game: smashing gramophone records over the nearest head. Everyone joined in willingly and the game soon had to be suspended for lack of ammunition.

The rain persisted, and the mess games became even more destructive. There was a nightly uniform-tearing contest. The rules were simple: the aggressor sneaked up behind his victim, grasped his collar firmly, gripped the flange of the uniform coat, and ripped the garment neatly up the back seam. The only members of 60 Squadron who were less than enthusiastic about the game were the officers' batmen who were required to work overtime mending the ripped jackets.

Old Young's garments suffered irreparably. He insisted on wearing the tartan trews of his erstwhile Highland regiment as part of a colourful but unauthorized flying uniform, and those plaid trousers—or portions thereof—became coveted prizes of the game. (When flying weather returned Young had to go into battle in his tennis flannels for several weeks until replacements arrived from a London military tailor.)

On a murky afternoon toward the end of the week of foul weather the occupants of Filescamp Farm heard the drone of a plane overhead and all hands hurried outside. Perhaps the Germans, knowing that all the Allied machines were grounded, were staging a hazardous surprise raid in retaliation for Bishop's recent stunt. But the plane that dropped hesitantly through the overcast bore French markings. The pilot landed smoothly.

He explained that he had taken off from his own aerodrome with the intention of flying around for a few minutes at low altitude to test repairs to the plane's controls which had been damaged by anti-aircraft fire during a patrol the previous week. But the clouds

had descended and swallowed his plane, and soon he became
hopelessly lost. He had flown around aimlessly for hours, seeking a
break in the clouds. Then with fuel running low he had been forced
to come down and take a chance on finding a reasonably level place
for his forced landing. By merest chance he had emerged directly
over the Filescamp aerodrome.

The French pilot was ceremoniously conducted to 60 Squadron's mess and established as guest of honour of a riotous party. He
was introduced to—and thoroughly approved—the squadron custom of pouring part of each bottle of champagne into the mess
piano's works "to improve the tone." With the instrument thus
lubricated, the assembled pilots serenaded their guest with the
squadron's favourite toast, a somewhat lugubrious ballad rendered
to the tune of "The Lost Chord":

We meet neath the sounding rafters,
The walls around us are bare;
They echo the peals of laughter—
It seems that the dead are there.
So, stand by your glasses steady,
This is a world of lies.
Here's a toast to the dead already;
Hurrah for the next man who dies.

Cut off from the land that bore us,
Betrayed by the land that we find,
The good men have gone before us,
And only the dull left behind.
So, stand by your glasses steady
This world is a web of lies;
Then here's to the dead already,
And hurrah for the next man who dies.

More champagne, and suddenly the "game" erupted. Bishop selected the French officer for the ceremony, whereupon the latter cheerfully but firmly declared that the honour of his country's uniform had been despoiled, and challenged Bishop to a duel in the form of a flying contest. Everyone trooped on to the field and, the French pilot's plane having been refuelled, he and Bishop took off into the early dusk. Each tried to outdo the other in a series of wild manoeuvres which were all the more hazardous because they had to stay within a couple of hundred feet of the ground for fear of losing their way in the low clouds—as the Frenchman had done once before that day. The latter climaxed his performance by scraping a wingtip through the grass of the field, but even he admitted that Bishop outdid him by rolling his wheels on the roof of the mess building as he came in for his landing. Honour having been satisfied, the squadron repaired to the mess to resume the party.

One of the more disciplined pastimes in 60 Squadron mess was a ritual instituted by Jack Scott: that of speech-making at dinner. Each night one of the pilots would be called upon to give a peroration on anything, from his current combat experiences to his latest adventures in Amiens. Scott (who at this time was still on leave) regarded speech-making as part of moulding a man's character. Serious though this intention was, the inevitable highjinks became a part of the ceremony. If a speech was poor or dull or pompous, it was celebrated with a derisive round of jeers, and a shower of buns, cutlery, and even plates when the occasion seemed warranted, all of which were aimed at the errant orator of the evening.

Jack Scott returned from leave just in time for the resumption of combat flying with the return of good weather, at the end of the first week of July, 1917. He brought Bishop word from London that Lord Beaverbrook was increasing his pressure on the government to form a separate Canadian air force. Scott also reported what was good news for himself, bad news for 60 Squadron: he was to be promoted to command an RFC wing. In one way it was bad news for Scott too. With his new and increased responsibilities as wing commander his flying days would be over.

As leader of a squadron Scott was under orders to confine himself to test and "recreational" flights on his own side of the front lines. General Higgins had to try to suggest diplomatically, because Scott's legs were severely crippled, that he refrain from *all* flying. But Scott ignored both the order and the suggestion, and from time to time he joined one of his flights, either as an extra man or to replace a regular pilot who might be ill, injured or on leave. No matter how many fights he got into he always logged his flights as "recreation" so that on several occasions pilots received full credit for victories to which Scott had contributed.

As a leader Scott was bold and aggressive, but as a fighter pilot he lacked blood lust, the killer instinct. On one "recreation" sortie with Bishop, Scott manoeuvred a German Albatros directly into his gunsight, but did not fire, and the enemy escaped. Afterward Bishop asked him:

"Why didn't you shoot? You had him cold."

Scott grinned. "I was interested in his head."

"In his *head*?"

"Before the war I studied in Germany, and I'm interested in Germans—anthropologically, I mean. You know, I'd swear that pilot was a Bavarian."

Now that Jack Scott had only a week or two left with 60 Squadron he joined one or more patrols every day. A little after eight o'clock on the evening of July 10 the klaxon horn at Filescamp blared. The observer corps had reported that twelve German planes were attacking ground forces near Monchy-le-Preux. Bishop and Soden, a new arrival at the squadron, who was nicknamed "Mongoose," were playing tennis with two other pilots. They dropped their racquets and scrambled for their planes, wearing flannels and tennis shoes.

Scott, who had been watching the match from the comfort of a deck chair, grabbed his canes and hobbled out to his Nieuport, shouting to Bishop that he was joining them. Five planes took off in no semblance of order, then closed into formation at a thousand feet. They reached Monchy just as the enemy planes were turning for home. In a moment seventeen planes were swirling around in a vicious dogfight perilously close to earth. Bishop singled out one of the green enemy scouts and had sighted on the head of the pilot when a burst of machine-gun bullets tore into his own fuselage just behind him. He turned on his attacker, only to have another Albatros pounce on him from the other side. He was trapped. But before the German pilot could open fire a Nieuport dived out of nowhere and set his plane afire with a stream of tracer bullets. As the plane that had rescued him flashed by, Bishop recognized the grinning pilot as his squadron commander.

"Thank God the Hun pilot wasn't a Bavarian," Bishop muttered to himself. Another Albatros dived at him and bullets ripped into the Nieuport's tail. Bishop pulled straight up and as the German flashed under him he pushed the stick over and went into a rough stall turn that put his Nieuport directly behind the Albatros. Bishop had a dead shot. His burst ripped the German's fuselage apart. It fell, streaming smoke and shedding splintered wood and torn fabric. That ended the fight. The remaining Germans scattered, using their superior speed to outdistance the Nieuports.

When Bishop landed at Filescamp, Scott's plane was already on the ground and he hurried to the mess to thank him for saving his life. Scott wasn't there, and Caldwell had bad news: Scott had been wounded in the arm and the same burst had badly damaged his motor. Scott, becoming increasingly weak from loss of blood, had barely been able to coax the sputtering machine back to Filescamp. Mechanics had pulled him from the cockpit and rushed him to a makeshift hospital at Izel-le-Hameau.

That was gallant Jack Scott's last combat flight. As soon as the report of his injury reached Colonel Pretyman, the latter ordered Scott's transfer to his new post immediately he recovered from the wound. Bishop blamed himself for Scott's mishap, since he had been shot while his attention was occupied in saving Bishop from almost certain disaster. But Scott, cheerfully convalescing in a lounging chair in 60 Squadron's mess, laughed scornfully at Bishop's melancholy brooding.

"I was fighting my own fight," he insisted. "I didn't even know you were in the vicinity."

The day after Scott's departure, an exciting event occurred at Filescamp: the first of 60 Squadron's S.E. 5 scouts arrived. It was assigned to Bishop.

"A most tremendous thing," Bishop described the event in a letter to Margaret that night. "It's forty miles an hour faster than our present machines and has two guns. It will be wonderful to be able to catch Huns instead of watching them disappear."

THE BEST
MACHINE IN
THE WORLD

THE NEW PLANES took a lot of getting used to. The controls felt heavy and awkward after the small Nieuports. They landed at much higher speed, and in one most important way they were a thorough disappointment to the pilots: the guns would not work.

Like the Nieuport, the S.E. 5 mounted a Lewis gun on the top wing. But it also had a more rapid-firing gun, a Vickers, on the engine cowling directly in front of the pilot. It was equipped with an interrupter gear designed to permit it to fire safely through the propeller, an advantage German pilots had enjoyed for several months. It was this device that caused most of the trouble.

"I am thoroughly fed up with life tonight," Billy wrote to Margaret. "Yesterday we did our first job on S.E. 5's and my gun was the only one that fired. It shot holes through my propeller. Tonight I put nine holes through the propeller so that makes two machines I have done in. It will take days to get a new one. Tomorrow an expert is supposed to come over about the gear."

Bishop remembered unhappily that Albert Ball had spoken scathingly of his own S.E. 5 a few weeks before. Actually the planes

60 Squadron received were improved models, and the interrupter gear, which needed only expert adjustment to work perfectly, was a superior design to Fokker's synchronizer, which was activated by a series of arms and rods. The S.E. 5's interrupter gear was operated by a simple, smooth hydraulic mechanism that automatically went into action when the gun button was pressed. It was the invention of an eccentric genius, a Romanian named Georges Constantinescu, who worked on it for many months in a laboratory of the War Office in London.

While the factory expert sent from England worked on the S.E. 5's guns at Filescamp, 60 Squadron's pilots continued their patrols in the faithful old Nieuports. On July 12 Bishop fought the highest battle of his career—nineteen thousand feet above Vitry—against an Aviatik two-seater. His Nieuport wallowed in the thin air and barely responded to the controls. Worse, Bishop's hands were numbed by cold and he became dizzy from lack of oxygen. Twice he got the enemy within ten yards' range but his shots went wild. The second time his plane stalled and went into a spin and he had to struggle hard to regain control.

"I'll never fight again at that height," Bishop vowed.

Later on the same patrol his flight encountered a formation of Albatros fighters that showed no inclination to avoid battle, but turned savagely on the Nieuports. Bishop took aim at an Albatros in front of him just as another of the vivid green-and-yellow enemy planes started a loop directly below. Bishop shifted his sights quickly and raked the belly of the Albatros as it turned on its back at the top of the loop. For a moment it remained poised in its upside-down position. Then its nose dropped and it fell in a vertical dive, streaming smoke, into a field eight thousand feet below.

Another Albatros closed in behind Bishop and got him in his sights. But before the German pilot could fire, and before Bishop could turn away, a British triplane sent the Albatros spinning down in flames with one short burst. Bishop knew his rescuer must be a pilot from a land-based Royal Naval Air Service squadron—only the RNAS was equipped with triplanes. The three-decker followed Bishop's flight back to Filescamp, and when the navy pilot introduced himself Bishop realized that the recent dogfight had been a minor historical event. The navy pilot—who explained that he had "just been sightseeing" when he ran into the mêlée of Albatros and Nieuport scouts—was Robert Little, a New Zealander who was second only to Bishop in air victories among living British pilots. In the fight northeast of Douai, Bishop had scored his thirty-third kill and Little his twenty-fifth within seconds of each other.

That night 60 Squadron's new commanding officer arrived. He was C. Kennedy "Pat" Cochrane-Patrick, a tall boyish Scotsman who had been flight commander with 23 Squadron. General Trenchard, commander of the RFC, regarded him as the most brilliant pilot at the front, and that appraisal was borne out by the fact that Pat wore the same decorations as Bishop, the D.S.O. and the M.C. Like Jack Scott, Pat completely disregarded orders prohibiting squadron commanders from flying across the front lines.

His skill as a pilot was soon demonstrated. Cochrane-Patrick put the new S.E. 5 through its paces, in a series of intricate manoeuvres the other pilots could not hope to duplicate. What he learned he passed on to the pilots of 60 Squadron: "You'll have to treat her roughly, she's a heavy-handed machine. Rely on speed for advantage and remember to use all your strength on the stick when you turn or pull out of a dive."

Pat's study of the new machine made the transition from the slower but more responsive Nieuports easier for his pilots. Bishop in particular was happy at his commanding officer's appraisal of the S.E. 5's characteristics. For one thing, he was a naturally heavy-handed pilot and for this reason he had never achieved perfect accord with the Nieuport. For another, the method of fighting he had developed needed speed more than manoeuvrability. He could learn how to horse a plane around in the air, but speed was something that was built into a plane. However, the pilots of 60 Squadron could not yet fly their S.E. 5's into combat. The guns were still not working properly.

On July 17 Bishop in his Nieuport shot down two enemy planes within twenty minutes of each other on an after-dinner sortie south of Cambrai—not far from the scene of his aerodrome raid two weeks before.

The synchronization gear was ready on July 20, but the impatient pilots were under orders not to use the new planes. There were other minor adjustments to be made to other equipment. Bishop took off on a lone patrol—his last flight in a Nieuport. He attacked a formation of five Albatros scouts and shot the lower left wing off one. It fell to earth like a dead leaf. The rest of the formation scattered in all directions, leaving Bishop, as he complained later, "standing still." The frustration of fighting an enemy who could escape almost at will, which he had experienced many times before, made him all the more eager to get his hands on the S.E. 5. When he landed Corporal Bourne told him that his new plane was finally ready to the last detail—a freshly-painted blue nose.

The S.E. 5's had been made operational just in time for the Third Battle of Ypres. The offensive was to be launched on the last day of July, and as usual with major attacks the tactical air support began more than a week in advance. Although the 13 Wing was far from Ypres it had a role to play. All along the line a curtain of offensive patrols had to be maintained as an integral part of the order of battle.

On one of these patrols Bishop made his first score in his new machine. It was July 28, three days before the attack at Ypres started. Bishop, Young and Soden were assigned O.P. duty in the vicinity of Drocourt. Their orders were to maintain vigil just over the lines and not to venture into enemy territory, because of their unfamiliarity with the new planes. As they flew up and down their patrol area they sighted three enemy planes. The Germans hovered a mile and a half behind their own lines, as if aware of the British pilots' orders and taunting them to pursue. Bishop endured this impudence for half an hour, then signalled Young to take over the patrol and turned

toward the enemy planes. He pushed the throttle all the way forward and gloried in the magnificent surging power of the Hispano
engine. Two of the enemy pilots turned tail when they saw the S.E. 5
headed in their direction, but the other attacked head-on. Neither
pilot scored a hit as they rushed toward each other at a combined
speed of more than 250 miles an hour, but Bishop took pleasure in
the rhythmic clatter of his twin guns, which he later described as
being "like the unleashed power of a three-inch cannon."

The German swerved away just before the planes collided.
Bishop turned hard around and discovered that the S.E. 5 did
indeed respond to rough handling. The manoeuvre put him on the
enemy's tail—not as nimbly as the Nieuport would have slipped
into place a dozen yards behind the quarry, but at the respectable
range of fifty yards. Twin streams of bullets set the Albatros afire
and it fell trailing smoke and debris.

Bishop had never felt so elated over a victory, so sure of superi-
ority in combat. That night he wrote home: "I've never enjoyed
myself so much since I've been over here. This is positively the best
machine in the world."

Bishop was, in fact, so excited by the performance of the S.E. 5
that next morning, even though it was his day off, he teamed up on a
three-man patrol with Grid Caldwell and Bill Gunner, a pilot from
Grid's flight. At ten thousand feet over Beaumont, just east of the
Switch, they spotted a two-seater Aviatik that seemed to be flying
nowhere in particular. Long and bitter experience of such innocent
behaviour by an enemy pilot had made Bishop and Caldwell suspicious, and they approached the Aviatik cautiously. Their alertness
was rewarded when four Albatros scouts dived at them out of the sun.
At that moment Gunner's engine went dead, and he was forced to
turn into a glide that would carry him to safety behind his own lines.

The German pilots swerved to attack the helpless S.E. 5, and
Bishop and Caldwell turned into them to head them off, firing
from extreme range. Suddenly both of Caldwell's guns jammed,
and he pulled away from the fight to work on them. Bishop was left

alone to face four Albatros scouts—and suddenly there were seven. They boxed Bishop in so that escape was impossible. It was only a matter of time—of very short time, he knew—before one or more of the German pilots, who were firing wildly every time the S.E. 5 came anywhere near their sights, got in a fatal burst. Bishop kept his own guns blazing in short bursts, in hope of preventing the German pilots from closing in for the kill.

Suddenly Caldwell, whose guns were still dead, burst into the midst of the swarming Germans. He darted in and out among them and the surprise appearance caused them to scatter. Bishop saw a gap and dived to escape, just as an unlucky German pilot crossed his sights. Bishop's guns were firing to clear a path for his departure. A double burst of bullets sliced through the Albatros amidships, cutting it almost in two, and it fell out of control.

Bishop and Caldwell flew back to Filescamp side by side and landed just as a heavy storm broke. In the hangar Bishop and Corporal Bourne closely examined the precious S.E. 5 and made an incredible discovery: not a single bullet had struck the plane. Bishop walked through the rain to buy Caldwell a drink and say a simple "thanks, Grid." Caldwell was always impatient at gratitude. Later Bishop wrote home: "It was the bravest thing I have ever seen, but typical of him. He's always getting shot up helping others out of scrapes."

Bishop's second victory in an S.E. 5 was almost his last. After lunch the worst of the storm was over but rain still fell in gusts and the overcast was low. Bishop took off alone, intending to cross the lines north of Monchy-le-Preux to avoid the hated anti-aircraft concentration at that point. But he sighted a pair of two-seaters over Monchy and forgot caution. He flew toward them at five thousand feet, an ideal height for anti-aircraft gunners, who promptly threw a murderous barrage at their favourite target, the blue-nosed British plane.

Bishop threaded his way among the puffs of exploding shrapnel shells and was almost out of their range, and gaining on the two-

Billy Bishop's mother and father.

Bishop as a Royal Military College Cadet.

LEFT:
Bishop as an observer in the Royal Flying Corps.

BELOW:
With 60 Squadron at Filescamp Farm in 1917. From left to right: Mongoose Soden, Bishop, Grid Caldwell, Moley Molesworth and Spencer Horn. Photo: *Imperial War Museum, London*

With King George V and other officers at Windsor Park in 1918.

Spencer Horn.   Arthur Benbow.

Bishop sighting through his Lewis gun on the Nieuport.

TOP: An Albatros D.V.: British soldiers looking at the German plane in Allied hands. Photo: *Royal Canadian Air Force*

BOTTOM: German Fokker D.V. II. Photo: *Royal Canadian Air Force*

TOP LEFT: The S.E. 5A. Photo: *Royal Canadian Air Force*

TOP RIGHT: Sopwith triplane of the R.N.A.S. Photo: *Royal Canadian Air Force*

BOTTOM LEFT: The R.E. 7. Photo: *Royal Canadian Air Force*

BOTTOM RIGHT: Farman Shorthorn. Photo: *Royal Canadian Air Force*

The wedding of Billy Bishop to Margaret Burden at the Timothy Eaton Memorial Church in Toronto, 1917.

TOP: Billy Bishop and Margaret in 1917, soon after their marriage.

BOTTOM: Bishop beside his Nieuport at Filescamp aerodrome, 1917.

LEFT:
Baron Manfred von Richthofen.
Photo: *Imperial War Museum, London*

BELOW:
Bishop with group at Hounslow, 1918. Larry Callahan is second from right.

TOP:
Some of Bishop's decorations and trophies. Note the windshield with bullet hole in it the day he became an ace by shooting down his fifth enemy plane.

LEFT:
Eighty-five Squadron at St. Omer, France; formation of S.E. 5A's with Bishop's plane in the foreground. Photo: *Royal Canadian Air Force*

Combats in the Air.

Squadron :   60

Type and No. of Aeroplane : Nieupprt Sct. B.1566

Armament : 1 Lewis Gun

Pilot: Capt. W.A. Bishop D.S.O. RC.

Observer :   none

. 456 Locality : **Either ESNES aerodrome or ANOIGNT.**

Date :   June nn . 17.

Time :   4.nn – 5 a.m.

Duty :   ....

Height :   50 ft. – 7.0.0°

Remarks on Hostile machine :—Type, armament, speed, etc.

Albatros Scouts.

—— **Narrative.** ——

I fired on 7 machines on the aerodrome, some of which had their engine
running. One of them took and I fired 15 rounds at him from close range
60 ft. up and he crashed. A second one taking off, I opened fire and
fired 30 rounds at 150 yds. range, he crashed into a tree. Two more
were then taking off together. I climbed and engaged one at 1.000'
finishing my drum, and he crashed 300 yds. from the aerodrome. I
changed drums and climbed E. A fourth H.A. came after me and I fired
one whole drum into him. He flew away and I then flew 1.000' under
4 scouts at 5,000' for one mile and turned W. climbing. The aerodrome
was armed with one or more machine guns. Machines on the ground were
6 scouts (Albatros type I or II) and one two-seater.

                 (Sgd)   W.A. Bishop Capt.

Capt. Bishop had been encouraged to catch the H.A. referred to in
VII Corps Daily Intelligence Summary No. 151. His method was not
quite what I intended. He was several times at a height of 50 ft.
over this enemy aerodrome at least 17 miles E. of the lines. His
machine is full of holes caused by machine gun fire from the ground.

OPPOSITE:
Combat report of the attack on Estourmel aerodrome that won Bishop the Victoria Cross.

LEFT:
Barker (left) with Bishop in the H.S. 2L at Muskoka Lakes, 1919.

BELOW:
Bishop with German air aces in Berlin, 1928. Goering is on Bishop's left with his arm around him. Ernst Udet is third from right.

TOP: My father in front of our Montreal house with three of his favourite breed of dogs—chows.

BOTTOM: Air Marshal Bishop with Prime Minister Winston Churchill at 10 Downing Street during the Battle of Britain.

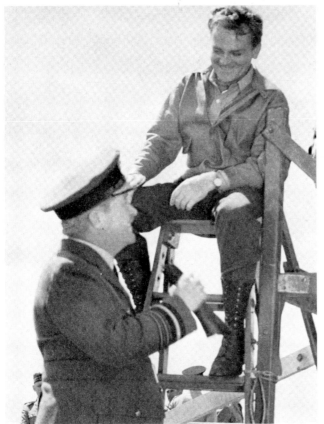

ABOVE:
With Hollywood stars at a party given in his honour at the Warner Bros. Studios.

LEFT:
With James Cagney during the filming of "Captains of the Clouds."

My father pinning my pilot's wings on my tunic, July, 1942.
Photo: *Royal Canadian Air Force*

seater, when a shell burst under his plane. He heard a sharp clang, felt a sickening lurch, and immediately his engine spluttered and slowed.

He turned quickly toward his own lines, losing height. With relief he saw that he was out of anti-aircraft range. The engine was barely idling, providing less than enough power for the long glide back to Filescamp. He pushed the throttle cautiously open, hoping to coax a little more power from the damaged motor. Instead it vibrated violently—and suddenly flames enveloped the plane's nose and were blown back toward the cockpit. The smoke and heat choked Bishop. Quickly he kicked the right rudder bar roughly and pushed the stick to the left. The effect was to throw the plane into a sideslip and sweep the flames away from the cockpit. But it also pushed the plane close to the ground, and Filescamp was still more than two miles away.

The flames licked at the fabric of the lower wing and charred pieces tore off. The earth was now only five hundred feet below. Bishop looked over the side in search of a field level enough to give him a chance of landing a crippled and unfamiliar machine. Drenching rain was falling again and Bishop could barely make out a field below, beyond a barrier of poplar trees.

Two hundred feet, one hundred feet. One of the struts was on fire. When it burned through the wing would collapse and drop the plane like a stone. Twenty-five feet. Bishop pulled back on the stick in a desperate effort to gain enough altitude to clear the trees. He ducked his head as flames swept around the cockpit; with a violent shudder the plane stopped in mid-air, turned on its side and crashed into the poplar trees.

In the sudden silence he remained conscious only long enough to feel a rush of blood to his head and to realize he was hanging upside down. Then he fainted.

Someone was trying to jab a cigarette between his lips.

"Thanks, but I don't smoke," Bishop said, and it somehow sounded a little ridiculous.

"You all right?"

Bishop focused his dim sight on a large, worried face staring down at him. Memory broke through the blur. The aeroplane . . . the fire . . . the trees. It was vivid, frightening. He tried to stand up but a heavy hand clasped his shoulder and held him down. "Take it easy," the voice said. He looked around and discovered that he was sitting with his back against the trunk of a tree. It was raining hard and the foliage above dripped streams of water on his head and shoulders.

"What a mess," someone said, and Bishop's eye followed a pointing hand upward. What remained of his S.E. 5 was a mangled mass of fabric and wire dangling carelessly between two tall poplars.

The rain of course had helped save his life. It drowned the fire that would surely have burned him to a cinder. But he might still have been hanging upside down in his harness if some soldiers driving along the St. Pol-Arras road by the edge of the field had not seen the blazing aeroplane stall and crash into the trees. One man climbed on another's shoulders to pull the unconscious pilot from the cockpit. When the soldiers were sure he had suffered no broken bones or internal injuries, they drove him the two miles to Files-camp. The amazing fact was that Bishop did not receive so much as a scratch or the trace of a burn. But his nerves were badly affected. He wrote to Margaret:

"I don't suppose my nerves will last more than three months out here. They are getting shaky now. I find myself shuddering at chances I didn't think anything of taking six weeks ago."

Cochrane-Patrick sent him to Amiens for two days' rest, and in that friendly and relaxing atmosphere he soon felt refreshed and calmed. When he returned to Filescamp Farm his S.E. 5 was, incredibly, ready to fly. He was amazed that Corporal Bourne and his mechanics had even been able to salvage enough of it to turn in for scrap. But the S.E. 5 was a sturdy job and it had not been as badly damaged as Bishop had thought. The wings had been smashed and burned but were easily restored. The only thing that had to be completely replaced was the burned-out engine.

Bishop decided that he had better get into the air as soon as possible. He had heard fearsome stories of pilots who had crashed, survived, taken a long rest, only to find that they had lost their nerve for flying—and for fighting.

The day after he returned to Filescamp Bishop took off on patrol with Molesworth and Horn over his favourite hunting ground, the Drocourt-Quéant Switch. The three-plane patrol had been introduced because the enemy had been resolutely avoiding the usual six-plane patrols. Ten minutes after they crossed the front lines eight Albatros scouts dived on them. The leader was in a bright silver machine. The rest were bright green. Bishop singled out one of the green machines and opened fire on it head-on. The Albatros burst into flames. Molesworth and Horn both opened fire on another Albatros, and it too went down in flames.

Bishop glimpsed the leader's silver plane overhauling him from the rear. He looked about for Horn and Molesworth. They had disappeared. Later he learned that the guns of both their planes had jammed and they had been forced out of the fight.

Bishop now had all six Albatros fighters to himself, and he was interested only in escaping. But the silver plane kept darting at him from behind and from the flanks. Finally Bishop tried a desperation manoeuvre. He flew head-on at the enemy plane. The German pilot had no appetite for such an attack and swerved aside. This gave Bishop the opportunity he had been seeking—to concentrate on the other machines in the hope that he could bring one down and so frighten the rest. He hurled his plane around and got under the belly of one of the green fighters. Then his guns jammed too. He dived out of the battle and fumbled with the unfamiliar firing mechanisms of the S.E. 5's guns.

Presently they started firing again (Bishop never did figure out what he had done to get them back into operation) just as one of the enemy planes crossed his sights. He fired a short burst and the plane's fuselage disintegrated and it fell out of control. The silver Albatros dived out of the action and the rest of the German planes followed. Bishop did not pursue them. Gratefully he returned to Filescamp—just in time. When he landed it was almost dark, and his motor was sputtering from lack of fuel.

That night Bishop wrote home: "Tonight I got two more Huns. One in flames and another that spun down and crashed. That is forty for me. Eight more and I will have the same as the French flyer Guynemer who is the highest. And I might even be able to beat his record and lead the Allies. I am only three behind Albert Ball."

He came close to his objective on August 5, when he followed a decoy enemy plane into a trap east of Monchy-le-Preux at seven thousand feet under clouds, and shot down one of the three Albatros scouts that ambushed him.

Two to go to catch Ball. Shooting down enemy planes became an obsession with Bishop, and he did not try to conceal it from Margaret. He wrote to her, three nights after his forty-first victory: "I am due for leave in a fortnight but I don't think I'll take it as the last few days have been dud and there had been no flying. I am sufficiently rested from loafing around to do another six weeks here. If it is clear tomorrow I'll shoot down every Hun in the sky."

August 9 did dawn clear, but Bishop shot down only half the Huns in the sky—but then, only two showed up. Next day it rained again. Horn watched Bishop pacing about the mess until he could stand it no longer. "There's a cavalry regiment up at the lines," he told Bishop. "Let's drive over and see if any of your old pals are there." They borrowed a car and as Bishop reported, "darned if Horn's hunch hadn't been right. The place was overrun by Royal Canadian Dragoons, and Royal Canadian Horse Artillery. I had a merry reunion with Gordon Cassels, John Crerar, Ham Roberts and a dozen other Royal Military College people."

Horn and Bishop got back to Filescamp late—very late. Corporal Bourne was waiting for them: "C.O. wants to see you—no matter how late you get back. He's in the mess. And by the way, Sir, congratulations."

"What for?" asked Bishop.

"Don't know, Sir. At least, it's only a rumour. C.O. will tell you."

Late as it was, all 60 Squadron was in the mess. Cochrane-Patrick told Bishop: "Old Boom Trenchard has been trying to reach you all afternoon. You're to phone him right away."

Bishop lifted the telephone nervously. In a few seconds he was speaking to the General Commanding.

"That you, Bishop?" he bellowed.

"Yes, Sir."

"Good! Allow me to be the first to congratulate you on winning the Victoria Cross."

The celebration of Bishop's award of the highest honour the British monarch could bestow was to go down in history as the most frantic ever held on the Western Front. At some time during the proceedings Jack Scott showed up, and so did Colonel Pretyman.

Before it was over [Molesworth reported in the only coherent description of the event], Boom Trenchard may have joined the proceedings, for all we knew, to say nothing of Sir Douglas Haig himself. There was a dinner at which several people made speeches and the piano received about as much champagne as we did. After dinner we had a torchlight procession to the other squadrons, led by our Very light experts. Luckily for us the night was very cloudy or the Huns would probably have come over to see what was going on.

We charged into the other messes and threw everything out of the windows including the occupants. We bombarded the messes with Very lights, the great stunt being to shoot a Very light through one window and out the other. I can't imagine why the blessed place didn't go up in flames. After annoying these people for a bit we retired to our mess, where we danced and sang till the early hours of the morning.

Next day Bishop, red-eyed and in delicate health, was summoned to lunch with General Trenchard. The general told Bishop—and everyone else within earshot—that the Victoria Cross was for "the aerodrome show." He also informed Bishop he was recommending him for the post of chief instructor of fighter pilots at a large new air school the RFC was organizing in Britain. He would probably not return to 60 Squadron after his forthcoming leave.

"I'm sure he thought he was giving me good news," Bishop said later, "and I had to pretend it was. But I hated the thought of leaving Filescamp Farm and 60 Squadron, which had become home and family to me." But the biggest disappointment was that he might not be able to catch up with Albert Ball's leading Allied score of forty-three enemy planes downed. He still had one plane to go—and one week of operations left. As a pilot instructor in England he might never get into combat again.

But next afternoon, August 13, ten thousand feet over Drocourt he tied Ball's score by shooting down an Albatros—and seconds later he became the leading Allied airman by downing another Albatros. He took particular satisfaction in the fact that the first of his victims was the shining Albatros that had eluded him in several dogfights; the plane he had dubbed "old Silversides." In one surprise dive through a formation of three enemy scouts he got in short bursts at two and watched them crash into a field one after another.

With only three days of flying left, Bishop was determined to stay in the air from dawn to dusk. But that night Cochrane-Patrick told him he was grounded for the following day. "Orders from headquarters," he said with a grin. "The official photographer chaps are coming over to see you." Bishop described the ordeal in a letter to Margaret: "They were here today taking all kinds of pictures, and of course I am being ragged to death by the others. To add to this something has already appeared in the London papers about me, aged 19 and V.C., D.S.O., and leading British airman with a lot of other rot. I'll never hear the last of it. Surely they could have checked the official records and found out I'm 23."

The Canadian newspapers were full of Bishop's exploits, too, and his father wired him to be cautious during his last days with the squadron. Bishop replied: "I now know the fighting game well and I am successful at it because I fight with my head. Worry not about me, I am playing a safe game although it may not sound so. Believe me, I feel the days of risk have passed. This life is too good to leave. I never felt better in my life."

At dusk on the evening of August 13 Bishop shot down his forty-fifth plane over Hénin-Liétard, further behind the enemy lines than he should have strayed. It was, he told Cochrane-Patrick on his return to the mess, the easiest kill he had ever made. He used that as an argument against being required to return to England before his new duties.

"It seems damned silly," he complained, "to let someone get competent at his business and then switch him to something else." Pat made sympathetic noises and pointed out to Bishop that he couldn't countermand Trenchard's order if he wanted to. Pat knew that Bishop would be horrified if he told him the truth: the Allied brass considered him more valuable as a symbol—Victoria Cross winner, top-scoring airman, and a colonial to boot—than as a pilot who took his life in his hands every day.

On his last day at Filescamp Bishop took off at dawn, determined to add to his score before he was grounded. There wasn't another plane in the skies. But over toward Lens there were flashes of artillery fire and clouds of smoke. He flew in that direction and circled, a lone spectator of an attack on Hill 70 by the Canadian comrades he had visited a few days before. The battle seemed to be going well for the Canadians, and since there was nothing he could do to help, Bishop took up the hunt again. With only a pause for lunch and refuelling, he quartered the sky in a vain search for a scrap. After dinner he went up again, and with less than an hour of daylight left he met his first enemy planes of the long day, a pair of Albatros scouts. They turned and fled, helped by a strong west wind. After a short pursuit Bishop realized that he could not hope to close in on them without going deep into enemy territory. He opened fire at almost hopeless range—two hundred and fifty yards. He had never shot down a plane at such a distance, but the plane at which he aimed lurched and went into a spin. He thought it might be the old German trick of throwing off pursuit by pretending to be damaged, but the Albatros did not pull out of its spin. Instead it crashed into a building near Drocourt and vanished in a cloud of smoke and debris.

Number forty-six. Half an hour of daylight left. Not another plane in sight. Bishop mentally closed the ledger of his career as a fighter pilot as he turned toward Filescamp. Then, in the dusk, a lone Aviatik two-seater flew toward him. Bishop instinctively dived under it and came up under its belly. His bullets struck the enemy plane under its engine at a range of twenty yards. The plane simply came apart. Pieces of wing, fuselage and engine showered to earth. The two crewmen tumbled free from the wreckage. Bishop knew they had probably not been hit by his bullets. By some strange accident of aerodynamics their plane had collapsed around them and they were falling, fully conscious, to certain death. It was a sight that Bishop had never seen in all his scores of encounters with sudden death in the air, and it horrified him. For an instant he had the urge to follow the tumbling bodies and try to put them out of their terror by giving them a quick death in mid-air. But he immediately realized it was impossible, and he turned his plane toward Filescamp, away from the sight of the falling bodies.

That night Bishop was not noticeably melancholy at the hilarious farewell party in 60 Squadron's mess. But for the first time he felt no regret at being done with killing—for weeks, or months, or for the rest of his life.

FIFTEEN

INVESTITURE

I N LONDON Lady St. Helier was able to tell Bishop his program for the next week before the War Office informed him. She wrote Bishop's mother:

Billy is going to the investiture on Wednesday. While he feels rather nervous about it, being his first time, I am so glad he has not been before, because Princess Marie Louise told me last week that the King said the *one* thing he wanted was to give the V.C., D.S.O., and M.C., at the same time, preferably to a Colonial officer and now Billy is the first person who has won them all and the King is very pleased as he has heard so much about him from the Princess. He is very well, although he looks a little older perhaps, and one could never believe all he has gone through.

Bishop himself could not believe what he would have to go through at the investiture. To begin with he arrived late at Buckingham Palace. Then he was not sure just where he had to go, and an equerry shunted him into the anteroom with those who were to receive the M.C. A call then came that a D.S.O. appeared to be missing and Bishop, feeling conspicuous, had to admit to the assembled gathering that he was a D.S.O. He was escorted into a second room. Then it was learned that a V.C. was missing. Once more he was identified as the culprit and he finally was led into a third room where he was severely admonished by a staff officer for delaying the proceedings.

What happened next he described in a letter to his father: "I had learned the investiture drill thoroughly—ten yards across to the middle of the room, and then turn left and bow. Imagine my consternation when during those first ten paces one of my boots began to squeak."

His embarrassment mounted when the King turned to the staff officer who held the medals on a satin cushion and instructed him to show them around the room, since this was the first time all three had been awarded to one man at the same time.

"It was too awful for words," Bishop wrote, "for fifteen minutes the old boy talked to me in front of a huge crowd. I nearly died."

A week later—and it was almost anticlimax—Bishop was notified that he had been awarded a fourth decoration, a bar to his D.S.O. The citation read: "For conspicuous bravery and devotion to duty while engaging hostile aircraft. His consistent dash and fearlessness have set a magnificent example to the pilots of his squadron. He has destroyed no less than 45 hostile machines within the past five months, frequently attacking enemy formations single-handed and on all occasions displaying a fighting spirit and determination to get to close quarters with his opponents which have earned him the admiration of all in contact with him."

Again Bishop was acutely embarrassed. Even the citation for the Victoria Cross, the world's top decoration for bravery, had largely been a relatively terse and factual description of his raid on the airport. Now his picture appeared in all the papers, and the captions conferred on him various titles, including one that made him wince most painfully: the Lone Hawk.

Bishop had tasted fame in a small way during his previous leave in May, but now he was a major celebrity and eminent Londoners were pulling strings to get invitations to Portland Place. Granny St.

Helier hugely enjoyed the embarrassment of her protégé for a week (shrewdly divining that he too was finding the discomfiture not entirely unbearable) then packed him off with another of her "lodgers" on a tour of country houses owned by her friends.

"The most perfect place you can imagine," Bishop wrote his father from their first overnight stop. "The Thames runs right in front of the house and is most restful to the nerves." He added a postscript: "By the way, thanks awfully for the fifty dollars. It came just in time and thank the Lord for it. Being a V.C. is just too expensive on a captain's pay."

At the end of his trip, though, he could no longer plead the poverty of a captain's pay. At Portland Place notice awaited of his promotion to major. He was also requested to call on Lord Hugh Cecil on the following Monday, when his leave expired, to discuss his new duties.

It was Bishop's first meeting with Lord Hugh since the casual peer had admitted him into the air force two years before. "You've done rather well, I hear," Cecil said. "You know, I wasn't at all sure you were the type."

He explained that unexpected difficulties had been met in the construction of the aerodrome at Loch Doon in Scotland where Bishop was to be the chief instructor of fighter pilots. Huge stone formations had to be excavated to make a level field. Where there was no stone the earth became deep mud under the frequent rains and heavy construction equipment bogged down. It would be weeks, even months, before Loch Doon was ready.

"Good," said Bishop. "Then I can go back to France meanwhile."

"That doesn't seem to be on the cards," said Lord Hugh. "In fact there isn't a job for you just now."

"Good," said Bishop, "then I can get leave home to Canada."

"Not my end, I'm afraid," said Lord Hugh. He explained that although Bishop was attached to the RFC and leave in England was under RFC jurisdiction, authority to grant leave to Canada

was the responsibility of the Canadian officials. Bishop, a little baf-
fled at this red tape, thanked Lord Hugh and called at Canadian
military headquarters, where he made formal application for leave.

Back at Portland Place, Granny St. Helier listened to his tale of
woe and, as usual, had the answer. Dick Turner was back in London at Canadian military headquarters. He had been at her house,
as a matter of fact, while Bishop was traipsing about the country-
side. She had known him for years, ever since the Boer War, in fact,
when he won the V.C., and he had led the Canadians at Ypres during that dreadful gas attack by the Germans.

It dawned on Bishop that Granny was referring to General Sir
Richard Turner, now in command of Canadian troops in England.
She dashed off one of her famous letters, and in two days it produced results. But it was obvious to Bishop that after the order for
his leave had left Sir Richard's desk it had fallen into the hands of
the economy-minded staff officers. The letter authorizing his leave
read: "Approval is given for leave of absence until November 1st,
1917, subject to the proviso that he not receive any pay or allowances
after one month."

Bishop's financial prospects were not entirely bleak, however,
as he explained to Margaret in a letter two days before he left London for Liverpool to board ship for Canada: "Lord Beaverbrook
may publish a book on my combats. The royalties might mean
thousands of dollars, even pounds."

UNEASY HERO

AMONG HIS FRIENDS—Lady St. Helier's friends—in London the Victoria Cross was a bearable burden. In the confines of a Canada-bound ship Bishop learned for the first time what winning the world's premier award for valour entailed. On the first day out he strolled into a salon where a boxing tournament was being held. The two men in the ring stopped pummelling each other. The spectators stood up and cheered. Bishop reddened, turned on his heels and left.

On September 27 he stepped off a train in Montreal's old grimy Bonaventure station. His mother and Margaret were waiting for him at the gate, and behind them a reception committee of military and government dignitaries and a milling mob of reporters, photographers and spectators.

Bishop panicked. He leaned over to Margaret and said, "For heaven's sake let's get away from here." His mother was beaming with pride and enjoying herself hugely. Margaret patted his hand and said soothingly: "Cheer up. You'll have to get used to it—there's more to come."

How much more there was to come neither Margaret nor Bishop could imagine at that time. The newspaper stories of Bishop's return to Canada as the most decorated airman of the war made eight million Canadians suddenly realize for the first time in the half century Canada had been a nation, they had an authentic international hero on their hands.

In the early autumn of 1917 Canadians badly needed an escape from grim reality, and they found it in this slim, unassuming twenty-three-year-old pilot. They were remote from the battle front on which thousands of their countrymen were fighting and hundreds were dying. At home the newspapers were full of news that cast doubt on Canada's contribution to the struggle in Europe. "Is Canadian nickel being shipped through the United States to make armament for use against Canadians at the front?" one influential newspaper demanded insistently. French-Canadian voters showed a distaste for conscription, and so did the farmers who wanted their sons exempted from compulsory service. Income tax had just been introduced in Canada to help finance the war effort. At the same time doubts were being cast on the competence of the Canadian leaders.

Bishop did not fit easily into the role of hero. The Toronto *Globe* in a special article headed "Seeing a Hero" described his first encounter with mass adulation thus:

> If I am any judge of expressions I should say that Bishop would rather be most anywhere else than where he was at that moment. He was more rattled at meeting that enthusiastic, admiring crowd than he would have been suddenly meeting an enemy aviator while turning a corner among the clouds. Though I had seen many receptions of this kind I admit that this was the first one that gave me a real thrill and I cheered for all I was worth. Come to think of it this was the first time I had ever seen a young hero—and heroes should always be young . . . This knight of the clouds was fresh from his triumphs, and his cheeks are still bronzed from voyaging through "lucent solitudes." No wonder we cheered, and just because he looked so modest we cheered all the more.

Bishop faced flag-waving, frenzied demonstrations from Montreal, through towns and villages en route to Toronto. There he was saluted by his old regiment, the Mississauga Horse, and the most fervent, if not the largest, reception came in his home town of Owen Sound.

His mother, who was present with his fiancée at all the receptions, was no help. In vain he tried to restrain the proud little Margaret Louise from relating tales of his boyhood ("he was a born pilot") to the receptive press.

"Mother, I told you—don't say anything," Billy reproved her.

"I wasn't," she replied with typical Irish reasoning and a twinkle of her blue eyes, "I was only telling them."

Bishop visited Royal Military College at Kingston and was duly embarrassed at his reception at the august establishment which had been on the verge of expelling him in disgrace just three years before. In Toronto he made a speech on behalf of the Red Cross war fund and the society's objective of $500,000 was surpassed by one third of a million dollars.

The major personal event of Bishop's leave in Canada was his marriage to Margaret Burden on October 17, 1917, at Timothy Eaton Memorial Church in Toronto. Bishop's best man was Earl Smith, Margaret's brother-in-law. Smith called for Bishop with time to spare for the drive to the church, but en route Smith mentioned to Bishop that, of course, the reception would be "dry." So they decided to stop off for a little fortification, and were late in arriving at the church. They were refused entry to the vestry by two members of the honour guard who did not recognize them.

Finally Smith told the stolid guards in exasperation: "Let me put it this way—if we don't get in there isn't going to *be* any wedding!"

Thousands lined the four blocks between the church and the Burden residence on Avenue Road to cheer the handsome young couple as they rode to the reception in an open car. And there were still some hero-worshipping onlookers gathered outside the house and at Toronto's railroad station as the couple left for their honeymoon at Yama Farms in the Catskills.

Bishop expected to return to England at the end of October as chief fighting instructor of the Gunnery School at Loch Doon, and intended to take Margaret with him. The problem of obtaining passage for his wife on a ship in wartime was easily overcome by the fact that Margaret qualified for overseas service as a V.A.D. (Voluntary Aid Detachments). But there were still difficulties in finishing the aerodrome and when he returned from his honeymoon he learned that it might be the end of the year before Loch Doon was ready. Meanwhile he was assigned to the British War Mission in Washington as assistant to the American staff in building an air force.

The United States was justly proud of the Lafayette Escadrille, a group of American volunteers who had joined the French Foreign Legion to fight in the air alongside the French. In the Somme battles of 1916 the Escadrille destroyed more than thirty enemy planes in bitter fighting against the formidable Boelcke formations. But American eagerness to join the fight was handicapped by a serious drawback. Not enough fighting machines were available. It was all the British could do to manufacture enough planes to supply the demand for more squadrons at the front. And the French had already reached the limit of their resources.

Even with its reputation for mass production the United States had been unable to keep pace in the manufacture of aircraft, and to help in this respect a British War Mission was set up in Washington in the summer of 1917 with Lieutenant-Colonel L. W. B. Rees, V.C., as the aviation representative.

When Bishop was attached to the staff in November he was joined by Major F. G. Blomfield who had commanded 56 Squadron, the unit in which Ball had been killed. Soon after his arrival in Washington Bishop and Blomfield went to Dayton, Ohio, to test the new American Liberty engine. It had been designed in 1917, shortly after the United States entered the war, with two objectives:

to produce an engine superior to the German Mercedes, and one that could be produced in quantity. American ingenuity and enthusiasm lacked at that time only one thing—experience with combat aircraft.

The host of Bishop and Blomfield at the Dayton Wright Company was that legendary figure of aviation, Orville Wright. But what they saw made them pessimistic. Production lagged far behind prediction and it would obviously be a long time before the United States could make an important contribution in the fight for supremacy of the skies in Europe.

These duties, while interesting, were not onerous or too time consuming. Bishop, in fact, found time to write an account of his experiences which he titled *Winged Warfare*. It quickly found acceptance by the noted publisher George Doran, and Bishop for the first time was able to cash in on his notoriety to the tune of a tidy advance against future royalties.

At the end of 1917 Bishop was informed that he would be returning to England at the end of January, when it was expected that the new Scottish aerodrome would be ready.

Before he departed for England with his bride he took it upon himself to express his views of the development of United States aircraft production in a speech to the Canadian Club in Montreal on January 11, 1917, which the American Press duly reported:

Germany will have nothing to fear from the United States airfighting forces during the coming spring because the American aircraft program is far behind schedule. . . . Major Bishop characterized as "unfortunate" the advertising which had been given the United States' aircraft program. He said that while France would find it impossible to enlarge her aeroplane fighting forces during the coming half year, Germany, knowing America's intention, had greatly expanded her flying corps in an effort to gain supremacy in the air warfare. Consequently, he declared, during the next few months Great Britain will have to face the most terrible time she has faced and especially from the point of view of war in the air.

When Bishop and Margaret disembarked from the troopship they were greeted by two items of bad news: the gunnery school project had finally been abandoned. And he was under arrest. True, it was an open arrest, which meant he was not behind bars. Nevertheless he was required to appear before Admiral Sir Godfrey Paine, Master General of Personnel for the British Air Council, which controlled all air policy. Theoretically Bishop faced a court-martial, but he was unabashed.

"Well, I'm really back on active service again," he grinned to Margaret when he received the news of his arrest.

THE FLYING
FOXES

FLANKED by a senior officer on each side, Bishop stood silently and nervously before Sir Godfrey Paine, who scowled at him for a full minute without speaking. Then suddenly the admiral barked:

"Bishop! You have behaved like an impertinent idiot. Your conduct is unforgivable. You have exceeded your authority. You have disgraced yourself as an officer. You have abused the hospitality of a friendly country and given comfort to the enemy by revealing the weakness—er, the alleged weakness, of an important ally ..."

It lasted for at least ten minutes. To Bishop it seemed an eternity. Then suddenly it was over. Bishop braced himself, for what he did not know.

Sir Godfrey shifted his penetrating gaze to one of the escorting officers. "What shall we do?" he asked sternly. "Severely reprimand him?"

The escorting officer smiled uneasily.

"Right then. Bishop, you are severely reprimanded," Sir Godfrey said with blessed finality. "Dismissed ... but not you, Bishop—wait here."

The escorting officers made their exit. "Sit down," Sir Godfrey said. It was an order, not an invitation.

Sir Godfrey towered over him, peering down at him and, Bishop thought, still very angry.

"You know you *were* a fool, Bishop," Sir Godfrey said.

"Yes Sir."

"But damn it—you were *right*," Sir Godfrey said. "The Americans won't have enough planes ready to matter a damn before next summer. But you shouldn't have said so. Tell me what you saw."

The subject was no longer his undeniable misconduct. Now he became part of a discussion on the serious matter of American aircraft production with a senior member of the Air Council. Sir Godfrey listened attentively, nodding in agreement from time to time. Finally he said: "We were afraid there would be production problems in the States, and it couldn't have happened at a worse time. The situation on the Western Front is that the Germans can now concentrate all their strength there. The collapse of the Russian forces on the Eastern Front has let the Huns send forty-two divisions into France and Belgium, and we'll undoubtedly face an offensive as soon as the weather clears in the spring and the enemy will undoubtedly have their best chance of breaking our lines. Our own best chance of preventing this is a greatly reinforced air force."

The abandonment of the costly air fighting school at Loch Doon was a serious setback to the need for a stronger air force, but it was the only possible decision in the circumstances. Thousands of pounds and, more important, many months had been wasted because of inadequate planning. Apart from the unsuitable terrain, it was discovered that fog and mist could prevent the Loch Doon establishment from being used as an aerodrome for more than half the year.

But the dire need for additional Allied air power meant that Bishop was no longer an unemployed airman. He was assigned forthwith to form a fighter squadron of his own. Lord Hugh Cecil conveyed the good news and added blandly, "Of course, you'll have to learn how to fly all over again."

Bishop thought Cecil was being unnecessarily jocular about his traditional shortcomings as a pilot. But he obliged with a smile and said, "Oh, I'll have to take a couple of flights to get into practice again."

Cecil shook his head. "You haven't been in a plane for more than six months," he said, "and don't think we've been standing still in that time. The planes are more highly powered, get more altitude, are more manoeuvrable and all that sort of thing."

But the principal change was that pilots were better trained. They went to the front with greater knowledge of their machines and more understanding of the dynamics of flight. This marked change was due to new methods of instruction, and the man who contributed most to this was Bob Smith-Barry, a crippled pilot who in 1916 had been the commanding officer of 60 Squadron. He gave Bishop a refresher course at Gosport Flying School near Portsmouth. It was a far cry from the cursory instruction of a little more than a year earlier in the clumsy and antiquated Shorthorn. Two weeks later, when Bishop—and his instructor—were satisfied that his sense of timing had been sufficiently recaptured, Bishop left for Hounslow aerodrome, just outside London, to take up his post as commanding officer of the newly formed 85 Squadron.

Bishop had a free hand in selecting pilots, so naturally he sought out the comrades with whom he had fought at Filescamp Farm. Not many were still around. Grid Caldwell had also been given command of his own unit, 74 Squadron, and had already snaffled most of the best available pilots. However, Bishop ran down Spencer Horn in Scotland, instructing at the Ayr school for fighter pilots, and he did not need much persuasion to join Bishop as a flight commander of 85 Squadron. He enlisted two other flight leaders, both veteran air fighters. One was Arthur "Lobo" Benbow, who wore a monocle in his eye and a Military Cross on his breast. The other was C. B. A. Baker, a soft-spoken youngster who had won both the Military Cross and the French Croix de Guerre. Next came Beverley MacDonald, known as the "Bull Pup," who had been the battalion sergeant major in Bishop's class at Royal Military College, and a fellow Canadian, Roy Hall.

At Ayr, Horn had been training American pilots, and he recommended three of them. On March 30 Horn introduced the "Three Musketeers" to Bishop, and that marked the beginning of a memorable international comradeship. They were Larry Callahan, a tall youth from Louisville, Kentucky, and two Princeton graduates, Mac Grider and Elliott White Springs. Springs, a short voluble man, was by all odds the most unusual personality of the trio. He was the son of a millionaire textile manufacturer with mills in South Carolina and New England. Springs and his father were not on good terms, and when the young airman brooded on this unhappy situation he became almost suicidally depressed. But most of the time he consoled himself by inventing new combinations of drinks for the refreshment of himself, his friends, and anyone else, male or female, who happened to be in the vicinity. In later years Springs inherited his father's mills, expanded them, became a civilian test pilot and amateur aviator, wrote several books, and concocted naughty advertisements for his Springmaid fabrics (which caused protests from moralistic groups and soul-searching on the part of publishers of national magazines who coveted Springs' lucrative advertising but deplored the sensuality of his words and pictures).

Mac Grider kept a diary which Springs later edited and published (and probably contributed to from his own memories). It gives vivid glimpses of Bishop, Squadron 85, wartime England and France, and the confusion that existed between the United States and Britain in the early attempts of the two countries to mesh their war establishments.

Grider's diary describes their first meeting with Bishop:

Springs and Callahan came down from Ayr with me and Captain Horn, who is a flight commander at Hounslow in the squadron that the great Major Bishop, V.C., D.S.O., M.C. etc., is organizing to take overseas, took us out to see him. He wants the three of us to go with him. They are letting Bishop pick his own pilots and he went with us to the U.S. headquarters to try and arrange it. A Colonel Morrow told us it couldn't be done. The whole staff nearly lost their eyes staring at us when we strolled out, arm in arm with the great Bishop. He has a very pretty chauffeur. . . .

In other ways, too, Bishop was enjoying the fruits of authority. To be near the airport where he was organizing 85 Squadron, he and Margaret rented a house at Osterly Court which immediately became the informal headquarters for members of the squadron.

Margaret at first found the life of an air force squadron commander's wife a little perplexing. As a member of a wealthy and ultra-conservative family she had led a sheltered life before she married Bishop. Certainly she had never been exposed to the extraordinary outlook of English and American youths engaged in an exciting adventure and coloured by the knowledge that sudden death was likely to be their fate.

"Don't they ever sleep?" she once asked Bishop plaintively. She gradually became reconciled, a process hastened by her own brother, Hank Burden, a tall, handsome, curly-haired lad whom she idolized and who, like Bishop, had transferred from the army to the Royal Flying Corps.

By the time Bishop and Margaret arrived in England Hank was already an ace with six enemy machines to his credit. On his first visit to Osterly Court, Margaret rushed out to greet him as he opened the white gate at the end of the path. He sauntered jauntily toward the house with a broad grin on his face and a bottle of champagne in each hand.

Margaret, who never had seen her brother take more than a sip of sherry, was surprised. But Bishop was highly pleased. Hank's high-spirited entrance earned for him the right to celebrate in the honoured custom of the flying fraternity. But what finally convinced Margaret that the boisterous proceedings at Osterly Court were socially acceptable was the good-humoured approval with which Lady St. Helier and Princess Margaret Louise, frequent visitors to the Bishop home, regarded the high-spirited behaviour of the members of 85 Squadron.

Soon after his return to London from Canada, Bishop took Margaret to Buckingham Palace to receive his fourth decoration, the bar to the D.S.O. King George V made a gentle joke. "If you win any more honours we will have to place them before your name instead of after it—we will have to call you 'Arch Bishop.'" After the investiture Princess Marie Louise showed the entranced Margaret through the palace apartments in which she had once lived. After that experience, Bishop and his friends could do no wrong in Margaret's eyes.

The Princess took a special interest in Larry Callahan, the youngest of the Three Musketeers. Perhaps it was because he always addressed her, in his slow Kentucky drawl, as "Ma'am"—which happened to be the correct way to address royalty. Bishop was about to compliment Cal on his surprising knowledge of English protocol when Cal asked him casually: "Who's that old babe that always hangs around your house?"

Bishop grinned, but did not explain. He enjoyed the situation too much to spoil it. Grider in his diary entry of May 17 describes how the Three Musketeers learned the identity of "the old babe."

We had a bunch of Brass Hats from the War Office down at Hounslow today and we put on an exhibition of formation flying and stunting for them that was pretty good—except for Springs' landing. His wheels hit a soft spot and he turned over on his back and his head was shoved into the mud. He was a great sight when he walked back to where all the generals were standing. He had on slacks and a white shirt and wasn't wearing helmet or goggles and his face and head were all covered with mud.

Mrs. Bishop had a lady with her and she invited us to tea with them. We explained that we were all pretty dirty but she said never mind. The lady proved to be very nice and very much interested in Americans. She was the most patriotic person I've ever met because she always talking about the King. When I told her how much all the Americans liked serving with the British, she said she was glad and she knew the King would be delighted. In fact, she knew the King was hoping to decorate an American airman soon. All this sounded pretty far-fetched, but we got on fine with her, we told her some funny stories and she nearly died laughing. We had a taxi waiting and offered to take her back to town but she said she'd rather take a bus and get the air and it would take her right by the palace.

As we went out we met the mother of Cunningham-Reid one of the Squadron members, and she nearly broke a leg curtsying, and I noticed Mrs. Bishop do the same when we left to take the lad to the bus. I asked Cunningham-Reid why the gymnastics and he told me the lady was Princess Marie Louise. All three of us have been trying to remember whether we cracked any jokes about the King. Mrs. Bishop must have been laughing merrily. She's a peach. We're all crazy about her. Well, I have pressed the flesh of royalty now. My hand has gotten accustomed to the grasp of nobility and now I know the feel of the real thing. Who says we were democrats? We're all snobs underneath the cuticle.

Bishop needed all his connections in high places to straighten out an unpleasant tangle of red tape that was having an unfortunate effect on the morale of his three American pilots. At first Springs and Cal were refused reassignment to 85 Squadron, and they returned to Ayr, as Grider noted in his diary, "after a very unsatisfactory conference with a major at headquarters, who is an officer all right but even an Act of Congress couldn't make him a gentleman."

Bishop and Grider organized a plot to kidnap the other two members of the Three Musketeers for 85 Squadron.

Early in April, 1918, Springs and Cal came to London from Ayr under orders to join another squadron for service in France. Meanwhile Bishop pulled strings, and when the two men reached London they found to their bitter disgust that they had been judged "not yet competent to fly combat."

In 85 Squadron's mess at Hounslow, Springs told Bishop and Grider: "Show me the son-of-a-bitch who declared I wasn't ready to fly and I'll wring his neck."

"But only after I strangle him," said Cal.

Grider pointed at Bishop. "He did it." And both men roared with laughter. Springs and Cal joined the merriment after Bishop explained that it was a ruse to delay their departure and give him time to wangle them into 85 Squadron. He succeeded in doing this a few days later.

But the situation was still unsatisfactory. Although the American pilots took their duty orders from Bishop, their discipline was still under the U.S. Army control. The three Americans were particularly galled at having to wear American uniforms which were uncomfortable in comparison with the casual RFC clothing. Another entry in Grider's diary reads: "I'm an American and proud of it but I'm damned if I can take pride in the boobs that are running our flying corps. For instance how can we fly when our necks are being choked off by these 1865 model collars?"

Bishop diplomatically arranged things so that eventually the Three Musketeers were fully under his control, and Grider could write joyfully: "Bishop says he doesn't care where we stay, so we have a house in Berkeley Square! A friend of a friend is a Lordship who has this four-story place he is willing to rent us for ten pounds a week. We also have a cook and butler."

They celebrated by throwing a memorable dinner party, which Grider duly recorded thus:

> Major Bishop, Horn and the rest of the squadron came in from Hounslow, and Colonel Hastings and Col. Hepburn of the Canadian General Staff were there too.
>
> We found out too late that we couldn't get any meat without ration coupons, and there was little else we could buy. However, we got around the food problem easily. All we had cooked was soup and fish, but Springs made a big tub of eggnogg and a couple of big pitchers full of mint julep. To make sure no one got beyond the fish course we shook up cocktails too.
>
> Springs was at the head of the table and served. Everybody had a bottle of port and a bottle of champagne. The butler brought in a big platter of fish and Springs served them by picking them up by the tail and tossing them to the guests as if they were seals. At the end of the fish course I was alone at the table. The rest were chasing each other all over the place.
>
> Before going to the theatre, where we had a box, all these ruffians armed themselves from His Lordship's wonderful collection of ancient weapons—swords, machetes, shillelaghs, maces, clubs, bayonets, pikes, flintlock pistols, and assorted daggers and dirks. It's a wonder they weren't all arrested, especially when Cal dropped a club on a bass drum in the middle of the show.

Somehow the serious business of preparing 85 Squadron for war continued. Someone pinned the name "Flying Foxes" on the squadron and the pilots asked Bishop's permission to attach foxtails to their wing struts. Bishop decided to make this a privilege of pilots who shot down two enemy planes.

When Princess Marie Louise heard this, she presented 85 Squadron with a mess-table centrepiece in the form of an inscribed silver fox. In a sense the squadron had royal sponsorship.

But the Flying Foxes were still far from ready for front-line duty. All the squadron pilots agreed that the Sopwith Dolphins with which they had been equipped were "pigs." The Dolphins had been designed for high-altitude work, with a 200-horsepower Hispano motor which made it very fast—and very unmanoeuvrable. In addition, it had a feature that was frightening from the pilot's viewpoint: the top wing had no centre section so the pilot's head protruded over the wing surfaces. This gave excellent visibility, but in a crash it could be hazardous. In mid-April a young Indian pilot on his first landing in a Dolphin tipped over and broke his neck. Bishop appealed for new planes and the improved S.E. 5A's were supplied with unusual alacrity—possibly because additional air power was desperately needed at the front.

A German offensive had started on March 21 and the Allies had been forced to retreat. The attack began along a fifty-mile front between Cambrai and St. Quentin in a drive toward the Maine River and Paris. Lacking adequate reserves, the Fifth Army was nearly annihilated. Thousands of guns had been lost and scores of thousands of prisoners taken. What was left of the battered British contingent retired in disorder toward Amiens. Farther north in the Ypres area a second attack was aimed at the Channel ports of Calais and Boulogne.

Jack Scott, Bishop's old 60 Squadron comrade, gave Bishop a first-hand report. He was now based in England, but characteristically he had borrowed a plane and flown out to the front to study the situation.

"It looks bad, Bish," he said glumly. "From what I can see there seems to be no question that the Huns will break through."

In a special order of the day on April 11, Field Marshal Sir Douglas Haig said: "Many among us are tired. To those I would say that victory will belong to the side which holds out the longest.

The French Army is moving rapidly in great force to our support. There is no course but to fight it out."

During that critical month of April the Royal Air Force had been formed, combining the Royal Flying Corps with the Royal Naval Air Service. This meant that the separate Canadian air force was postponed. The urgent need for more squadrons in France and the consolidation of aerial forces under one control made impractical the proposal to diversify this force by the formation of a separate Canadian section. Even the proposal of two distinctly Canadian squadrons was bluntly refused. Every available man was urgently needed at the front and this was no time for the delay that would come with the organization of a new unit.

In the midst of all this bad news from the front came a piece of news that should have been regarded as good by the Allied Air Force, yet somehow the death of Baron Manfred von Richthofen caused more sorrow than joy among his bitterest enemies. And it brought with it a controversy that has never been resolved to this day: who killed Richthofen?

Strangely enough, no one has ever been given official credit for the kill. Most people—certainly all Canadian airmen—credit Roy Brown, a Canadian serving with the RFC, with bringing down the German ace who not only claimed the highest score of World War I, but was certainly his side's most inspirational leader in air combat. On the other hand Australians have always maintained that Richthofen was brought down by a single lucky shot fired by Robert Buie, an Australian infantryman.

Twenty-five years after the war Bishop, who had fought several exciting but inconclusive air battles with Richthofen, expressed his thoughts on the controversy:

Richthofen was shot down over a sector held by Australians. When infantrymen reached the scene of the crash they noted that the great German pilot had been brought down by one bullet which had pierced his heart. His machine was unscathed, save for the effects of the crash. At the time of Richthofen's death Roy Brown had been in a dogfight with the German and when last seen he had been on the Baron's tail and firing at him.

When Richthofen's body was examined it was agreed that the killer's bullet had entered the German's body from the direction in which the shots fired from Brown would have pierced him. Troops on the ground in the immediate vicinity, however, vowed that Richthofen had been killed by a bullet fired by an Australian officer.

Well, the chances in favour of Brown are infinitely greater than those of the Aussie making a chance shot at a man who was going across the sky at a speed of at least 140 miles an hour, hundreds of feet above the marksman's head, in which case he either set an all-time high in marksmanship or a new record in miracles.

Brown, on the other hand, was in an ideal position to do exactly what he seems to have done. His speed and Richthofen's would be approximately equal—target and marksman virtually stationary in relation to each other. If Brown had had a reputation as a good shot people would have wondered what happened to all the other bullets in the burst he fired. But as he was never a great man with a gun, no fellow flier has ever been the least surprised to know that the rest of the burst failed to get on any part of the target.

My own belief is that Roy let go pretty much all over the sky, probably while skidding, and that Richthofen was so unfortunate as to fly directly into the path of one bullet. Nobody will ever convince anybody who flew in World War I that anyone but Roy Brown shot down Richthofen. Brown was never given official credit for the kill. Had he been in any other air force he *would* have been given credit and would probably have received half a dozen decorations from his own and other Allied countries, for to destroy Richthofen could be described

as the equivalent of shooting down fifty enemy machines—
with one bullet. But the British are a conservative crowd and
they don't give away credits for knocking down airplanes as
long as there is any possible vestige of doubt. In short, the
killer must be in possession of substantiating evidence which
would stand up in any court in the world.

Actually Robert Buie never tried to exploit the possibility that
he had shot down Richthofen. When he died in the spring of 1964
at Calga, New South Wales, the press report of his death stated:
"Buie, of the 53rd battery, Australian Field Artillery, did not boast
about the claim that he had hit the German plane with ground fire,
but it was widely supported by others."

If Bishop sounds a little bitter in his comment about the strict
rules imposed by the British for giving credit for planes shot down,
I am able to testify he felt no such bitterness. In later years when I
was old enough to talk with him about his war experiences, my
father expressed little interest in the statistics of his fighting days,
even when he was most relaxed and unrestrained, which was frequently. It is true that in 1917, when Bishop returned to Canada
after his first tour of duty, the British War Office admitted that in
addition to his 47 confirmed victories he had 23 "probable but
unconfirmed" kills.

It is almost certain that Bishop, between his first lucky victory
on March 25, 1917, and his final incredible twelve minutes over
Ploegsteert Wood and Neuve Eglise, when between 9.58 and 10.10
a.m., he caused the destruction of five German planes, shot down
more than one hundred enemy aircraft.

On the other hand, even Richthofen's admiring biographer,
Floyd Gibbons, admitted in his compilation of the German ace's
score that some of Richthofen's claims—he headed them "Request-
ing acknowledgment of my victory"—were in error, or involved
such a minor triumph as scarcely to constitute a "victory." For instance, Richthofen's twenty-first kill was characterized by Gibbons

as "two unidentified occupants [who] probably escaped uninjured behind the British lines." His twenty-fourth claim is listed
as "mistake—no English casualty records." The pilots involved in
Richthofen's eighteenth, thirtieth, thirty-first, thirty-sixth, forty-
fourth, sixty-first, sixty-fourth, sixty-sixth, and seventy-second
"victories" were forced down and made prisoners. Three others
were forced down behind the British lines and escaped uninjured.

To close this digression, here are Bishop's comments on
Richthofen as a fighter pilot:

> Richthofen's fighting methods were typically German. That is
> not said to belittle the Baron's qualifications, but it is certainly
> not said in admiration of his qualities either. Richthofen did
> not compile his score as hundreds of young men who flew
> for Britain, America and France acquired their credits. He did
> not fly with the devil-may-care abandon of a Barker, a Ricken-
> backer, a Ball or a McCudden. He flew with a cold calculat-
> ing skill and his great trick was to withhold from battle himself
> until his flying mates had set up the target for him. Then
> Richthofen would come whisking down out of the sun for the
> kill, pop off the lame duck, and fly away home with another
> great victory under his belt! In following this system he not
> only kept himself out of harm's way, but sacrificed many fine
> pilots from his own circus, the lads who did the dirty work
> before the great man jumped in.

In later years Bishop was indifferent to the scoring of air victories, but there is no doubt that in 1918, when he was a mere twenty-
four years old, he reacted to the challenge of combat much as an
eager young hockey or baseball player would. Certainly he did not
laugh off the fact that while he had been on extended leave, and
later while he was organizing 85 Squadron, his own record on the
British side had been broken. Jimmy McCudden, a flight comman-

der in Hank Burden's 56 Squadron, had returned to England after bringing down fifty-seven enemy machines.

"There's something to shoot at, Billy," Hank wrote from the front. "Better get out here while there are still some Huns left."

By the last week of May, 1918, the Flying Foxes were ready for overseas service. Their final days in England were memorable and fully lived up to the traditions they had quickly created for themselves. The night before they left they took over the Criterion restaurant in London for a farewell dinner. One of the pilots, Roy Hall, recalled that two hundred bottles of champagne were consumed and that only his physical restraining influence prevented Benbow from trying a solo flight from the third-storey window. But such antics by this time were accepted by Londoners as a matter of course.

There was, however, open relief over their departure. On the night they left a leading actress at a theatre, which more than once the squadron had virtually appropriated, expressed it in no uncertain terms.

"Thank God," she said as the curtain rose and the overture subsided, "Bishop and his crowd have finally gone to France."

EIGHTEEN

PETIT SYNTHE

FINALLY 85 Squadron went off to war—and no squadron ever did it in quite the style of the Flying Foxes.

Security be damned. Everyone knew that they were leaving anyway. And not since the departure of the Light Brigade for the Crimea, which had all the gaiety of a group of vacationers setting off on a cruise, had a British force gone to battle with such fanfare and revelry.

Princess Marie Louise was present, and, of course, Margaret and Lady St. Helier, plus assorted friends, relatives and acquaintances of 85 Squadron's members. Neatly assembled in front of the hangars were the nineteen machines, facing into the wind, arranged in three flights of six, with Bishop's plane in front. The pilots of 85 Squadron stood in line in front of Bishop facing the crowd. None was suffering from excessive sobriety. "We will fly to Lympne on the coast first," Bishop announced loudly so that the audience, and any spies present, could hear every word. "There we will refuel before taking off for Boulogne, where we will receive instructions as to our final destination.

"We will take off to the west. Look at the . . ." he pointed at the wind sock but called it by the time-honoured RFC name which referred to its fancied resemblance to an article of prophylactic equipment. When he realized what he had said his face turned bright red. Hurriedly he kissed Margaret goodbye, tried to avoid the shocked stare of the Princess and the other ladies present, and dashed for his plane.

An hour later the Flying Foxes landed at Lympne, minus one pilot. Larry Callahan's engine overheated soon after takeoff and he made a forced landing south of London to wait until it cooled off. A second casualty occurred after the squadron left Lympne. Another pilot, Brown, crashed on takeoff and had to remain behind.

Two more pilots crashed when the squadron landed at Marquis aerodrome near Boulogne. The first was Bishop's former RMC classmate, Bull Pup MacDonald. Seconds later Cunningham-Reid cracked up. Neither was injured, but the squadron was already short four pilots and four machines by the time they set off for their final destination at Petit Synthe, near the seaside town of Dunkirk.

Perhaps a clue to the reason for the high casualty rate was Grider's description of the Channel crossing: "My motor was missing a little and I kept picking out trawlers and destroyers below to land beside in case it gave out. On the way across Springs signalled me to come up close to him. I flew up to his wingtip and he took out his flask and drank my health. I didn't have a thing with me but a bottle of champagne and that was in my tool box so I couldn't get at it."

Bishop wrote to Margaret shortly after they arrived.

We shall probably be here only a month (it is a very quiet part of the lines) before moving to a livelier sector. A naval bombing squadron here on the aerodrome has been awfully good to us, putting us up and being very nice in every way. Of course we have nothing at all of our own. I will be sleeping in one blanket on an army mattress. The men and transport, with a bit of luck, should arrive tomorrow.

Darling, my machine is really a wonder, seems reliable too. Goodnight, darling, you were a real brick and it made my heart ache to see tears so near your eyes.

By the time he had finished the letter, the drone of German raiders was overhead. The nightly hate had begun. Bishop added a hasty postscript: "It's somehow good to get back closer to the war."

Petit Synthe was an easy target for the German bombers even at night. Dunkirk harbour and the canal were good landmarks, particularly by moonlight. For protection against regular raids, dugout shelters had been built all around the edge of the field. On that first night at Petit Synthe, after Bishop finished his letter, he walked over to the nearest dugout just as the German bombers arrived overhead. Near the entrance of the dugout an air force sergeant stopped him and reminded him that the wearing of steel helmets was mandatory during an air raid. He insisted that Bishop take his own helmet. Bishop impatiently jammed it on his head. Before he could take a step toward the dugout he heard a sharp "clank!" and felt a severe jolt that wrenched his neck. A jagged piece of anti-aircraft shrapnel had smashed into and dented the helmet Bishop had donned only a few seconds before. It was probably his narrowest escape. Without the helmet his skull would have been cracked open.

For the first few days after their arrival, the Flying Foxes accustomed themselves to their new surroundings, both in the air and on the ground—but especially on the ground, since the squadron was not supposed to cross the front line until the pilots had undergone two weeks of familiarization with the terrain.

An early entry in Grider's diary recorded that "today we bought a piano and have a phonograph so the mess is very cheery and excellently equipped with furniture. We are allowed so much cash by the government for furnishing and then have a private fund. Springs is vice president of the mess—officer in command of drinks.

We took a truck and went up into Dunkirk to stock up our cellar. We got Scotch, Benedictine, Cognac, Champagne, white and red wine, and port. We decided it was too much trouble to sign chits for drinks in the mess, so all drinks are to be free and each man will have to see that he gets his money's worth. P.S. Major Bishop got a Hun today on the other side of Ypres. First blood!'"

Bishop enlarged on this laconic account of his first air victory in more than nine months in a letter to Margaret:

Well the total is now 48: I simply had to bring down a two-seater today: This morning I had my guns sighted and a lot of things adjusted, then went out to the lines with Horn and McGregor. We didn't cross, just played around to see what was doing, then came home. This afternoon at four I went out again only alone and crossed the lines after a fat two-seater. There were ten scouts higher up, so I got to 17,500 feet, to worry them from above. Suddenly 200 feet below me, coming toward me, there was another two-seater. He saw me at practically the same moment I saw him and he turned to give his observer a shot at me before he beetled off to the east. I peacefully slipped under his tail and he lost his head and put his nose down hard. So I closed to 125 yards and let him have ten from each gun. I think the first burst killed both. He sort of went out of control, skidding to the left and I closed to fifty yards and got in 25 more from each gun. Then his left plane followed by the right, folded back and he fell. In a second the other planes and tail came off.

Next day a gusty wind blew from the west. Three machines crashed on landing, smashed beyond repair. The squadron was now seriously handicapped and the possibility of a move to a more active sector would be delayed.

It was one of those days when everything seemed to go wrong. Several pilots, including Bishop, suffered from "the complaint."

They blamed it on Springs' cocktails as well as on engine fumes, but whatever it was it left them weak and irritable.

It did not, however, prevent Bishop from flying three and a half hours that day. Before lunch he spotted an enemy two-seater on artillery observation over the battered city of Ypres. Not a tree or building was left standing. It seemed to be the most ravaged spot on earth.

The two-seater eluded Bishop easily. The pilot saw him in plenty of time, dived quickly and sped off east. Even with the S.E. 5A's powerful Wolseley Viper engine Bishop could not catch him. At lunch he grumbled to Lobo Benbow about his upset and bad luck with the two-seater.

After lunch he took off toward Ypres and climbed to fifteen thousand feet before he crossed the lines. He had not lost his dread of anti-aircraft fire, but to himself he justified his extreme altitude by the argument that at this height the S.E. 5A delivered its best performance.

After circling for five minutes he spotted a loose formation of fighters three thousand feet below. He was surprised to find that they were the familiar Albatros model—his favourite opponents of a year earlier. Not only were the planes obsolete compared with the improved British aircraft, but the pilots obviously did not fly with any of the confidence of the Richthofen circus. Almost with pity Bishop dived at them out of the sun.

He singled out two of the Albatros fighters and took aim on the one on the right. A burst of twenty rounds smashed into the engine. The second pilot, seeing his comrade hit, tried to turn away. It was too late. Bishop shifted his aim quickly and from thirty yards he couldn't miss. The Albatros flew right into his sights as he opened fire. Twenty rounds sent it, too, spinning down in flames.

That night he wrote to Margaret at 52 Portland Place, Granny St. Helier's house, where she had moved after Bishop left for France: "That makes us 50—sounds a lot more than 47 doesn't it?"

Bishop took the next day off and drove south to Clairmarais where Grid Caldwell's 74 Squadron was stationed. He found Grid cockily cheerful. "Since old Richthofen went down the fight seems to have gone out of the Huns," he told Bishop over a drink. He introduced one of his flight commanders, a slender Irishman named Edward "Mick" Mannock.

"Mannock now has more than 30 Huns," Bishop wrote later to Margaret. "He is a marvel from all accounts. I'm always glad when a man like Mannock does so well. He is such a good fellow and everyone likes him so much."

Bishop did not know, when he wrote his admiration for the lean impassioned Irishman in a private letter, that after the war newspaper and magazine writers would involve him in a controversy over whether he or Mannock (who by then was dead) had more air victories—in other words, who was the top fighter pilot in the service of Britain.

When Bishop met Mannock on May 29 the latter had, as Bishop noted, more than thirty victories. A month later Mannock was dead. He died because, in winning his fiftieth victory, he broke the cardinal rule: do not pursue an enemy plane closer than a thousand feet from the ground. Mannock dived after a mortally wounded Albatros to make sure it went down, and was killed by a thousand-to-one shot: a bullet fired by a German infantryman.

The citation for Mannock's posthumous Victoria Cross credited him with fifty victories, but first one journalist, then another, referred to Mannock's seventy-three victories—one more than Bishop's official score at the end of his fighting career. Bishop, who rarely lost his temper, did so when he realized that other journalists, for the sake of a story, were trying to draw him into a dispute over Mannock's record. But he controlled his anger and answered with a grim coolness:

"I wish to God Mick had shot down a hundred and seventy-three planes. That would have left a lot fewer Huns to kill our pilots. What the hell does it matter *who* shot them down?"

The controversy soon died down, largely because Bishop refused to become embroiled, but his attitude was significant. He took a healthy competitive interest in his score in comparison with that of other Allied pilots, exactly as if they were all players in some apocalyptic game. But it would never occur to him to envy the success of a teammate.

When Bishop wrote about being "glad when a man like Mannock does so well" he was referring to the extraordinary variety of difficulties Mannock had encountered in his life. His father deserted his wife and five children when Mick was twelve years old and he had to leave school to help support the family, first as a grocer's delivery boy in Canterbury, where the Mannocks lived, later as a barber's apprentice, and finally as a telephone lineman.

Mannock joined the British army before the war as an ambulance attendant. Unlike most men who became pilots and fought with a grudging admiration for his counterparts on the enemy side, Mannock hated the Germans so bitterly that he asked to be transferred from the hospital corps when war came, fearing he would not be able to give fair treatment to a wounded enemy prisoner, as the rules of war required. So he was referred to the Flying Corps and, incredibly, was accepted. Mannock was an unlikely air hero for two reasons: he was over thirty years old when he got to France with the RFC, and he was handicapped in the highly competitive game of aerial warfare by severe astigmatism of the left eye. Only because medical examinations were perfunctory in the extreme (as Bishop had discovered earlier) was Mannock in the air force at all.

He differed from the typical RFC in other ways: the youngsters who fought in the air were fun-loving types who lived for the moment and regarded politics as a dull game played by old men. Mannock was a militant socialist and he despised the English caste system and the pretensions of high society only slightly less than he hated the Germans.

Unlike Bishop, who was a rough pilot but a deadly shot, Mannock started off as poor a marksman as he was a pilot. Only by

endless practice did he become proficient enough to shoot down fifty enemy planes.

When Bishop got back to Petit Synthe bad news awaited him. Lobo Benbow had become the squadron's first fatal casualty. The day had started well. Benbow, Horn, McGregor and Carruthers on practice patrol had run into a large formation of German planes east of Ypres, and McGregor had shot down one. But later in the day Benbow, in battle with four enemy planes, had had his wings shot off and had crashed to his death. His plane came down just inside the British lines, but Bishop would not let his men attend the funeral.

They grumbled that it was heartless to let Benbow be buried and mourned only by strangers. But Bishop for once was curt in his decision.

"It's the first time they've lost one of their number in battle," he explained to Horn, his deputy. "It might be too unnerving. I hope if they stew a bit about it they'll go out and knock down a few Huns."

That afternoon, sixteen thousand feet aloft over Roulers, Bishop stalked a formation of Pfalz two-seater scouts, the new German fighters. When two of the pilots turned to attack him, he downed both in a three-minute dogfight.

Curiously enough, Bishop believed that he had not hit the second Pfalz with a single bullet.

"I scared him to death," he told Springs over a few of the latter's famous cocktails before dinner. He explained that after the first Pfalz had crashed in flames, the other tried to escape in a power dive. Bishop jammed his throttle all the way forward and began to overhaul the enemy. At one hundred and fifty yards he opened fire but shot wide. Seeing the tracers darting by his wingtips the German pilot steepened the angle of his dive until he was going down almost vertically. Bishop followed, and his airspeed indicator showed two hundred miles an hour. He fired a short burst again, but was still off the target. Then the enemy machine started to fall apart. The wings folded back a pair at a time until only the fuselage was left, floating for a moment like a huge war canoe out of its element. Then it plummeted to earth.

After dinner Bishop went up alone. In three days he had brought down five enemy planes, and the obsession to fly, to fight, to kill—which had sometimes seized him at Filescamp—was there again. He flew over toward Armentières. Across the lines, two thousand feet below, he spotted two Albatros scouts. The sun was too low for Bishop to use it as cover. So he dived under them and attacked from the rear. Both went down, billowing smoke. The second plane disappeared into a cloud bank and Bishop did not see it crash. When he landed he learned that the nearest anti-aircraft battery had reported seeing only one plane crash in flames. Although he was sure he had killed the pilot of the second plane with a double burst of machine-gun fire at twenty yards' range Bishop philosophically accepted the verdict: three confirmed kills in one day wasn't bad hunting, his squadron mates pointed out not without irony.

Bishop's one-sided score, in comparison with that of his men, aroused the latter into flying overtime in an effort to get "a Hun of their own." On May 31, when Bishop and Horn each got a Pfalz on afternoon patrol, Springs "got all full of enthusiasm and went out by himself to do battle," as Grider noted in his diary.

His ambition was rewarded and he managed to find six Hun scouts south of Courtrai. They chased him all over the sky and he had a time getting away from them. He finally just put his tail plane forward and dove wide open. Nothing can hit you while you're doing two hundred and fifty miles an hour, so if your plane stays together you're all right. But it's not easy to come out of a dive like that alive. Springs tore all the fabric loose on his top wing doing it.

He was so excited when he landed that he ran into the major's plane and locked wings with it on the ground. The major was all set to bawl him out but Springs walked up to him and ran his finger across his row of ribbons and said, "You see these medals?"

Bishop nodded.

"Well," says Springs, "I just want to tell you that you are welcome to them." With this he walked off to the bar. Bishop laughed, although he wasn't pleased about having his machine smashed.

Actually, Bishop put a high value on Springs' antics, his laconic humour, and above all his inventiveness in the mixing of drinks, as a safety valve for the tensions of other members of the squadron. But periodically Springs himself suffered from moods so black that it was all Bishop and the rest of the squadron could do to keep Springs from committing some reckless act.

But most of the time life in 85 Squadron was both merry and luxurious. "I don't think Bishop is sorry he brought us along," Grider commented. "We are the only outfit at the front that has ice cream for dinner every night. Springs went down to Boulogne and got a freezer. He has taught the cook to make Eggs Benedict and we breakfast well. In fact, although 'in the midst of life we are in death,' we manage to have a hell of a lot of fun—chicken livers en brochette, champagne and Napoleon brandy."

High living and late hours did not make dawn patrols popular with the pilots of 85 Squadron, but Bishop was adamant. He was, quite possibly, the most lenient squadron commander in the Royal Air Force in the matter of what his men did with their spare time (and, for that matter, what he did with his own). But he insisted that his pilots earn their freedom of action by rigid discipline during "office hours."

Not that Bishop's pilots—and particularly his American trio—complained of their fate. Grider acknowledged: "We seem to be the only Americans in Europe that are really enjoying this war. All the others I have met seem to be having to work, or sleep without sheets, or eat out of mess kits, or do something unpleasant to spoil their holiday."

Moreover, not only was Bishop leading the same rigorous life as the others, but in addition to flying patrols he had to perform an unpleasant amount of administrative work. Nevertheless, he was outscoring his squadron mates by an almost embarrassing margin.

On May 31 when he shot down a German scout at dusk, near Hazebrouck, he wrote his father: "That makes ten for the squadron. Not bad when we still haven't officially gone into combat yet." He failed to add that he had shot down eight of the squadron's ten planes, and that his score was now fifty-five, just two behind the leading RAF pilot.

ST. OMER

NEXT MORNING, at 52 Portland Place, the pretty house-maid, white-faced, knocked on Lady St. Helier's bedroom door to report a rumour that was spreading through London: Major Bishop was missing in action and it was feared he had been shot down.

"Not a word to Mrs. Bishop," Granny warned, and she got on her bedroom telephone to various high officials who, denying any information of Bishop's fate, were ordered to take steps to find out. But for the rest of the day the rumour proliferated in the city, and Lady St. Helier had to take extraordinary steps to keep Margaret unaware of it. Late that night one of Lady St. Helier's War Office cronies telephoned that he had got a query through to 85 Squadron, and Bishop was safe. Margaret was surprised when Granny threw her arms around her and said emotionally, "My dear, I'm so happy it wasn't true."

For most of that day Bishop didn't even fly. He had been informed only that morning that 85 Squadron was officially to go active immediately. From the point of view of the pilots the change of status was an anticlimax—they had already been in combat several times, had shot down ten enemy planes and had penetrated deep behind the enemy lines. Now they were assigned to line patrol between Nieuport on the coast and Ypres, and were still restricted, in theory, from crossing the enemy lines.

Nevertheless, the new order required a great deal of paperwork that kept Bishop at his desk, and it was not until half past seven that evening that he finally finished his chores as commanding officer. It was the part of his duties that irked him most, and he used to say that an hour of administration tired him more than several hours in the air. He went up alone, but near Armentières he saw three other S.E. 5A's flying in a neat *V* formation. From the numbers on the machines he knew the trio were Elliott Springs, McGregor and Horn. The four machines turned south toward Lille, well behind the enemy lines. South of Lille a formation of six black Pfalz scouts darted beneath them, and the four S.E. 5A's dived to the attack. The dogfight that immediately developed ended in a result that would have seemed far-fetched even in a moving picture script: RAF pilots shot down one enemy plane each, in rapid succession.

It was Bishop's fifty-sixth kill. It placed him one victory short of McCudden's score. Next evening at precisely the same time and place, he caught up with his friendly rival. That night he wrote his father: "This afternoon the man in charge of gunnery on General Salmond's staff came over and he was full of buck about the squadron. He said GHQ were all talking about it, so our reputation is growing."

At eleven o'clock the next morning the Flying Foxes escorted a flight of bombers to Zeebrugge on the Dutch coast to raid the submarine pens.

The bombers flew at twelve thousand feet three miles out to sea to avoid the fire of coastal batteries, and the S.E. 5's cruised two thousand feet higher. Halfway between the ports of Nieuport and Ostend Bishop saw a formation of Albatros scouts approaching from the north. One of the enemy straggled behind the formation. Bishop needed only ten rounds from each gun to send the Albatros flaming into the ocean. It was his fifty-eighth kill, the first plane he had shot down into water, and the second time he had taken the lead as high-scoring ace of the British air service.

By now well behind the formation of bombers and fighters, Bishop dived to gain speed and catch up—and ran into a formation of eight Albatros fighters. He fired a burst of thirty rounds at the nearest. Its top wings flew apart and the plane spun down out of control.

"The Squadron total is now 18, and 12 for me," Bishop wrote to Margaret that night. But it was his last victory for eleven days.

For the first few days the weather was so bad that there could be practically no flying. Then on the morning of June 8 he was awakened by an urgent telephone call. (It was mid-morning, but there had been a party the night before, featuring an enormous bowl of champagne punch mixed by Springs.) The news was that the Flying Foxes finally had a home of their own. They were to move without delay to an aerodrome near St. Omer, where Bishop had been stationed when he first arrived in France as an observer two and a half years earlier.

Grider wrote admiringly in his diary:

You can't appreciate the British airforce until you see a squadron on the move. I was taking a nap when my batman shook me and said, "orders have come, Sir, that we are to move at twelve o'clock." It was then ten a.m., but at noon our baggage, transport, equipment and dogs left and at four we flew to our new airdrome. We hoped to pick up a Hun on the way so we had a squadron show, with Bish leading, but we had no luck. Our new beat is from Ypres to Nieppe. At one place near Hazebrouck the ground for about three square miles is a dull yellow. That's where there has been a gas attack.

It took several days to get properly settled. Necessary furniture— a piano, a gramophone with records (some profane, none sacred)— were secured. At the end of three days the mess was completely decorated, even to a proud array of purple garters with names and addresses of local belles. Bishop acquired another item of coveted equipment. A pilot he had known in his 21 Squadron days, who now issued all equipment for the area, wangled him a new and faster airplane.

"It is an absolute beauty," he wrote Margaret excitedly. "And I will be able to get 130 miles per hour on the level. It will take a good Hun to catch me now."

But for another two days he was unable to test it. The weather remained dull, and Bishop busied himself with decorating the new machine, painting it in gay colours, with an Indian crawling along the side, giving the nose the inevitable coat of blue.

His first flight in his new plane was nearly his last—and all because of the cherished helmet Margaret had given him. It was an expensive model from André's in Piccadilly. Bishop's head was large, so Margaret had picked out the largest model. It was comfortably lined with soft zebra skin, but was still a very loose fit.

In his new plane and wearing his new helmet, Bishop climbed to fifteen thousand feet over the Flying Foxes' new sector. Over Estaires he sighted four Pfalz scouts diving to attack him. At this critical moment the loose helmet slid around, covering his face. He was blind to the enemy's attack, his face wrapped in a blanket of soft zebra fur. At that moment the German opened fire. Bishop's plane was out of control. With his left hand he pulled his helmet around, and peered cautiously around, not knowing what he would see but afraid that it would be four enemy scouts in close attendance. Instead, the enemy planes were far below. If they had realized that Bishop was blind and helpless, they would have pressed home the attack, but instead when Bishop pulled up they continued diving. His efforts to evade them now turned to his advantage. He was well above and closing fast.

When Bishop neared them he realized he was being led into a trap. A thousand feet below a group of twelve Albatros fighters awaited him. He decided to make a fast attack, then escape. Twin streams of bullets set one enemy scout afire. It fell through the midst of the rest of the German planes, which scrambled to escape. By the time Bishop levelled off his fifteen surviving opponents had disappeared. He wasted no time, but swiftly returned to his aerodrome at St. Omer.

By way of celebrating his first victory in over a week, Bishop took Springs, Grider and Callahan on a visit to his old 60 Squadron, now based a few miles to the south. The squadron's losses had been heavy during the spring, and some of the spirit had gone out of the group, but the visit of the Flying Foxes developed into a exuberant "rag." Springs, of course, took over the cocktail bar with the assistance of Grider, and Callahan presided at the piano which Bishop remembered so well. "It was a good party," Grider noted in his diary. "And I think we won because when we left their C.O. was doing the Highland Fling with a couple of table knives as swords."

When the Flying Foxes got home an air raid was in progress. The raid was an unusually long one, and it was almost dawn before

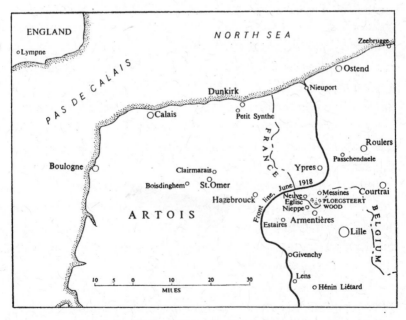

85 Squadron sector in 1918

the Flying Foxes got to bed. Horn took the dawn patrol while
Bishop, as squadron commander, slept soundly until noon. He
pretended to be annoyed, but was actually delighted when he
learned at lunch that Horn and Callahan had each shot down an
enemy plane on that early patrol.

Later that morning Cunningham-Reid brought down an observation balloon. The day that started off well for the Flying Foxes
had still more glory to come. That evening, a time of day which had
become his favourite hunting period, Bishop shot down two more
planes in the span of eight minutes.

He was in high spirits when he landed at St. Omer. The two victories brought his score up to sixty-two, well ahead of McCudden,
who was still in England. In only nine days of actual fighting he had
accounted for fifteen enemy machines and all fifteen had been
destroyed with approximately three hundred bullets, an average of
twenty rounds per enemy destroyed. Not once in those nine days
had Bishop's plane been struck by an enemy bullet.

But ten minutes after he climbed out of the cockpit, his mood
was abruptly changed. He received a telephone call from General
Webb Brown, the brigade commander.

"You have been recalled to England to help form a Canadian
flying corps," the general told him. Bishop said nothing of his keen
disappointment in the mess that evening, but before he went to
bed he wrote to Margaret: "I've never been so furious in my life.
It makes me livid with rage to be pulled away just as things are getting started."

Next morning, still angry, Bishop went up after a late breakfast
and in half an hour shot down three planes. It was the third time in
his career that he had scored a triple on one patrol. But he thought
it worth no more than casual mention in his next letter to Margaret.
He was much more concerned at his imminent transfer.

No more news today. I went over to see the Colonel and he
is furious that I am likely to go. By the way, as a sideline I got

three more Huns today. I went out this morning and carefully searched the sky, finding a two-seater at 18,000 feet.

Him I sent down in flames.

Then I found a scout.

Him I crashed.

Then I found another two-seater and sent him down. He crashed.

Cunningham-Reid also got a Hun and Springs, Gilder and Canning got one between them. That's five today. Squadron total 30. Mine 65.

If Bishop was annoyed, his pilots were apprehensive. A rumour circulated through the squadron that McCudden was being considered as Bishop's successor—and McCudden had a reputation for being not only an exceptional pilot, but very discipline-minded and "regimental." The Flying Foxes were an easygoing crew, and they feared there would be friction.

Bishop's own choice was the slender Irishman he had met with Grid Caldwell—Mick Mannock of 74 Squadron. He was a superb aerial tactician who would probably be popular with the Foxes— and all hands were delighted when Bishop's recommendation was accepted by headquarters. With the appointment settled, Bishop knew that his own transfer was imminent.

"I imagine I'll hear this afternoon," Bishop told his brother-in-law, Hank Burden, glumly at lunch. "Anyway I got two more this morning, and if this damned weather clears I'll go up again this afternoon."

But the weather did not clear. It got worse. Hank decided to get back to his own aerodrome before it closed in completely. It was a wise move. By mid-afternoon a storm swept in over St. Omer and all machines were grounded. To add to Bishop's gloom the news he had been dreading came at tea time: he must leave for England at noon the following day. That still left him the evening and the next morning in which to have one more look at the war. But the weather was even worse by evening, and it seemed that Bishop had already had his last look at the war.

So instead of flying, the Foxes organized the most glorious party of their career in honour of Bishop's departure. Springs and Grider excelled with their finest and most lethal cocktail bowl. Callahan proved worthy of his renown as a pianist and Bishop's tap dance on the piano was surely his most spectacular. After the second encore the overburdened instrument collapsed, and even a generous quantity of Springs' punch couldn't revive it. The clothes-tearing ceremony was notable—Grider lost his shirt as well as his tunic—and there was not a single record left intact by the time the celebration ended at half-past three in the morning.

The morning of June 19, 1918, barely dawned in the gloom of a heavy drizzle. It had rained all night. The field was soaked. It was as rotten a day for flying as Bishop had ever seen when he looked out the window of his quarters. His head pounded from the festivities of the night before, but he had to leave the airport by noon and it was past nine when he sat down to bacon and eggs and tea.

One last flight? Why not? After all, you could get to a thousand feet and it might be clearer to the east—the wind was blowing from that direction.

"It's probably worse over the lines," Springs said, "and chances are there won't be any Huns up in this stuff anyway."

Bishop shrugged and sloshed his way across the field to his plane. At half-past nine he climbed into the cockpit of his gaudily decorated S.E. 5A for the last time. Once aloft, visibility was not nearly as bad as he had anticipated. As he headed east towards battered Ypres, Bishop could see the ground distinctly. Then at the trench lines, the broken ditches that scarred the landscape, he climbed into the clouds at eighteen hundred feet to hide from the ground fire.

He casually decided to fly to Passchendaele, seven miles east of Ypres, before coming down from the clouds to cut a wide arc to the north. After ten minutes he dropped out of the clouds to check his position. He had not paid enough attention to his compass, and his plane had veered south. He was directly over Ploegsteert Wood—the landmark the pilots called "Plug Street." And he was not alone.

Three hundred yards to his left, flying away from him, were three Pfalz scouts with black and white tails. The German fighters began to turn as Bishop swept in behind them. From one hundred and fifty yards he took aim—then the Aldis sight oiled up. He shifted to the auxiliary ring and bead sight, which was not as accurate, but better than a blind shot. But by then he was too late. The Pfalz scouts had come halfway around in a turn and now they dived head-on at him. Ugly orange flashes blossomed from the muzzles of their guns and Bishop heard the bullets streak past. There was a rending crunch as his left lower wingtip was shredded by tracers. Bishop got away only a short return burst as the enemy fighters slipped by underneath him. He banked left to try to get behind them again, meanwhile taking a quick look behind. It probably saved his life. Two more Pfalz scouts were diving out of the clouds at nearly two hundred miles an hour.

The three enemy planes in front were now only four hundred yards away. Bishop decided to risk a quick attack on them before the two others could join in. He had no time to get at close range, and opened fire at one hundred and twenty yards. The burst was brief but destructive. It struck the rearmost plane and killed the pilot. The machine turned over and fell nose-forward in a vertical dive. Bishop had no chance to see it crash, then the second pair of Pfalz scouts began to fire at him.

He slammed the left rudder bar hard and pulled into a steep turn. His attackers slipped past and below.

The other pair of Pfalz machines had begun to climb. Bishop knew they intended to hide in the clouds until he was fully occupied with the other two German planes, then pounce on him. But they never made it to the clouds. Just under the layer, where it was misty and hard to see, they drifted too close to each other, locked wings with a splintering crash, and for a moment hung there suspended. Then the planes fell apart. Bits of wing, fuselage and tail fluttered away, and they joined the first Pfalz, which was burning on the ground a mile east of Ploegsteert.

It had all happened in the space of three minutes. The remaining pair of enemy fighters now tried to climb into the security of the clouds. But one was too slow making his escape and he presented a perfect target. Bishop had a dead shot from fifty yards. From behind and below, he watched his tracers hurtle toward the belly of the Pfalz and tear a gaping hole in the wings. The plane nosed forward, went into a spin, and crashed.

Bishop, now alone in the sky, noticed that the clouds had dropped lower, and the ceiling was now less than a thousand feet. His compass was not working—the violence of his manoeuvring in the dogfight had put it out of kilter, and Bishop had only an approximate idea of his location, somewhere between Ploegsteert Wood and Neuve Eglise.

As he flew in the misty drizzle, the outline of another machine emerged, a ghostly apparition. Then the outline became clearer. It was a two-seater with black crosses.

It wallowed in eccentric shallow turns and the observer in the rear seat peered over the side. Both pilot and observer were obviously unaware that they were seen and pursued. Bishop easily slipped into the ideal position—the blind spot, behind and beneath. When he got within forty yards of the enemy machine he tilted his nose upwards and took aim. The tail skid, the two wheels, the crossbar between them, all seemed to be within grasp. Bishop aimed at the spot where the pilot's backside would be. Ten rounds from both guns tore into the bottom of the enemy plane. It wobbled for a second, then skidded violently. One of the wheels fell off and spun past Bishop like a huge twirling plate. Then the two-seater fell earthward, and Bishop could see that the pilot he had aimed at was alive and fighting to keep the plane under control, while the observer was slumped limply in his seat. Seconds later the plane crashed into a hillock and burst into flames.

Bishop circled once, watching the tumbling pall of smoke rise from the hillock. The sky was now clear of planes. He knew he had fought his last fight in the air. He knew he should be feeling some strong emotion—triumph at his seventy-second victory, resentment at being recalled from the front, pity for his final victim, burning to death on the earth beneath. But he felt nothing—only a dull automatic reaction that made him turn toward his home airport for the last time.

He was barely aware that he had achieved his greatest triumph—five planes within fifteen minutes. Only later would he learn that his final month in France had earned him yet another decoration, the Distinguished Flying Cross, an award he could not have won before because it had only recently been created. The citation read:

> A most successful and fearless fighter in the air whose acts of outstanding bravery have already been recognized by the award of the V.C., D.S.O., a bar to the D.S.O., and the M.C. For the award of the D.F.C. now conferred upon him he has rendered signally valuable service in personally destroying twenty-five enemy machines in twelve days ... five of which he destroyed on the last day of his service at the front. The total number of machines destroyed by this distinguished officer is seventy-two and his value as a moral factor to the Royal Air Force cannot be over-estimated.

Soon after Bishop left France, General Morrison, commanding the Canadian artillery in France, wrote to General Turner, Chief of the Canadian Forces in England: "I was particularly interested in meeting Major Bishop and am glad that he has been selected for an administrative appointment. The more so because Major

McCudden, V.C., was killed yesterday afternoon. While Major Bishop's services were invaluable to the army as a fighting man, I believe he can do more good by training others than continue to risk the almost inevitable on the firing line."

Bishop became the first commanding officer designate of the Canadian wing with the rank of lieutenant-colonel. The wing was to be composed of two squadrons, which in turn were to be part of a tactical force in support of the Canadian Corps in France. Selection of pilots and observers presented no problem. There was an abundance. Finding suitable men to be trained as ground mechanics, however, was another matter. They were to be recruited from Canadian army units in England. But Bishop soon discovered that the applicants fell into two categories: those who were decidedly unhappy in their regiments, and others whose commanding officers wanted to get rid of them.

By mid-August, however, a school for the technical training of Canadian "volunteers" had been formed and an extensive training program made it possible to select suitable applicants. But the role the Canadian wing was expected to play appalled Bishop. General Sir Arthur Currie, the commander of the Canadian Corps in France, believed the wing could help win the war by strafing ground troops. He had been immensely impressed by the success of the RAF in killing and pinning down surface forces during the summer offensive. But Bishop, who had a horror, based on his experience in the Arras and Vimy battles, of getting any nearer to ground fire than was absolutely necessary, protested bitterly against this idea, and it was abandoned. Next it was proposed that Bishop lead a bombing raid against Berlin. Bishop was tempted. At least the project would get him back into combat flying. But he remembered the arduous reconnaissance of his days as an observer, back in 1916, and he said bluntly: "I don't want the job." (Among the jobs he *did* want was designing the insignia of the Canadian wing. He sketched the maple leaf emblem which became the symbol of the flying Canadians.)

Meanwhile with Margaret, Lady St. Helier and Princess Marie Louise, Bishop returned enthusiastically to the social life of London.

During a Canadian military demonstration at Windsor Park, Bishop had his third meeting with King George. The monarch looked at him quizzically and said, "Bishop, I've been telling everyone that you shot down seventy-two planes, and now I read in your own book that you shot down forty-seven. Are you a liar or am I?"

"Neither of us, Sir," answered Bishop. "When I wrote the book I had forty-seven, since then I have added twenty-five."

The King seemed satisfied with the explanation, and for his part Bishop was gratified that among the readers of his book, *Winged Warfare*, was George V.

But Bishop had little cause for satisfaction in other respects. It was becoming more and more obvious that the war was coming to a close, that the German armies were beginning to crumble and the Allies were preparing to deliver a death blow. But the Canadian wing was not ready to participate. Bishop was ordered to return to Canada to report to the prime minister, Sir Robert Borden, on progress, and at the same time assist in recruiting. He and Margaret left England in October, 1918.

His homecoming this time was, if anything, even more enthusiastic than his reception the previous year. The newspapers did not fail to headline the fact that he was the leading killer of German pilots and was, moreover, the most decorated fighting man alive (the French government had added to his laurels the Legion of Honour and the Croix de Guerre with two palms, bringing his total awards to ten).

After a meeting with government leaders and a series of speeches urging enlistment in the air force, he was again ordered to return to England. This time he decided to leave Margaret behind. He did not think his absence in Great Britain would be a long one. The end of the war was obviously imminent. In November he went to New York to sail for England. During his three days in Manhattan he met Lee Keedick, an enterprising booking agent, who suggested a lecture tour on air fighting throughout the United States. Bishop agreed to the attractive terms Keedick offered.

He was halfway across the Atlantic when the ship's wireless brought the news of the war's end. "How did I react?" Bishop recalled many years later. "I thought of how the boys at the front and in England would be celebrating the news. And here were we sailing under war regulations—which meant that there wasn't so much as a blasted bottle of beer aboard."

THE TWENTIES

THE FIGHTING was over—but not for Bishop. When he took off his uniform at the beginning of 1919 he was immediately involved in a struggle to readjust and stay on even keel. As a soldier he had achieved something of the acclaim accorded a Wellington, a Nelson or a Marlborough. But there was a shuddering difference. Bishop was twenty-five, and in many ways immature and unsophisticated. When he started his lecture tour, Carnegie Hall and Lexington Hall in New York were packed to capacity. The audiences were comparatively as large as the tour moved through the eastern states, but it was a gruelling trip. Bishop would often lecture in one city at night and by noon the next day would be addressing an audience two hundred miles away.

It was tiring, but the money was good. And sales of *Winged Warfare* were at their peak, perhaps because Bishop managed to mention the book casually in his lectures. But the money was spent as fast as it was earned. Bishop was simply continuing the habit of not counting the cost—a habit he and thousands of other men who daily faced sudden death had come to accept as a way of life. Why ask the cost of a meal, a drink, a hotel room, an automobile, a suit of clothes, a gift, a tip—when money might have no value next day because its owner had joined the company of the dead?

The answer to that collective question came to Bishop with stunning impact. In March, 1919, he collapsed on the stage during a speech at Roanoke, Virginia. He was publicized as the first patient admitted to the new Jefferson Hospital in Roanoke. The doctors diagnosed appendicitis, and operated. Bishop's war service and the rigours of the lecture tour had taken a toll that even he was unaware of, and it was a month before the Roanoke doctors would let him resume his journey. But by then it was too late. In a month too much had happened in the world of mid-1919 for the Canadian air ace to maintain his popularity. On the first night of his resumed lecture tour exactly ten persons were in the audience.

Margaret was dismayed, but Bishop was philosophical. "It had to end sooner or later," he told her comfortingly, "and perhaps it was better sooner."

He cancelled the rest of the speaking tour, took the several thousands of dollars he had earned, and returned to Toronto. Characteristically, he rented a large house on fashionable Poplar Plains Road before giving serious thought to how he would pay the rent, to say nothing of supporting himself and his wife in the manner she had always—and he had recently—become accustomed to.

Upper Canada College, a well-endowed private school, offered him a teaching post, and Bishop was seized with the romantic idea that his future might lie in the training of the next generation. But when he heard the modest figure the job offered he turned it down. An enterprising automobile dealer decided he could cash in on Bishop's fame by making him a super-salesman. "I'll give you a salary of three thousand and commission," he told Bishop.

"A month?" asked Bishop.

"Hell no, a year," said the auto magnate, and Bishop walked out of his office in scornful silence.

Bishop was still living on the avails of speech making (and not to put a fine point on it, had no compunction about using his wife's allowance from her wealthy family if his own funds were sparse) when a Canadian air hero of stature second only to Bishop blew into Toronto. He was William George Barker, a tall, rangy man from Brandon, Manitoba, whose exploits deserve a book all of their own. Although the two men were physically as dissimilar as could be imagined, they shared a few important things. Both were winners of the coveted Victoria Cross. Less important historically, but possibly more significant in the subsequent events involving the two men, they both were dedicated to the proposition that champagne, cognac, Scotch or old rye whiskey were superior beverages to tea or coffee.

The Bishop-Barker Company was best remembered for two things: it was a commercial failure and it was a great deal of fun.

To finance the undertaking, Bishop and Barker appealed to leading businessmen in Toronto and Montreal, liberally offering stock in the enterprise. More out of sentiment for the two young V.C. airmen than from cautious financial judgment, many of these giants of commerce generously proffered substantial sums to get the business started.

In the winter of 1919–20 the partners sold aircraft for the Sopwith Company of England. In the spring of 1920 they acquired for their own company three clumsy pusher-type seaplanes known as H.S. 2L's, which had been used in the latter stages of the war for submarine hunting. As surplus war material, Bishop bought them for $1,000 each.

By June of 1920 the Bishop-Barker Company was ready to operate as passenger carriers. The seaplane was designed to carry three persons in addition to a crew of two. But Bishop and Barker managed to crowd in five. Behind the passengers the two pilots operated the machine jointly. Barker manipulating the controls, Bishop the throttles.

The airline route was from Toronto harbour on Lake Ontario to the Muskoka Lakes vacation area one hundred miles north. The first flights were heralded with much publicity. Wireless stations along the route telegraphed reports of the progress of the lumbering machine. There was nothing unusual about the flights other than the celebrity of the pilots and the fact that it was the first time an aeroplane had flown that exact course. True, there was the constant hazard of a seaplane having to come down on land if the engine failed at a point too far from one of the numerous lakes for a glide-in. The partners acknowledged this danger by a solemn ceremonial which the passengers, fortunately, were unable to witness. As the plane climbed north from the safety of Lake Ontario, Barker would produce a flask, announce "over the land, brother," and share the contents with his copilot. Bishop's tongue was at least partly in his cheek when he advertised his airline in the Toronto newspapers as offering "safe and sane flying."

And what Bishop and Barker did next scarcely carried out the theme of safety and sanity. They bought a pair of Martynside two-seaters and offered to put on exhibitions of aerobatics, or, to put it bluntly, stunting. In the summer of 1920 they signed a contract with the Canadian National Exhibition to stage a daily show. One of the provisions of the contract was that the pilots must not stunt over the site of the exhibition itself, but must perform their aerobatics over the waters of Lake Ontario which bordered the area.

But the partners decided they should give the customers more for their money. On the second evening Bishop, stunting over the lake, suddenly broke off and dived toward the grandstand. At a height of fifty feet—"I could see thousands of frightened faces," he recalled later—he pulled his plane's nose up, turned on its back, and executed a loop that brought the roaring machine even closer to the crowd.

Barker quickly followed, and dived even closer to the grandstand before pulling up. Then Bishop did another loop, and so did Barker. One eyewitness insisted that they repeated the manoeuvre "nearly one hundred times."

On the ground there was pandemonium. Many people fled the stands in fright. The noise of the stunting Martynsides drowned out the band and the stage performance came to a halt. Three horses reared and one of them jumped the rail in front of the spectators. One woman fainted from fright and another claimed she had suffered a miscarriage. "It was," one spectator declared flatly, "the most frightening thing I have ever seen."

Further performances were cancelled by the directors of the exhibition. Bishop and Barker paid dearly for their fun. The company could ill afford to lose the contract. It already faced bankruptcy. A substitute pilot had crashed one of the H.S. 2L's, the government's flying certification branch was investigating the accident and meanwhile, in view of the Canadian National Exhibition performance, officials were considering suspending the Bishop-Barker licence to operate. Among the evidence against them was something that had nothing to do with their conduct aloft, but was indicative of their status as "safe and sane" citizens: between them they had collected more than one hundred traffic tickets and summonses for various driving offences including recklessness. The accumulated fines could have amounted to thousands of dollars—and jail terms if they were unable to pay the fines. Bishop's own account of what happened next (and anyone is entitled to doubt it) was this:

> We arranged a cocktail party to which we invited various civic dignitaries, magistrates, judges, aldermen and the like. The first drink to each was free, but after that there was a price—a cancelled summons for each drink. Fortunately, the dignitaries entered into the spirit of the thing, everybody had a good time—and the summonses were disposed of.

The partners decided, however, that there was no immediate future for them in aviation. But before they could liquidate Bishop-Barker they must raise enough money to pay off the businessmen who had financed them. The only business they knew well enough for the purpose was, of course, flying. They would abandon passenger flying and solicit air freight, which they felt would be both less hazardous and more profitable. But before they could get the cargo business started another disaster struck the partnership.

Tom Sopwith, the English aircraft manufacturer for whom Bishop-Barker had been serving as Canadian sales agents, sent out a new model, a Dove two-seater. Bishop was eager to test it, and as soon as it was assembled he took it up with a passenger, Andrew Maclean, son of a Toronto magazine publisher.

Bishop put the plane through its paces with a practised hand. It was fast and manoeuvrable, and the only fault he could find was that it was somewhat nose-heavy. But that, combined with Bishop's traditional difficulty in executing smooth landings, very nearly ended his career and that of his young passenger.

As Bishop levelled out the machine to touch down, the wheels struck a deep rut on the edge of the field. The machine nosed over, struck the ground hard and came to a violent stop. Bishop's face smashed against the cowling above the instrument panel and his knees dug into Maclean's back. Both men were knocked unconscious.

Barker, who had been watching from the other side of the field, rushed across in a car. With the help of bystanders he pulled the two men from the wreck. When Bishop regained consciousness Barker leaned over to him and said calmly: "I've just talked to the doctor—you mustn't blow your nose." However, the truth was he had practically no nose to blow. It had been flattened across his face. Maclean had not been any luckier. His back had been broken in two places and for a long time he had to wear a support.

With his head swathed in bandages Bishop lay for three weeks unable to see. But what bothered him most was a pain in the toe of his right foot. It throbbed continually. Actually it had been broken but no one paid the slightest attention when Bishop complained of it. Everyone was too concerned about his shattered nose, afraid that he might be permanently blinded.

When the doctor removed the bandages no one knew what to expect. Everyone stood anxiously around. But a smile appeared on Bishop's bruised face. "I'm not blind anyway," he announced happily. "In fact I can see twice as much as anybody. Everybody is double."

The double vision gradually disappeared, although occasionally when Bishop became tired it would return. But his nose, even after surgery, never looked the same again. Once straight, it was now and for the rest of Bishop's life squat and bulbous.

By February 1921, Bishop had recovered and could go back to work. But he was not allowed to fly. There remained the danger that the double vision might return while he was in the air.

He now faced a major personal crisis. The one thing at which he had excelled, the thing he enjoyed most and for which he had become noted, had been shorn from him. Added to this, the Bishop-Barker Company continued to lose money in his absence and the shareholders still had to be paid.

Then the old "Bishop luck" returned. Looking for a new enterprise to which to turn his hand, he and the company's master painter experimented with a quick-drying paint, the most important new ingredient of which was the dope used to shrink airplane fabric. No sooner had the formula been perfected than an opportunity for its profitable use presented itself. At that time the Toronto city government had decided not to renew the franchise of the Toronto Railway Company. The cars were to be taken over by the Toronto Transit Commission, and the price paid to the railway company for its equipment would depend on the condition of the cars at the time of purchase. Therefore the railway company decided to have the cars painted.

Bishop submitted a tender of $300 per car, and in addition guaranteed to deliver one painted car per day, ready for service. Since the company's revenue lost while the cars were idle would be sharply reduced by such fast service, Bishop was awarded a contract to paint one hundred cars. He and his master painter had to do most of the work themselves, since the painters they hired objected to the acrid fumes of the dope. Both men were half-ill for months afterwards, but the venture earned $30,000 for the

Bishop-Barker Company. This added to the sale of assets and some profit which Barker accumulated flying cargo raised enough money to pay off the investors and liquidate the enterprise.

Barker decided to return to the air force and re-enlisted as a wing commander. He died not long afterwards in a crash at Ottawa. Bishop was tempted to return to the service, but remained a civilian and at the end of 1921 he was back in England, a situation brought about by an odd mixture of good fortune and personal tragedy.

Margaret gave birth to a son, who died not long afterwards. Grief, added to his own financial misfortunes, made Bishop decide on a change of scene. In England, Bishop had always been happy and confident, and when an opportunity arose to return there with good prospects of making a comfortable living, he did not hesitate.

The opportunity was provided by a Toronto friend, Gordon Perry, who was involved in a venture to sell foreign rights to a new method of producing iron pipe, invented by a Frenchman, Dmitri Delavaud. Perry needed someone who had wide contacts. Bishop's London friends, such as Granny St. Helier, made him the ideal front man. He became sales representative for the company, with headquarters in London. Bishop's friends and the celebrity of his war record helped his new career, but in addition he proved to be an unexpectedly shrewd negotiator. Gordon Perry said to Margaret, "In a business deal he has the face of an angel and the mind of a murderer."

Soon the Bishops' personal grief and frustration were forgotten. They settled into a house in Chester Terrace near Regent's Park and became Londoners. Granny St. Helier continued to exert her influence on their behalf. They soon became very much a part of the London set of the twenties.

And Bishop began to amass a fortune. In addition to the Delavaud dealings, he also represented Frank N. Pickett, who dealt in surplus scrap metal left at ammunition dumps in the Pas de Calais area in France. As an enjoyable sideline he bought and traded polo ponies for his employer.

All this allowed Bishop, still in his twenties, to live in luxury. He had plenty of money, and did not have to work too hard for it. He therefore had lots of time for recreation. He played polo and played it well, a four-goal handicap man. He captained his own team, the Birds, which in 1924 won the Cirencester Senior Cup matches.

One of his polo teammates was Winston Churchill, whom he had first met at Lady St. Helier's during the war. In his diary he noted an incident at Templeton in May, 1925:

> Scored the winning goal in the last few minutes of play with a right hand shot to the goal line from an impossible angle under my pony's neck. Because I was leaning out of the saddle, the correct backhand shot to keep the ball in play was almost impossible. Winston, who was playing back, was in a perfect position to receive a backhand from me. He was unguarded and shouting at the top of his Winstonian lungs: "Backhander, Bishop!"
>
> I reached out of the saddle and somehow hit the so-and-so ball. It sailed through the posts at an unbelievable angle. To say that I was pleased is putting it mildly, but as we rode off the field Winston said to me in no kind voice, "Why didn't you hit a backhander to me? your shot was not polo."
>
> Later in the dressing room when we were changing he said, "You know I was right, that shot was not polo. But my dear Bishop, who can criticize success?"

Churchill and Bishop became close friends. Churchill tried to interest him in politics, which he himself had entered successfully at an early age. But Bishop refused. His excuse was that his father, who was a minor political figure as an organizer of the Canadian Liberal party, had once advised his son: "Don't go into politics

unless you are absolutely sure you are going to be at the top of it."
Bishop did, however, stump for Churchill in the election of 1925.
Closer to the truth is that Bishop preferred the privileges of pros-
perous private life to the responsibility of political office.

In addition to polo, Bishop played golf in the low eighties. He
ran around the block each morning. He took boxing lessons from
a professional at his house twice a week. He never stopped proving himself, and exercise gave him a sense of being stronger, and
better attuned physically than others.

By night he was a man-of-the-world figure in café society, a regular visitor to such well-known places as the Embassy and Buck's
Club, to which he was driven in his Rolls-Royce by Percy Lethbridge, a quick-witted Londoner from Kentish Town, whom he
fondly called "Leffo."

He and Margaret holidayed at Le Touquet and Cannes. They
mingled with the celebrities of the "roaring twenties" and he soon
became a celebrity in his own right. He became friends with Hem-
ingway, Scott Fitzgerald, Josephine Baker. Through Princess Marie
Louise he mingled with royalty—the Prince of Wales and Prince
Albert. And this developed an almost unreasonable loyalty to the
Crown. He knocked down a man who announced to him in 1936
that King Edward VIII had abdicated. He felt it his duty to defend
the King's honour.

Bishop's maturity was late in developing, but this was belied by
the fact that before he was thirty his hair had turned completely
grey. It tended to make him look about ten years older. And he was
still haunted by memories, and one persistent nightmare plagued
him. It was a frighteningly clear re-enactment of the time he
crashed in flames in the S.E. 5 and was left hanging upside down in
the burning machine. Even the sounds were accurate: the clanking
of the engine, the crackle of the flames, the shearing, crunching
sound of the wings striking the trees.

In March, 1928, nearly ten years after the war ended, Bishop
met some of his former foes in Berlin. He had travelled to the Ger-

man capital in connection with the Delavaud interests. At first his visit was a lonely one ("Not one German invited me to his house") and he spent most of his leisure time in his hotel.

One morning he visited Mercy Cemetery where Manfred von Richthofen had been buried. The baron's remains had been taken there in 1925 from Bertangles, in France, where he had crashed and been buried with full military honours by Australian troops in 1918. At the cemetery gate Bishop registered, and the alert gatekeeper contacted the German Ace Association. The news that Colonel Bishop, V.C., was in Berlin was quickly transmitted to Ernst Udet, Germany's top living ace, with sixty-two planes to his credit.

That afternoon Bishop received an invitation to attend a special luncheon in his honour at the Berlin Aero Club the next day. It turned into quite a party. After several toasts had been drunk Bishop became the first and only foreign member of the German Ace Association and was presented with the emblem of membership—a tie pin with gold propeller mounted in a blue enamel roundel. Among those who applauded enthusiastically was a forceful, jovial man who had taken over command of Richthofen's circus after the baron's death, and had been credited with a score of twenty Allied planes. His name was Hermann Goering. Champagne flowed freely, and after a toast proposed by Goering, Bishop said with wry humour: "You honour me for having shot down more German planes than any other Allied airman. But I now ask you to honour me as *Germany's* greatest ace." When his former enemies looked puzzled, Bishop added with a grin: "I personally destroyed more Allied planes by my own method of landing than all of you combined!"

The party continued all afternoon and into the night. Old fights were discussed and compared. At one point Bishop told Goering, "I've always been curious to know what you called us. We always referred to you as Huns because it was the worst thing we could think of."

"Oh, we just called you Britishers," was Goering's good-humoured reply. "We always considered that quite bad enough."

The celebration might have continued all night if Bishop had not had to catch a train for Paris, where Margaret was waiting. Before he left for the station he phoned to say that he would soon be on his way. At the same time he thought it opportune to introduce her to his hosts. Somewhat aghast she listened as the effervescent Udet came on the line, buoyed up with the best of champagne, to announce blandly, "I speak no English. Haff a cocktail! Haff a drink!"

Three months later Bishop renewed another attachment with the past. In June, 1928, when he and Margaret were staying at Le Touquet on the French coast, they drove to Filescamp Farm, the old base of 60 Squadron. The church still stood intact and proud in the centre of the town of Izel-le-Hameau. But the other buildings were new.

"It was wonderful," Monsieur Tétus, who owned the farm, told Bishop. "After you left we were bombed and the government rebuilt all our houses."

When Bishop politely asked after Madame Tétus, the Frenchman replied: "Yes, she too was destroyed in the bombing. So me, I marry the maid."

Later that summer Bishop returned the hospitality of his German hosts by giving a festive dinner for them in London. "Colonel Bishop's breaking of bread with his old foes is an example to us all," editorialized the influential *Ottawa Journal*. "It would be a great pity, and a great loss if this spirit were retarded by acts of Germany's conquerors. A far better and wiser course has been shown by Colonel Bishop."

But Bishop himself had developed an uneasy feeling about the Germans which he could not explain. But he was certain of one thing. He did not trust them.

On the black day in November, 1929, when the New York stock exchange crash was heard around the world, Bishop was playing golf. When he returned to the clubhouse there was a telephone call from his broker informing him that he had been wiped out. Apart from a few thousand dollars he possessed in cash, he had lost nearly a million dollars in paper assets. He had no debts, however. His only outstanding obligation was a new record player, one of the first with a remote control, that he had allowed to be installed in his house on a demonstration-and-trial basis. When he got home he walked over to this coveted instrument, leaned over and kissed it solemnly, and said, "Well, it was fun while it lasted."

It was the second time Bishop had gone broke since the end of the war. But now his responsibilities were greater. He had a six-year-old son (me) and a three-year-old daughter. He had set a high standard of living for himself and his family—and certainly he was extremely reluctant to exchange his *bon vivant* mode of living for anything less pleasant.

Bishop had an unshaken faith in the wisdom of Gordon Perry. who had been responsible for bringing him into the Delavaud ventures. It was Gordon to whom he now turned for assistance and advice. And for the second time it was Gordon who rescued him from financial jeopardy.

Among other posts he held, Gordon was a director of McColl-Frontenac Oil Company, whose head offices were in Montreal. The oil business was thriving. McColl-Frontenac, an amalgamation of several companies, was keen on establishing itself as a leading contender in the market. "People will always buy oil and gasoline, no matter what they have to do without," Perry told Bishop, offering him a vice-presidency in charge of sales promotion. The salary and expense account were generous enough for him to maintain his style of living—minus the polo ponies and the chauffeur-driven Rolls-Royce.

By the summer of the following year, 1930, the Bishops moved back to Canada. The man who by this time had become a part of the family, "Leffo" the chauffeur, came with them.

In 1931 they moved into a large roof-garden penthouse on the slopes of Mount Royal overlooking the city.

TWENTY-ONE

MY FATHER

I DID NOT, of course, know Billy Bishop, the war hero. Nor did I know the heedless, free-spending *bon vivant* sportsman of the twenties.

As a small boy I was not conscious of Billy Bishop or what he had done. Traditionally, young boys learn the intimate facts of life from playmates a year or two older. So did I learn the facts about my father from boys who were old enough to be interested in reading the legends of World War I. But my recollection is that I was impressed by my father only because he impressed others, and I was actually quite unable to connect Bishop, the hero, with the man who was my father. How could I, when he behaved so much more like a friend than like a man whose fame rested on killing?

Once when my sister and I were confined to bed with colds we got bored and decided to hurl all our books out the window. We lived on the seventh floor of the apartment building, and our window faced the courtyard.

Downstairs my father said to my mother: "It's nice that the children are quiet for once, instead of quarrelling." But in a moment the doorman came up to the apartment to complain that "it's raining books down there."

My father stormed into our bedroom ready to stop us and probably give us a stern lecture. But when he saw the fun we were having (my sister was throwing the books out two at a time) his mood changed abruptly. "All right," he said with a twinkle, "just one more each—and I get the first throw."

Bishop set strange standards for himself and others. He approved of gaiety, even vulgarity, but they had to be disciplined. Few people have ever possessed such a repertoire of ribald jokes. ("The shorter the better—long jokes are boring.") But they had to be told at the proper place and time.

Appearances and dress were a fetish with him. The juvenile dandy at Owen Sound became the adult Beau Brummel of Montreal. His clothes were always made by the Savile Row tailors, Anderson and Shepherd. His shoes were especially built by Tucsec of London. He had his ties cut for him. He wore dark, striped double-breasted suits, starched collars, a dark homburg and always carried a cane. He would never allow a barber to use the clippers, and held to the notion that "a gentleman always wears his hair a bit long."

He was a master of flattery. To pregnant women, who in that condition welcome compliments, he would say, "I can tell, there is a joyful look in your eyes." He often confided mischievously, "They always believe it—it's the nicest thing you can say."

More than once he also said: "Never say anything about anybody unless you have something nice to say." And he would not tolerate gossip, but would simply walk away from such conversation. In his mid-forties, he was a massive man, with bulging biceps, a barrel of a chest and a growing girth. We called him "Fatty"—and he loved it.

But in some respects the rules he laid down for me were unreasonable and illogical. For example although he gave me flying lessons in my early teens, he never allowed me the use of the family car, even when I was old enough to get a driving licence. "When you can afford your own car, then you drive," he said.

He also believed in inculcating an early appreciation of the value of money. Thus he put me on a monthly allowance at an early age.

I had to buy my own clothes, pay my own transportation to and from boarding school, buy my own books, necessities and sports equipment. He did not believe in owning property, and all his life he lived in rented houses. "You only tie yourself down," he maintained, and refused to argue the point.

He never severed his connection with the Royal Canadian Air Force—the force which finally came into existence in 1924, six years after the war, and more than six years after he had been pulled back from the front line to organize it. In 1931, he was appointed Honorary Group Captain of the RCAF, but it was not an honour that gave him any great pleasure, because he was heartsick at what he considered to be the neglect by the government of the armed forces in general and the air arm in particular. By 1934 the activities of the RCAF had been reduced to the point where Canadian pilots were putting in barely a thousand hours a month of total flying time.

In this year of 1934, when Canada's preparedness was at its lowest ebb, my father had a strange and blood-chilling experience that finally convinced him that war with Nazi Germany was inevitable. Early that summer he was in England on business, and on impulse he wrote to Hermann Goering, with whom he got along well during that convivial evening in Berlin six years before. In 1928 Goering had been, as far as my father was aware, a friendly ex-enemy with some vaguely unorthodox political leanings. Now he was Hitler's right-hand man and head of the resurgent German air force.

Goering replied immediately. He would be delighted to see his distinguished former antagonist once more. Would Herr Bishop dine with him at the Berlin Aero Club on June 30?

My father accepted. But at the last moment he decided not to go. After an exhausting week of business appointments, an invitation to spend a weekend at a friend's country house seemed far more attractive than the long trip to Berlin. He wired his regrets to Goering and he and my mother drove down to the Sussex coast where a friend, Norman Holden, owned "The Priory," a lavish estate.

Next morning while my parents were playing croquet after breakfast, their host hurried out with the shocking news that had come over the radio: Hitler and Goering had staged the bloody night-long purge of their own party, starting with the murder of Ernst Roehm, head of the elite Nazi forces known as the Brown Shirts. It was an event that was to be stamped in the catalogue of Nazi crime as "The Night of the Long Knives."

My mother turned pale. "You might have been there!" she exclaimed. My father needed no reminder of the many unpleasant possibilities that might have resulted from his presence in Berlin that night. But that was conjecture, and more important was the certainty in his mind now that "The Night of the Long Knives" had demonstrated that the Nazis would use mass violence to gain their ends. If they would slaughter their own friends so ruthlessly, what would they not attempt against their chosen enemies?

My father returned to Canada determined to renew his efforts to arouse the Canadian government to action. It was a determination that was reinforced by what Winston Churchill told him on the eve of his departure: "You must do all you can to help us prepare, Bishop. *We haven't got much time left.*"

Later that year, partly as a result of my father's constant warnings that neglect of the nation's defences could be suicidal, the government reluctantly approved of pilot training via private flying clubs—"Sunday fliers." He decided to encourage this trend by joining one of the part-time flyers' clubs—the Montreal Light Aeroplane Club.

When this news reached an old London friend, Viscount Castleross, the influential London newspaper columnist, the latter had this to say about my father's resumption of flying:

"Why the devil have I got Billy Bishop on my mind?

"Oh, I remember.

"He is taking out a pilot's licence.

"The old idiot.
"He never could fly, although he gets angry if you say so.
"By that I mean he could never land."

It didn't take my father long to live up to that dubious reputation. One afternoon he landed a Fleet two-seater on its nose at Cartierville airfield. He climbed out, walked over to the pilot's hut and grinned.

"Haven't lost my touch," he said proudly to a group of flabbergasted students.

Spencer Horn, his comrade in 60 Squadron in the RFC, had described him as "a fantastic shot but a terrible pilot." This statement I can verify. Flying with him, you noticed his tendency to be ham-handed on the controls, his manoeuvres were jerky, his turns rough and hurried. He did not guide an aircraft, he pushed and pulled it.

In those days there were few restrictions on pilots. They did not have to file a flight plan, and there were apparently no laws against erratic flying.

One afternoon when he knew some friends were playing golf at nearby Laval, north of Montreal Island, my father decided to put on a special show for them. He invited me to go along—without, of course, telling me his plans. We flew over the golf course until he spotted a foursome, dived at them, swept across the green at a height of no more than ten feet, then pulled up. The golfers scattered in all directions.

That was only the warm-up. Next we flew west to Vaudreuil on the Ottawa River where another friend, Colonel Gustave Rainville, had a summer place. When we reached it my father pointed down at a raft moored a hundred feet from the shore. On it were a number of Rainville's guests sunning themselves. As we got close the swimmers plunged into the water and swam for shore. This gave my father an opportunity to execute a manoeuvre even more daring than the one he had originally intended. He bounced the wheels off the raft.

Strangely, I had utter confidence in him throughout. I was beginning to think of him as many others did—invincible.

TWENTY - TWO

GETTING READY

THOUGH THE WAR CLOUDS over Europe had considerably darkened by the mid-thirties, they were still almost totally ignored. But more people were more active in preparing for war—limited though that activity was—than was generally known at the time. In Canada my father was one of them. Circumstances brought this about.

Shortly after the Liberal government came to power in Canada under William Lyon Mackenzie King in 1935 my father was created an Air Vice-Marshal of the RCAF. He became close friends with the new Minister of National Defence, a tall, burly Scot, Ian Mackenzie. They were a strangely assorted pair. My father was short, no more than five feet seven inches, and by now quite portly. Mackenzie, lean and standing well over six feet tall, towered over him. They differed more seriously in another respect. Mackenzie firmly believed that the air force should be assigned primarily to the protection of Canada's shores. My father insisted that it should be an offensive weapon, on the ground that defence could best start at the battle line. Both agreed, however, that the air force should be expanded as rapidly as possible.

This was the reason, or at any rate one of the reasons, for the appointment of my father as Honorary Air Vice-Marshal, with full powers to assist the government in the appropriation of more funds for the air force by wooing public support. As an honorary, non-serving officer he was not restricted by military dictates, and the prestige of his high rank and his own fame gave authority to his propaganda activities.

Not all the newspapers agreed with the theme he kept repeating in speeches across the country ... "We cannot close our eyes to the possibility of war, in which event our most valuable contribution would be a trained air force. I plead with the government to devote more adequate funds to the expansion of the Royal Canadian Air Force...." For more than a year speeches like that made him a controversial figure. But in March, 1936, the need for preparation was clearly spelled out when Hitler reoccupied the Rhineland in violation of the peace treaty. In England Churchill warned: "All this means that the Nazi regime has gained a new prestige in Germany and in all the neighbouring countries. But more than that, Germany is now fortifying the Rhine Zone."

At this time not by any means all of my father's time was taken up with air force matters. They were, after all, extracurricular (and without pay) and the business of making a living as an oil company executive came first. His employers recognized, though, that his role as a World War I hero and crusader for air power increased his value to the company, and they gave him all the time off his secondary role required.

A typical entry in his diary in those mid-thirties days read:

Very tired tonight. Rode on Mount Royal this morning then walked to the office because it was clear. At noon sat for Jongers for an hour. Portrait coming along well. Lunch at the Ritz. Ross Malcom tells me Sladen leads the market. I bought another four hundred shares. Phoned Ian Mackenzie about my Ottawa speech. Sent him a copy. This afternoon played golf with Paul Rodier at Laval. It rained and I played atro-

ciously. Later at the club saw a Mr. O'Brien who wants to write
some sort of book about me for American school-children.
Margaret and I had cocktails at the Bells then dined at home.
I spent two hours at the piano practising. Phoned Ian again
about changes in my speech. At 11 p.m. George and Fiorenza
Drew came in and stayed until 3 a.m. It was hilarious.

This typical entry indicated that he was still busily engaged in
proving himself. For example, he learned to play the piano in three
months and played surprisingly well. But he practised as much as
four hours a day. He did the same thing with table tennis, in which
at that time he became keenly interested. For many weeks we lived
with the Ping-Pong table in the living room so that he could practise at any time the mood came upon him.

This relentlessness concealed and to a great extent overcame
his inner frustrations and anxieties. This is the impression he
made on Quentin Reynolds who wrote:

> It is very disappointing to meet ex-champions twenty years
> after. They are fat and dull and they are living in the past—
> looking at the present through the glamour of the past. Bishop
> was different. Bishop lives in the present and the past to him is
> merely a record of time—a record that he is too busy to look
> back upon.
>
> He is an intelligent, cultured gentleman, a *bon vivant*, and
> extraordinary host and one of the keenest businessmen in
> Canada. But to me he's the toughest man in the world—the
> only living person to whom one can point and say "There is a
> man without fear."

On one point Reynolds was entirely right—my father was an
extraordinary host. He entertained lavishly, and everything was
done correctly—up to a point. Beyond that point his ingenuity—

and often his eccentricity—took over. At one party he had the
entire meal served backwards—coffee first, then dessert, entree and
then soup, followed by cocktails. Leffo entered into the spirit of
things by entering the room backwards to serve the meal. On one
St. Patrick's Day he held a party patterned on an old "rag" at the
mess in France. He even poured champagne into the piano and
danced on it. For another party he rounded up all the organ grinders
in Montreal, so that guests were greeted in the apartment foyer by
a dozen grubby organ grinders (some complete with monkey) all
churning out different tunes.

But on another point Quentin Reynolds was dead wrong.
Bishop was far from being the most fearless of men. For one thing,
he was terrified of the very element of flight—altitude. Once he
pointed to a window a few floors above the street and told me with
a shudder: "If I leaned out of that window, I'd faint."

He never got over the memory of a pathological fear of ground
fire. And while he seemed to seek out enemy planes with an eagerness far beyond the call of duty, he once confided to me that every
time he sighted an enemy plane his heart pounded and his throat
went dry.

Even the confident, almost aggressive air he assumed as a busi-
nessman sometimes masked black moods of depression. Once
he terrified my mother by telling her, "There are so many things
buzzing around in my mind I sometimes wish I could stop them
by blowing them out with a bullet." But it is doubtful that he ever
seriously considered suicide. He was too interested in the "things
buzzing around" in his head.

The thirties were drawing to a close, and so was peace in
Europe. Hitlerism cast its shadow over Czechoslovakia, and in
England Prime Minister Chamberlain was timorously advancing
the view that war could be averted through compromise. Churchill
continued to thunder warnings of danger. His was the only strong
voice that cried out and for the most part it was tragically ignored.

In Canada my father's voice became an echo of Churchill's, and for the most part it too was ignored.

But progress was made. Defence Minister Ian Mackenzie persuaded the Canadian government to increase its expenditure for building the air force. On August 10, 1938, he appointed my father Honorary Air Marshal, the highest rank in the country at the time. He also became head of the Air Advisory Committee, made up of a group of Canadian war pilots including his brother-in-law Hank Burden.

Ian Mackenzie and my father still pretended that they were at odds on the role of air power. "I'm making an Imperialist out of Ian," my father boasted. And the Defence Minister retorted, "I am making an isolationist out of Bishop."

At the end of September came the brief false respite of Munich. What happened next is history, but the Bishop family had a private view of it from the exiled President Edouard Beneš of Czechoslovakia himself, when the latter was a guest at our house.

"If I had been allowed to fight I could have beaten Hitler. Hitler was bluffing and wasn't prepared for war!" Beneš declared.

My father's own reaction to Munich was recorded in a letter he wrote at the time: "There's no use kidding ourselves. We are in for a war and this Chamberlain thing has only postponed it. War is coming. I dread the thought but we are going to have to prepare for it quickly. My guess is that it is less than a year away."

He now devoted all of his time to air force matters. One outgrowth of his anxiety was an impulsive scheme that turned out to have great foresight. He was convinced that Canada's earliest and most important role in case of war would be to provide aircrew material—and unlimited space in which to train additional airmen. An essential part of this effort, he realized, would be U.S. citizens—like the Lafayette Escadrille of World War I.

My father telephoned a former war pilot, Clayton Knight, who since the war had become a noted illustrator. Clayton was dining in Cleveland at the house of an old comrade-in-arms, Thomas J. "Tommy" Herbert, who had become the Attorney General of Ohio. After Knight was summoned to the telephone, he returned to the table shaking his head in bewilderment.

"That was Billy Bishop," he told Herbert. "He wants me to help him in a plan to smuggle pilots up to Canada if war starts."

Herbert almost choked on the food he was chewing. "As Attorney General I should be the last to know about this," he complained. "It's illegal to solicit an American citizen to fight in a foreign war if America is neutral."

My father set about trying to make it legal. On March 27, 1939, he visited the White House to discuss plans for enlisting American flyers in the RCAF with President Franklin D. Roosevelt. And as an indirect result, the Clayton Knight Committee was set up to handle voluntary enlistments. Offices were established in centres throughout the United States. As a memoir of his visit, Roosevelt gave him a picture autographed "To my great friend Air Marshal Bishop."

The next day when Knight telephoned the U.S. State Department to confirm the arrangements, the voice that answered said: "This is the German Embassy."

"Brother!" Clayton said afterwards. "That was the wrongest wrong number in history."

During that summer I accompanied my father and the defence minister on a tour of Canadian air force stations from coast to coast. In five years the activity of the RCAF had trebled. Britain had sent over new planes, including a squadron of the latest Hurricanes. By now the total strength was four thousand men. But more training planes were needed, and it was far easier for enemy observers to detect American breaches of neutrality in the matter of airplanes than of men. So my father devised a method of bringing United States' training planes into Canada. They landed at airports that straddled the border between the two countries, and were left "unattended" on the American side a few feet from the border.

Whereupon Canadian aircraftmen lassoed them and dragged them across the boundary line, without the military personnel of either nation "violating" the border of the other.

As the crisis in Europe mounted, the silver RCAF Grumman amphibian assigned to my father appeared more and more frequently over the Burden family's summer place in the Muskoka Lakes near Windermere to take him to Ottawa for conferences. Perhaps a little ironically, the Grumman's route was the same as that flown by the ill-fated Bishop-Barker airline. Every time the aircraft arrived, everyone in the area was sure it was a signal that war had started.

TWENTY-THREE

CALL TO
THE COLOURS

CANADA was not prepared when the war finally came. In the fall of 1939 an understaffed and under-equipped RCAF was numerically and physically incapable of handling the number of volunteers that lined up to enlist. In any case there weren't enough instructors to train aircrews. Thousands had to be turned away. But in December, 1939, the Canadian government agreed to a proposal by Great Britain that Canada become the training centre of the Commonwealth, and overnight my father's part-time job became a second full-time air force career. Men from England, New Zealand and Australia as well as Canada would be trained by the RCAF. The nation was to become a nursery of aircrews—its most important early contribution to the Allied cause, and a dream that my father had long nurtured and publicly predicted.

Now his hopes were realized, and on January 23, 1940, he became director of recruiting. In this job he had a completely free hand. His first step was to inject colour, drama and excitement into the quest for air force volunteers. He believed in bands, parades and lots of publicity. The fact that he himself was the focus of most of the publicity did not faze him. It was in a good cause.

Early in 1940 the Bishops moved to Sandy Hill, in Ottawa. It was a compact little operation he ran there. His aide-de-camp was Paul Rodier, another World War I pilot from Montreal. His secretary was Margaret Northwood, a strikingly beautiful girl from Winnipeg who had also been his secretary in his civilian job. The faithful but long-suffering Leffo enlisted in the Royal Canadian Air Force and was granted the rank of flight sergeant in order to become my father's chauffeur, batman and, as he himself put it, "his bloody wet nurse."

To complete the entourage, along with my mother, my sister and myself, there was always a couple of pairs of chows, a breed of dogs my father favoured because he considered them much maligned. "People call them vicious," he would say, "but actually there are no more intelligent and tractable dogs than chows."

Members of his entourage just had to adjust themselves to his habits. Once he decided that because of gasoline rationing everyone must learn to ride bicycles. There was no argument, for he immediately went out and bought four.

His decisions to take off on recruiting trips were often made on impulse, at a moment's notice, and invariably resulted in a domestic uproar. Lethbridge particularly bore the brunt, packing clothes and other travelling gear, particularly the large leather hatbox which was the sole relic of grandfather Eleazar Bishop's leather-making career. My father had had it converted into an ingenious carryall with compartments for an ice-bucket, glasses, bottles of tonic water and club soda, plus assorted liquors. "It's the only good use that has ever been made of it," my father used to say.

This active period was undoubtedly the happiest of his life since World War I days. Not only did it soothe his restless soul to be constantly on the move, but it kept him in touch with the important people of the day—Churchill, Mayor Fiorello La Guardia of New York, Edouard Beneš of Czechoslovakia, Prime Minister Mackenzie King, Princess Juliana and Prince Bernhardt of the

Netherlands, Alexander de Seversky, the aircraft designer, and many more, all of whom were guests at our house.

In September 1940 my father crossed the Atlantic on the flying boat *Clyde* at the invitation of the British Air Ministry for a conference on the Commonwealth air training plan, an ambitious program that had been given top priority with the fall of France, the evacuation of the British expeditionary force from Dunkirk, and the massive air assault against Britain launched by Goering's Luftwaffe.

No. 1 RCAF Squadron, formed partly of Sunday fliers, was already in action. The month my father spent in England gave him full confirmation that his celebrity was firmly established. He was pictured, full-page, in the magazine *Sketch*, under the caption, "Seventy-Plane Bishop Comes Home." He and Prime Minister Winston Churchill were photographed in the garden of the Prime Minister's residence at 10 Downing Street as bombers droned overhead and anti-aircraft guns barked. Of that memorable moment he recalled that "we had a most welcome drink of scotch and soda first, and Churchill said 'I suppose we better look like we're talking about something. But what will we talk *about*?'" Actually they had talked of my father's promise that the RCAF would send over a thousand trained airmen almost immediately.

He was received by King George VI in the room at Buckingham Palace where His Majesty had been sitting when the palace was bombed. The King pointed out the damage. "I told him," my father recorded, "that I thought the bombing was a good thing. He was very startled at this and said 'Oh you do, do you?' I replied 'Yes Sir, I certainly do, the bombing of the civilians has made everyone angry, but this puts the cap on it.' He laughed and said that I might not have been so cheerful if I had been there at the time."

In other ways it was a sentimental journey. Nostalgia flooded his sentimental soul on a visit to his old haunts at Northholt, where he arrived just as the pilots of No. 1 RCAF landed their Hurricane fighters after a scramble against German raiders in which two

German Dornier bombers had been brought down. Part of the tail of one of them was later retrieved and given to my father as a souvenir.

My father's visit was climaxed by a solemn ceremony at which he unfurled the RCAF flag for the first time on English soil, the blue ensign with the maple leaf in the centre of the roundel, an insignia that theoretically came into existence in 1918 when he had been named the first commanding officer of the Canadian Wing of the RAF. When he returned to Canada he said "I felt like a Victorian in a bustle watching a modern bathing beauty."

In 1941, the Wings Parade became a familiar part of the Canadian wartime scene. At these colourful ceremonies held throughout the country that year, fourteen thousand Allied airmen marched proudly forward to have the shiny emblem of training aircrews pinned to their tunics—their "wings."

At his own insistence my father frequently officiated at these parades. He knew how much the moment meant to every man who graduated. He would try to put each man at ease as he presented him with his wings. How did he like the service? How many hours had he flown? (It was about 150 hours compared to his own 18½ when Bishop got his own wings). Then—"the best of luck!"

At a graduation for observers, my father, for the first time since 1916, wore his own "O" with the outstretched wing in place of his pilot's wings, as a tribute to the men "who take enormous risks and seldom get any of the glory."

In his speeches to graduating classes of airmen and on other "patriotic occasions" in which he was continually asked to participate, he used all the dramatic tricks he had learned, first in the officers' mess speech-making game with Jack Scott at Filescamp, later on his fundraising tour of Canada in 1917, and finally in his brief but spectacular tour of the United States as a professional lecturer.

Oratory is not one of the more enduring art forms, unless it happens to be Churchillian. So my father's speeches that the newspapers described as, among other things, "the closest approach to great poetry," may not quite stand up to that billing when removed from the emotional context of Canada's war effort in the critical days of World War II. An example was a speech he delivered at a tri-services rally in Toronto in November, 1941:

> I have seen you go by and my heart is full and very proud. I have seen you lads of the Navy march past today as the lads of the British Navy have marched past the parade grounds of a very eventful history and have stood by their stations in angry waters. And I have watched you Air Force men go by. Yours it is and will be to blaze the trails of combat and of conquest amid the sounding battle-clouds. It is upon these that the freedom of mankind rests—the victorious squadrons of our indomitable youth. Yes—my gallant cloud crusaders—this is your hour. And you—the Army on feet and on wheels—a member of which I was for so many happy years of my life—I have seen you march by—proud and strong and stalwart—with shoulders squared and resolute eyes fixed fearlessly on the far objective—which is the salvation of men. Yours is the less glamorous and spectacular task, but yours is the more abiding duty. I know you of old, I think. I watched your forebears surging across death-ridden soil to gain precious yards for freedom. I watched their matchless gallantry from whilom hideouts in the skies. God speed you. God speed you in the skies, or upon the seas, or across unknown acres where, on the edge of destiny, you may test your strength.

As a relief from this type of expected eloquence, my father made himself the butt of his own wry wit when he accepted an honorary Doctor of Laws Degree at the University of Toronto: "As an airman I know no law and as a Bishop I know less theology. Memories of my own academic career force me to the conclusion that I would have a very hard time attaining a degree by legitimate means in this seat of learning. Every question was a potential nose-dive."

By now my father had such confidence in himself as a speaker and performer that when in 1942 Warner Brothers of Hollywood produced a film on the RCAF, *Captains of the Clouds*, and asked him to play a part, he readily accepted. The story concerned three bush pilots (played by Jimmy Cagney, Alan Hale and Dennis Morgan) who enlisted in the RCAF. Hale and Cagney were discharged for misconduct, and in retaliation they decided to dive on a Wings Parade at which Bishop was officiating.

The scene was faked, of course. No planes left the ground when Michael Curtiz photographed the episode at Uplands Flying School, near Ottawa. The graduation ceremony was produced in detail and required little rehearsal. My father talked to the graduates as at any bona fide ceremony. His only display of uneasiness was when makeup was applied to his face in full view of the airmen lined up in front of him. But the part in which Cagney and Hale were to buzz the field caused much anxiety, delay and tension. My father, standing rigidly at attention, was to appear startled and annoyed, yet to maintain military aplomb, as he watched two aircraft dive down, sweep across the field, and climb up.

The trouble was there were no aircraft to look at—only a stagehand holding a red flag running along an elevated ramp in front of him at a height above eye level. The man with the flag sometimes ran too fast, sometimes not fast enough and once he nearly fell off the ramp. The scene had to be shot over and over, until at the end of the warm day the exasperated Curtiz exclaimed, "This is the last take positively if I have to take an airplane up myself."

Camm Ship, a Warner Brothers executive, testified, "Bishop is a very remarkable man. He had a long speech to deliver and he did it splendidly without much time to learn it. It was all the more remarkable because we had to take the shots of the same thing several times over, and he has been better than our professional actors."

My father's liaison with Hollywood continued in a coast-to-coast tour with the film star Anna Neagle to raise funds for the Air Cadet League, of which he was honorary president. He had supported the League even before the war started, as one of the best sources of future aircrews.

In December, 1941, Prime Minister Churchill came to America for the first time since the outbreak of war. This journey eventually brought him to Ottawa and at his own behest to the Bishop residence in Sandy Hill.

The impromptu visit was arranged at the house of the Canadian Prime Minister, Mackenzie King, where my father was a guest at a dinner for Churchill, who remarked, "I understand your house is just across the street, Bishop."

My father assured him that it was less than two minutes' walk.

"Right," Churchill said. "After dinner we'll stroll over."

He stayed for an hour. Nothing among my father's souvenirs escaped the Prime Minister's searching gaze. But it was a china piece in the drawing room that intrigued him most—a group of hungry piglets all trying to suckle on the same sow.

"It reminds me," Churchill reminisced, "of a time when all my ministers came to me with demands. All wanted men or monies or priorities or equipment. I could only tell them, 'Gentlemen, the old sow has only so many teats and there are not enough to go around.'"

The china piece was christened "Winston" from that day on.

On December 7, 1941, the pattern of American interest in Canada's war effort changed abruptly. After Pearl Harbor the United States entered into the war. On balance the Allies benefited immensely, of course, by gaining as an open ally the most powerful nation on earth, but the transfer of American volunteers to the ranks of their own armed forces posed a formidable problem. Early in 1942, for example, my father was called to London to help in the reorganization made necessary by the transfer of most of the seven thousand American citizens in the RCAF to their own air force.

Interviewed in New York on his way to London, he remarked that although it cost Canada $30,000 to train each pilot, the investment had been amply repaid because the Americans had helped build up the training plan quickly. The advantage now enjoyed by the United States in being able to secure flyers at no cost he described as "casting bread on the waters and getting back frosted cake."

The United States began to pour men and aircraft into England. The Eagle Squadrons of the Royal Air Force, composed of United States volunteers, became squadrons of the U.S. Army Air Forces. Canada by 1943 had trained twenty-five thousand aircrews for the Royal Air Force and in addition had twenty-four squadrons of her own in action. Vast changes in command and organization became necessary with the planning of two new major operations—the landings in North Africa and the joint British-American round-the-clock bombing of Germany.

My father found London a different place from the beleaguered city he had left two years before, during the Battle of Britain. The drone of attacking German bombers had been replaced by the roar of Allied aircraft on their way across the Channel into the enemy's territory. Fighter pilots, instead of defending against the invaders, now made sweeps over northern France to St. Omer, Cambrai, Ypres, Arras, Lille—his old hunting ground.

My father found many of his old comrades were serving again. Elliott Springs was back in the uniform of the United States Army Air Corps. Grid Caldwell was back in the air force, as were William Fry and Frank "Mongoose" Soden. And Larry Callahan, now a lieutenant-colonel in the U.S. Army Air Corps in charge of intelligence for the planned North African landings, was a frequent visitor to my father's suite at London's fashionable hotel, Claridges.

Together they visited their old 85 Squadron, the Flying Foxes, which then was flying night fighters. In the office of the commanding officer, Wing Commander G. I. Raphael of Quebec City, they browsed through the squadron scrapbook to look at pictures of themselves in their fighting days. My father was a weekend guest at Prime Minister Churchill's country residence, Chequers. He reported, "Winston is in terrific form. But he stays up too late and kept everyone else up until three or four in the morning."

During one of these late discussions the Prime Minister paced the room, delivering one of his well-known discourses on war policy then abruptly stopped and waited for unanimous confirmation of his views. My father recounted: "Of course I had to be the one stupid ass to speak up and say I didn't agree with him when I could just as easily have kept my mouth shut. Winston immediately turned on me. Sholto Douglas and Harris and the others looked at me as if to say 'Thank God someone else is getting it for a change.'"

But it was the kind of language Churchill respected. Later that evening when he and my father were alone the Prime Minister fingered Bishop's row of ribbons somewhat in awe and said, "This row should be preserved."

Back on this side, he continued the relentless pace of travelling, inspecting and speaking. He was swamped with thousands of letters, all of which he insisted on answering. These were from parents whose sons had been killed in action, from young men wanting to enlist, others who wanted transfers, from well-wishers and from American critics who blamed propagandists like Bishop for their country's entry into the war. He arranged for appearances in the United States, notably as the principal speaker at a Veterans' Day in Chicago where his speech was credited with winning over two powerful newspaper publishers with isolationist leanings, Joe Patterson of New York and Bertie McCormick of Chicago, to the cause of American entry into the war.

My father had never before worked so hard. He kept going by sheer willpower, aided by the stimulus of convivial after-hours activities. It was obvious to his family and friends that the pace was taking a terrible toll. The pace finally caught up with him on November 7, 1942, as he made a speech to air cadets at Scott Park in Hamilton, Ontario. Midway through his talk he felt an agonizing pain in his stomach. He thought he had been shot, but continued the address.

When he had finished he quickly made his way out of the park, helped by another officer. The cramp in his stomach made it difficult to walk. He was near to the exit when a man with a maniacal look in his eyes stepped in front of him and in a hysterical scream shouted, "I'm going to kill you."

My father stopped dead as the man lunged, his fist aimed at his stomach. Just in time someone managed to push the assailant aside. It probably saved his life.

He was flown to Montreal and rushed to hospital semi-conscious. His condition was diagnosed as an acute inflammation of the pancreas. The family doctor, Guy Johnson, explained the situation to my mother: "If it bursts he will live only a matter of days. If we take it out, he will last at the most for six months. Only hope and a miracle will help him now."

TWENTY-FOUR

EPILOGUE

MY FATHER's critical illness was reported in the London papers and letters from old acquaintances poured into the hospital. Puddin', the flower man outside the Berkeley Hotel, from whom he habitually bought his boutonniere when he went out on London town, wrote laboriously: "I learned that you had been ill in the paper. I hope you will get better soon so that you can continue your great work."

Corporal Walter Bourne, his guardian angel of World War I days, wrote from an RAF base where he was serving out his second war: "Get well soon, Sir. Train us the men and we will beat them as we did in the old days. Here is good luck—I am enclosing something which has travelled with me all these years. Remember the time your gun jammed (April 30 1917 in the attack against the Gothas) and you had to get away. Well, Sir, here is the bullet that might have ended your career. You can see the mark on it where I gripped it in the vise to get it free."

My father, restless in confinement to bed, did his best to negate the "get well" wishes. Guy Johnson declared he was the most restless and unco-operative patient he had ever had.

One morning he decided to get up and shave himself. His knees felt wobbly at first but by the time he had finished he felt much better and decided he needed some exercise. He performed a few knee bends to loosen up a bit. Then he got down to serious business. From the door to the window he paced back and forth across the room, gradually gaining speed. He had just completed the third lap when the door opened. The angry face of Guy Johnson glared at him. He ordered him back to bed and warned him bluntly: "You are so near to being dead that it is a miracle you are breathing. We couldn't operate even if the thing burst—and you want exercise. You will stay in bed until I tell you to get up."

Reluctantly my father obeyed the doctor and endured a prolonged convalescence. And even by the time he was discharged from the Montreal Hospital in January, 1943, he was still in no condition to return to duty. He took a long period of sick leave.

He had been warned by Guy that any recurrence could be fatal and that the illness had taxed his entire system and had weakened his heart. Even when completely recovered he would never again be able to renew his previous pace.

But my father was just as contemptuous of this warning as he had been about anything that restricted or limited his actions. And soon after he returned from leave in March, 1943, he attacked the job of recruiting with more vigour than he had ever done. But inevitably it took a heavy toll.

On February 8, 1944, he celebrated his fiftieth birthday. He looked twenty years older. A certain vitality remained, and the cheerful manner. These concealed the fact that he was close to total exhaustion in body and soul.

But the task of recruiting was nearly over. After D-Day, although victory was still to be won, recruiting for aircrews ceased. My father, who had spent twelve and a half years in uniform and had devoted as many more to the cause of aviation, asked to be relieved of his duties by the end of the year. In accepting his resignation, Honourable C. G. Power, Canada's Minister of Air, wrote:

By your untiring efforts and your unbounded enthusiasm you have been singularly successful in accomplishing a very difficult and important task, the manning of the RCAF with the finest of Canada's young men. Your magnificent record in the First Great War fired the imagination of our Canadian aircrews in this war and has inspired them to deeds of courage to rival your own.

In the King's Birthday Honours that year he was made a Companion of the Most Honourable Order of the Bath—an award generally referred to as the C.B. This was a fitting climax to his military career in two wars, but he rather regretted that the C.B. ranked after the Victoria Cross, thereby breaking up his perfect "fighting row"—V.C., D.S.O. and Bar, M.C., and D.F.C. Officially this closed his career as an airman. But as a kind of epilogue to that career, he set out his views on the future of aviation in a volume entitled *Winged Peace*.

When the war ended in 1945 he returned to Montreal, to the oil business and to the large yellow stone house on Peel Street. But his resumption of business life—and normal family life—was frankly half-hearted. He could not readjust after the feverish activity and excitement of his role in building up the Allied air forces. He no longer had his old energy and enthusiasm. The great challenges which had inspired him in two world wars no longer existed.

In public, he went through the motions. Each year, in a uniform decorated with the incredible array of his honours, he attended the major military anniversaries, the Battle of Britain Day parades, Warriors' Day parades, Armistice Day parades.

In private life he lived in semi-retirement. He spent hours reading in his library. His reading was largely adventure stories and history. His favourite character was Napoleon. He read every book on the French emperor he could lay hands on.

In his library he could seal himself off from the rest of the family. The room contained a huge fireplace at one end, and at the other french doors that opened on a veranda overlooking the lawn. A few friends were admitted to the room, but mostly he preferred to be alone. Around the walls were hung framed maps he had used in his fighting days, as well as a collection of hunting prints. The entire room was dotted with trophies—the propeller and blue spinner of his Nieuport; the windshield with the hole in it that marked the day he became an ace.

Photographs by the dozens adorned the walls and his desk— pictures of him seated with Goering, talking to King George V., and autographed pictures of Roosevelt, Churchill, Beneš, Hedy Lamarr. One held a special place on his desk and in his heart. It was small, cracked and in a silver frame—a portrait of Jack Scott, his commander in the days of 60 Squadron.

Semi-retirement, however, did not end my father's proclivity for new activities. He took a correspondence course in typing, and practised diligently for four hours a day until he perfected it. He explored unusual hobbies. Ice carving was one. Everyone in the family had to participate. Half a dozen blocks of ice would be piled up on the veranda. Then all the family got together and began to whittle away with picks. Later we graduated to soap carving and wood carving. But as quickly as he started such pastimes, once he either perfected them or lost interest in them he gave them up—to the great relief of the Bishop family. And yet we regretted it each time one of his enthusiasms was abandoned. For these were the things, we knew, that kept him alive.

I am sure that many people thought that my father's irrepressible behaviour made life unhappy for my mother. Nothing could have been further from the truth. Certainly my father was not easy to live with, but what very few people outside the Bishop family knew was that although my father's eccentric antics often embarrassed her and sometimes even angered her a little, my mother understood and shared my father's moods in her own quiet way.

For example, if she were departing or arriving by train, my father would line up all the porters in advance and present her with a guard of honour—and she would smile through her blushes because she realized that my father was showing attentiveness to her.

She shared his emotions. When he cried (which was frequently, because many things touched him deeply) she cried too. Apart from his more outlandish practical jokes, what amused him amused her too. She never forgot a piece of advice Grandmother Bishop had given before her marriage: "Don't try to push Billy—you've got to lead him."

During these years following the Second World War my father and I became very close friends, more like pals than just father and son. Partly, I feel this was due to the fact that I had served as a fighter pilot in the RCAF and this established a comradeship between us.

Deep inside, he was sad but not rebellious at the knowledge that the years of activity he had so enjoyed were slipping away. Reaching for a last hope that those years could be recalled, he volunteered for duty in 1950 when the Korean War started. His services were politely but firmly declined. Thereafter, his health and his spirit steadily declined, and soon the strain of making business decisions became intolerable. After a series of brief illnesses he retired in 1952.

Disintegration came quickly. In the winters he lived in Palm Beach. He played a little golf and did a little writing. But he knew then that the days were running out. He watched the end approach without fear, indeed, almost with a sense of relief.

The summer of 1956 he did not spend in Canada, as was his habit. He was too tired and ill to undertake the trip from Florida. Early in September my mother came up to visit me in Edmonton, where I was working. My father, attended by the faithful Lethbridge, was nevertheless lonely. He always had been lonely when my mother was away. When he travelled without her, he would telephone, write or wire her every day. Sometimes he would use all those methods, even several times a day.

On the evening of September 10 he had a drink and dinner, then read for a couple of hours before going to bed. Lethbridge offered to help him, but my father declined.

"I'm feeling better than I have for weeks," he said cheerfully.

After midnight Lethbridge looked in on him before going to his own bed, as he always did. There was no faint sound of breathing, no slight movement of the body. My father had died painlessly and peacefully in his sleep.

Never before had the death of a Canadian been recorded at such length in the press of so many countries; never before such widespread retelling of the events of a few months in the life of one man, now four decades ago.

It was the largest funeral held in Canada within living memory. Thousands of people lined the route, and the procession took seventy minutes to pass. The service was held in Timothy Eaton Memorial Church, Toronto, where my parents had been married forty years before.

As I knelt beside my mother and sister and listened to Rev. Dr. Andrew Lawson begin his tribute, "Let us talk about great men . . ." I remembered something my father had confided to me: "I may not be a religious man as most people understand that term. But I never took the air on patrol without a silent prayer: 'God give me strength. God be with me now.'"

Of all the countless tributes that were published—some were in verse—the one that moved me most, perhaps because I felt that it would have secretly pleased my father too, even while it embarrassed him, was written by John Bassett, publisher of the *Montreal Gazette*:

"Death came to Billy Bishop in the early morning. He died at that chill hour before the coming of dawn—an hour when he must often have been making ready for his solitary flights.

"Perhaps the very core of his courage lies in this very fact—that he showed it most at an hour when men feel it least. For his courage was not a thing of sudden inspiration, the surge of the moment, needing the support and cheer of others. It was a solitary thing, lonely as the dawn itself.

"Perhaps if he had a choice, this would have been the hour he would have preferred. For he had that courage which Napoleon once said was the rarest—*the courage of the early morning.*"

LIST OF VICTORIES

1917

	DATE	TIME	HEIGHT	LOCATION	ENEMY AIRCRAFT
1	March 25	5.00 p.m.	9,000 ft.	Between St. Léger and Arras	Albatros
2	March 31	7.30 a.m.	15,000 ft.	N/E of Arras	Albatros
3	April 7	5.00 p.m.	300 ft.	E of Arras	Albatros
4	April 8	9.30 a.m.	4,000 ft.	N/E of Arms	Albatros
5	April 8	9.40 a.m.	10,000 ft.	E of Arras	2-Seater
6	April 8	10.10 a.m.	10,000 ft.	Vitry	Single-Seater
7	April 20	2.58 p.m.	8,000 ft.	N of Monchy-le-Preux	2-Seater
8	April 22	11.20 a.m.	8,000 ft.	E of Vimy	Albatros
9	April 22	11.21 a.m.	8,000 ft.	E of Vimy	Albatros
10	April 23	3.30 p.m.	2,200 ft.	Vitry	2-Seater

11	April 23	3.59 p.m.	6,000 ft.	Vitry	Albatros
12	April 29	11.55 a.m.	14,000 ft.	E of Epinoy	Albatros
13	April 30	11.15 a.m.	8,000 ft.	SE of Lens	2-Seater
14	April 30	11.45 a.m.	5,000 ft.	NE of Monchy-le-Preux	2-Seater
15	May 2	10.00 a.m.	6,000 ft.	E of Epinoy	2-Seater
16	May 2	10.02 a.m.	6,000 ft.	E of Epinoy	2-Seater
17	May 4	1.30 p.m.	5,500 ft.	Vitry	2-Seater
18	May 7	9.50 a.m.	11,500 ft.	N of Vitry	Albatros
19	May 7	10.50 a.m.	10,000 ft.	N of Vitry	Albatros
20	May 26	10.16 a.m.	10,000 ft.	NE of Vimy	Albatros
21	May 27	9.40 a.m.	9,000 ft.	E of Lens	2-Seater
22	May 31	7.11 p.m.	7,000 ft.	Epinoy	Albatros
23	June 2	4.23 a.m.	25 ft.	Estourmel aerodrome	Albatros
24	June 2	to	50 ft.	Estourmel aerodrome	Albatros
25	June 2	5.00 a.m.	200 ft.	Estourmel aerodrome	Albatros
26	June 8	12.10 a.m.	12,000 ft.	N of Lille	Single-Seater
27	June 24	11.36 a.m.	13,000 ft.	W of Douai	Albatros
28	June 25	10.00 a.m.	10,000 ft.	Dury	Albatros
29	June 26	10.55 a.m.	10,000 ft.	N of Etaing	Albatros
30	June 26	10.00 a.m.	11,000 ft.	N of Etaing	Albatros

31	June 28	9.00 a.m.	14,000 ft.	Drocourt	Albatros
32	July 10	8.10 p.m.	13,000 ft.	Midway between Vimy and Douai	Albatros (bright green)
33	July 12	8.15 a.m.	15,600 ft.	NE of Douai	Albatros
34	July 17	7.40 p.m.	12,000 ft.	Havrincourt Wood	Albatros
35	July 17	8.00 p.m.	10,000 ft.	SE of Quéant	Albatros
36	July 20	12.05 a.m.	13,500 ft.	S of Havrincourt Wood	Albatros
37	July 28	6.10 a.m.	10,000 ft.	E of Drocourt	Albatros
38	July 28	7.10 a.m.	10,000 ft.	Beaumont	Albatros
39	August 5	8.00 p.m.	12,000 ft.	E of Monchy-le-Preux	Albatros
40	August 5	8.20 p.m.	10,000 ft.	E of Monchy-le-Preux	Albatros
41	August 6	7.20 a.m.	7,000 ft.	Vitry	Albatros
42	August 9	9.00 a.m.	6,000 ft.	E of Drocourt	2-Seater
43	August 13	6.00 p.m.	10,000 ft.	E of Drocourt	Albatros
44	August 13	6.00 p.m.	10,000 ft.	E of Drocourt	Albatros
45	August 15	8.20 p.m.	11,000 ft.	N of Hénin Liétard	Albatros
46	August 16	8.00 p.m.	14,000 ft.	NE of Lens	2-Seater
47	August 16	8.10 p.m.	14,000 ft.	NE of Lens	Albatros

1918

	DATE	TIME	HEIGHT	LOCATION	ENEMY AIRCRAFT
48	May 27	4.23 p.m.	14,300 ft.	Passchendaele	2-Seater
49	May 28	3.00 p.m.	13,000 ft.	E of Ypres	Albatros
50	May 28	3.00 p.m.	13,000 ft.	E of Ypres	Albatros
51	May 30	3.42 p.m.	16,000 ft.	Roulers	2-Seater
52	May 30	3.45 p.m.	16,000 ft.	Roulers	Albatros
53	May 30	7.53 p.m.	15,400 ft.	Armentières	Albatros
54	May 31	3.05 p.m.	14,000 ft.	SE of Armentières	Pfalz
55	May 31	8.15 p.m.	11,000 ft.	E of Hazebrouck	Pfalz
56	June 1	8.10 p.m.	11,000 ft.	S of Armentières	Pfalz
57	June 2	8.10 p.m.	16,500 ft.	S of Armentières	Pfalz (black, white tails)
58	June 4	11.28 a.m.	14,000 ft.	Between Nieuport and Ostend, 3 miles miles out to sea.	Albatros
59	June 4	11.37 a.m.	15,000 ft.	5 miles inland	Albatros
60	June 15	6.55 p.m.	10,000 ft.	E of Estaires	Pfalz
61	June 16	8.20 p.m.	18,000 ft.	E of Armentières	Pfalz
62	June 16	8.28 p.m.	8,000 ft.	Armentières	Pfalz
63	June 17	10.25 a.m.	18,000 ft.	Staden	2-Seater
64	June 17	10.50 a.m.	4,000 ft.	Sailly-sur-le-Lys	Albatros

65	June 17	10.55 a.m.	2,000 ft.	Laventin	2-Seater
66	June 18	10.45 a.m.	9,000 ft.	NE of Ypres	Albatros (natural wood fuselages)
67	June 18	10.50 a.m.	9,000 ft.	NE of Ypres	Albatros (natural wood fuselages)
68	June 19	9.58 a.m.	1,100 ft.	E of Ploegsteert Wood	Pfalz
69	June 19	10.00 a.m.	1,100 ft.	E of Ploegsteert Wood	Pfalz
70	June 19	10.00 a.m.	1,100 ft.	E of Ploegsteert Wood	Pfalz
71	June 19	10.03 a.m.	1,100 ft.	E of Ploegsteert Wood	Pfalz
72	June 19	10.10 a.m.	900 ft.	E of Neuve Eglise	2-Seater

Index

RECYCLED
Paper made from
recycled material
FSC® C021757

Marquis Book Printing Inc.

Québec, Canada
2011

Printed on Silva Enviro 100% post-consumer EcoLogo certified paper,
processed chlorine free and manufactured using biogas energy.